"Paul Marcus has brought together a classic of wisdom literature, the Ethics of the Fathers, and psychoanalytic theory and practice in ways that mutually illuminate each other. Their co-nourishing interaction adds to our sense and feeling for life in depth and breadth. A welcome addition to our exploration of who we are and can be."

Michael Eigen, *Ph.D, author,* Contact with the Depths, Faith, *and* The Sensitive Self

"Paul Marcus brings a unique psychoanalytic perspective to the ethical teachings of the ancient rabbis. Readers will discover a completely different way of looking at familiar statements in the Ethics of the Fathers. This volume succeeds in bringing to bear a modern discipline for understanding a classic Jewish text."

Lawrence H. Schiffman, *Global Distinguished Professor of Hebrew and Judaic Studies, New York University*

"As a congregational Rabbi, I have read many interpretations of *Pirkei Avot, Ethics of the Fathers* to help guide me in offering effective pastoral care. What makes this volume uniquely intriguing is that it beautifully and seamlessly weaves together psychoanalysis with rabbinic interpretations of these wisdom teachings. Dr Marcus's expertise illuminates a psychological lens through which to understand *Ethics of the Fathers* that has been underappreciated in many traditional commentaries, as well as what psychoanalysis might learn from rabbinic wisdom. I recommend this book to clergy, pastoral caregivers, and all those interested in a psychological understanding of this Ancient Rabbinic masterpiece."

Rabbi Sharyn Perlman, *Temple Beth Israel*

Psychoanalysis and Wisdom

Psychoanalysis and Wisdom applies psychoanalytic insights into one of the great examples of wisdom literature, the Ethics of the Fathers, an ethical tractate of the Talmud.

Paul Marcus quotes key passages from the Ethics of the Fathers, providing a psychoanalytic commentary to enlarge and deepen our understanding of its contents, focusing primarily on what constitutes a flourishing life. Marcus then considers what psychoanalysis can provide in its engagement with this classic of the wisdom teachings, such as illuminating aspects of the Ethics that are overlooked or underappreciated, and how "pearls of wisdom" from the Ethics can be incorporated into psychoanalytic theory and practice. The book contains clinical material as well as the insights of philosophers like Martin Buber, Gabriel Marcel and Emmanuel Levinas.

Psychoanalysis and Wisdom will appeal to readers interested in psychoanalysis and psychotherapy and to academics and students of psychoanalytic studies, religious studies, Judaic studies and philosophy.

Paul Marcus is a training and supervisory analyst at the National Psychological Association for Psychoanalysis in New York City and Co-Chairperson of the discussion group Psychoanalysis and Spirituality at the American Psychoanalytic Association. He is the author of *Psychoanalysis and Toileting: Minding One's Business* (Routledge).

Psychoanalysis and Wisdom

Encountering 'Ethics of the Fathers'

Paul Marcus

LONDON AND NEW YORK

Designed cover image: ZU_09 / Getty Images

First published 2024
by Routledge
4 Park Square, Milton Park, Abingdon, Oxon OX14 4RN

and by Routledge
605 Third Avenue, New York, NY 10158

Routledge is an imprint of the Taylor & Francis Group, an informa business

© 2024 Paul Marcus

The right of Paul Marcus to be identified as author of this work has been asserted in accordance with sections 77 and 78 of the Copyright, Designs and Patents Act 1988.

All rights reserved. No part of this book may be reprinted or reproduced or utilised in any form or by any electronic, mechanical, or other means, now known or hereafter invented, including photocopying and recording, or in any information storage or retrieval system, without permission in writing from the publishers.

Trademark notice: Product or corporate names may be trademarks or registered trademarks, and are used only for identification and explanation without intent to infringe.

British Library Cataloguing-in-Publication Data
A catalogue record for this book is available from the British Library

ISBN: 978-1-032-59238-1 (hbk)
ISBN: 978-1-032-59240-4 (pbk)
ISBN: 978-1-003-45373-4 (ebk)

DOI: 10.4324/9781003453734

Typeset in Times New Roman
by Taylor & Francis Books

For Simone Devorah, welcome to the world

Contents

Acknowledgments		x
1	Introduction	1
2	The Ethics of the Fathers	8
3	Conclusion	119
	References	127
	Index	140

Acknowledgments

I would like to thank Rabbi Sharyn Perlman, a Conservative rabbi, for her reading and critiquing of my book and for her promotional blurb. Thanks also go to my wife, Irene, a child and adult psychoanalyst, for her helpful comments on the manuscript. I am also grateful to Michael Eigen and Lawrence H. Schiffman for their promotional endorsements of my book. Thanks also go to editor Susannah Frearson for her support of my writing project and to Saloni Singhania, her editorial assistant.

Chapter 1

Introduction

In two of my books, *Ancient Religious Wisdom: Spirituality and Psychoanalysis* (2003) and *Psychoanalysis as a Spiritual Discipline: In Dialogue with Martin Buber and Gabriel Marcel* (2021), I have made the claim that psychoanalysis is culturally aging, in that it is no longer regarded as the primary psychotherapy for those who are suffering from psychic pain. Psychoanalysis is also in conceptual disarray as a theoretical discipline. That is, as Marshall Edelson noted, it is a "theory in crisis", characterized by a "profound malaise" (1988, p. xiv), while Nathan G. Hale describes the psychoanalytic crisis as a "crisis of clashing theories, competing modes of therapy, and uncertainties of professional identity" (1995, p. 360). As Greenberg and Mitchell have noted in their seminal book (1983, p. 404), "Psychoanalytic models rest upon ... irreconcilable claims concerning the human condition" (and therefore psychopathology and treatment). Twenty-three years after Hale's comment, the editors of the impressive anthology *Psychoanalytic Trends in Theory and Practice: The Second Century of the Talking Cure* (Etezady, Blon & Davis, 2018) made a similar assertion, "Psychoanalysis has become a very diverse field with multiple schools of thought, each with its own theory and praxis... [there is no] unified theory of psychoanalysis" (ibid., p. 476).[1] A noteworthy example of the conceptual disarray in psychoanalysis is the Oedipal complex. As contemporary Freudian analysts Knafo and Moscovitz noted, "Today adherence to the Oedipus complex, even by contemporary Freudians, is a hotly debated topic, with some insisting that it is central while others believing the concept needs to be revised or discarded" (2018, pp. 13–14). Likewise, the core concept of transference neurosis is up for grabs. Says Vogel in his discussion of Loewald's work, "there are few concepts in psychoanalysis as controversial as this one. Contemporary theorists argue about its definition, its qualities and characteristics, its usefulness or necessity as a concept, and whether psychoanalytic process should be defined by it" (1991, p. 125). Also, as Israely noted, "analysts may share theoretical principles yet reach totally different practical conclusions" (Israely, 2018, p. 29).[2]

As Freud noted, psychoanalysis can be a useful tool for assisting us to comprehend what he called the "riddles of the world in which we live" (1927a, p. 253),[3] "a key to the explanation of human phenomena in general (and not only pathological symptoms)" as Chasseguet-Smirgel emphasized (1985, p. 120). Likewise, Freyer (2004) noted that "psychoanalysis is at its core a reading of how we live in the world, of our struggles with our past as it shapes our present and future" (p. 26). Thus, this book attempts to improve the aforementioned dismal landscape of contemporary psychoanalysis, a discipline and profession that is in a dire state both in the marketplace of ideas and in terms of clinical practice, by suggesting that psychoanalysis is still capable of being a robust interpretive framework as it applies its insights to understand one of the great examples of wisdom teachings,[4] the *Ethics of the Fathers* (henceforth, the Ethics), a tractate of the Babylonian Talmud.[5] Indeed, as William Berkson noted in his commentary on the Ethics, the Ethics "is an anthology of sayings of the greatest post-biblical Jewish sages" about what constitutes a good or flourishing life (henceforth, a good life).[6] It is comparable in its "timeless immediacy and power" to "the *Analects* of Confucius, from ancient China, the *Enchiridion* of Epictetus, from ancient Greece, and the Dhammapada of Buddha, from ancient India" (Berkson, 2010, p. 1).

While mainly focusing on what psychoanalysis can provide in its engagement with this classic of wisdom teachings, such as illuminating aspects of the Ethics that are overlooked and/or underappreciated, I will also attempt, where plausible, to suggest what "pearls of wisdom" from the Ethics can possibly be incorporated (in whole or in part) into psychoanalytic theory and clinical practice. Moreover, I will point out where the Ethics and psychoanalysis tend to agree with each other or at least are correlated. Before proceeding with the heart of this book, analyzing some of the more robust sayings contained in the Ethics, I should say something more about what is contained within the Ethics and how I view psychoanalysis.

What is the Ethics of the Fathers?

According to Lynn Somerstein (2014, n.p.) in the *Encyclopedia of Psychology and Religion*, the

> "Ethics of the Fathers", called in Hebrew, *Pirkei Avot* and more properly translated as "Chapters of the Fathers", is known as "Ethics of the Fathers" because of its content— a collection of laws, aphorisms, and guides to ethical behavior—wisdom literature that is over 2,000 years old [it is a 200 CE document]. It asks and tries to explain what makes a good person and how to get along with family members, teachers, and the neighbors. *Pirkei Avot* is concerned with down-to-earth, hands-on, practical living— like an early self-help book. The emphasis is on doing, embodying the religious life even in everyday actions. This accessibility makes it very popular, so it is included in many prayer books [and is customarily read during the summer months of the Sabbath].

A few noteworthy examples taken from the Ethics:

> If I am not for myself who will be? But if I am for myself only, what am I? And if not now, when?
>
> (Bokser, 1983, p. 242)[7]

> Who is wise? He who learns from all men.... Who is mighty? He who subdues his passions....
> Who is rich? He who is happy with his portion....
>
> (Ibid.)

> The day is short; the task is great; the workmen are lazy; the reward is abundant; and the Master is pressing.
>
> (Ibid., p. 237)

Thus, as Rabbi Dr. Bokser points out, the Ethics is part of the Mishnah (a written account of the oral law, part of the Talmud), an anthology of ethical teachings about life-conduction, "submitted in the name of the great teachers of Judaism, as fatherly [read parental] advice to the people they sought to educate" (ibid., p. 231). It was redacted by Judah ha-Nasi in about the third century CE. Ironically, considering the Ethics is a down-to-earth religious collection of sayings, Freud too, in his critique of religion in the *Future of an Illusion* (1927b), made "education to reality" (p. 49) one of the hallmarks of the adult as opposed to infantile outlook.[8] In essence then, says Rabbi Jill Jacobs, the Ethics provides a snapshot of the rabbinic worldview; it emphasizes rigorous learning, service to God, discipleship, ethical behavior, humility and equitable judgment (Jacobs, 2023).[9]

What is psychoanalysis?

Psychoanalysis can be conceived as a form of life, an affect-integrating, meaning-giving and action-guiding resource for individuals who can appropriate the life- and identity-defining narrative of psychoanalysis when they seek to understand, endure and possibly master the problems that affect, if not assault, the human experiences of, for example, conflict, anxiety, despair, loss and tragedy. Psychoanalysis can be viewed as what Michel Foucault called a "technology of the self": "an exercise of the self, by which one attempts to develop and transform oneself, and to attain a certain mode of being" (1989, p. 433). As philosopher Pierre Hadot notes about ancient Greek philosophy, psychoanalysis can be understood as a "spiritual exercise", a tool for living life skillfully, more fully and wisely (1995, p. 83). Erikson may have had this in mind when he wrote that "free association" was a "western form of meditation" (Hoare, 2001, p. 88),[10] while Symington explicitly states "that psychoanalysis has a spiritual function", such that "purifying motivation" becomes "the organizing center of his activities" (1994, p. 47). The aim of a spiritual exercise is to foster a deep modification of an individual's way of "seeing and being", a decisive change in how one lives one's practical, everyday life. Most importantly, the objective of a spiritual exercise is "a total transformation of one's vision, life-style, and behavior" in the service of increased personal freedom and peace of mind (Hadot, 1995, pp. 83, 103, 14), and, I would add, a less self-centric outlook and behavior. According to this view, as Levinas described "Jewish Humanism" at its best, psychoanalysis is "a difficult wisdom concerned with truths that correlate to virtues" (1990, p. 275). Psychoanalysis is a painful, deconstructive, demythologizing and defamiliarizing process for acquiring greater self-awareness and self-understanding, especially of one's destructive unconscious emotional activity, one that transforms moral consciousness by expanding and deepening one's capacity to love. Self-understanding leads to self-mastery, which leads to self-transcendence. In fact, Freud described psychoanalytic treatment as the "scientific cure by love" (McGuire, 1974, pp. 12–13).[11] In this sense, psychoanalysis is animated by both the "love of wisdom" and the "wisdom of love" (Levinas, 1981, p. 162), by Greek (metaphorically Athens, reason, philosophy, contemplation) and Hebrew (Jerusalem, faith, law, simple piety)[12] values and is a powerful tool for the art of living a good life, as one construes and fashions it.

The "art of living" is a phrase that deserves some clarification.[13] Foucault aptly defines the term as "those intentional and voluntary actions by which men not only set themselves rules of conduct but also seek to transform themselves ... and to make their life into an *oeuvre* that carries aesthetic values and meets certain stylistic criteria" (1990, pp. 10–11). With this definition in mind, psychoanalysis can reasonably be characterized as an art of living.[14] This is an important notion because the Ethics is a religious/ethical tractate of the Talmud that is also putting forth a grand narrative of subjectivity about what constitutes a good life. Following Wallwork, by ethics I mean "at its core, ethics is concerned with searching for and defending rationally our most basic general moral principles and virtues" (1991, p. 3). Wallwork (2005) further notes that ethics is "critical reflection about 'right' and 'wrong' actions and 'good' and 'bad' character traits and other states of affairs" (p. 281). In a word, ethics is practical morality (Rotenstreich, 1968). He also says that ethics is different than "*morality* in providing arguments on behalf of our most basic normative standards, whereas morality is a more descriptive concept referring to how people do in fact think and behave within particular cultural contexts" (ibid.).

My claim, then, is that psychoanalysis has its valuative attachments like love and work, and it can reveal aspects of the Ethics that are often overlooked and/or underappreciated and that have bearing on a secular (and religious) analysand's outlook and behavior. Psychoanalysis can also be enhanced as a technology of the self or spiritual exercise by entering into dialogue with the wisdom teachings, the Ethics, and possibly incorporating aspects of its pearls of wisdom. This is of special interest when we recall what

Freud wrote in a letter to American physician and neurologist James Jackson Putnam: "That psychoanalysis has not made the analysts themselves better, nobler or of stronger character remains a disappointment for me. Perhaps, I was wrong to expect it" (Hale, 1971, pp. 163–164).

The structure of the book is as follows: I will quote the passage from the Ethics, followed by a summary of what the Rabbis believed was its meaning, and then add some comments about what psychoanalytic insight can offer to enlarge and deepen our understanding of its contents, mainly in terms of the art of living a good life. I will then, when reasonable and doable, provide a psychoanalytic gloss and/or correlation on the passage, to put into sharp focus how psychoanalysis can be enhanced by incorporating aspects of the Ethics into its theory and/or practice.[15] I have "cherry picked" 43 (in no order) of what seem to me to be some of the most pertinent sayings worth considering, as there are about 128 sayings in total. I have also drawn, where pertinent, from three contemporary philosophers to help unpack some of the Ethics, namely Martin Buber, Gabriel Marcel and Emmanuel Levinas.[16] I have also inserted robust footnotes that further clarify and elaborate the body of the text, which I suggest the reader peruse.

Finally, it should be stated that the Ethics was written at a time and place that is very different than our current episteme, our socio-cultural reality. Therefore, one should take great care in assuming that what the ancient sages meant in a specific Ethic has applicability to the present. As the saying goes, "the bark of a dog is different from the bark of a tree" (Bagai, 2023, p. 110).[17] This includes the fact that I can only discuss the Ethics in terms of the historical and cultural stories that I am lodged in (hopefully respectfully without brazen psychoanalytic reductionism). While the Ethics is in part a socially situated moral code suffused with the meanings of the day, I believe that, following Berkson (2010) and others, one can reasonably find/create applicability to "modern life" (p. 11). Greenberg, too, notes that the Ethics has applicability to understanding its "'life wisdom'… from the contemporary perspective, with the goal of relating it to the challenges of life in today's world" (2016, p. xii). I have thus mainly relied on six modern commentaries on the Ethics, written by scholars who are steeped in religious tradition and the classical Jewish literature: Kravitz and Olitzky (1993); Twersky (1999); Berkson (2010); Sacks and Angel (2015); Greenberg (2016); Yanklowitz (2018).[18] For the interested reader, the historical context of the Ethics is provided in the aforementioned translations (especially in Greenberg), including about the particular sage who is being quoted and what he may have said elsewhere in the Talmud.[19]

Notes

1 Lichtenstein (2018), citing other authors, notes that there is a "crisis regarding the vitality of psychoanalytic thought", namely, "that something had gone missing in mainstream psychoanalysis, something of its mythopoeic possibilities" (p. 69). It should be noted that while "psychoanalysis as a discipline is not unitary (as Freud

has hoped)" (Sprengnether, 2016, p. 309), "The hope for an integral theory has not waned" (Elliott & Prager, 2016, p. 1). Some have claimed that there is in psychoanalysis a unified plurality. And to quote the great Jewish theologian Rabbi Abraham J. Heschel, "Pluralism is the will of God" (Fackenheim, 1987, p. 29).
2 There are some soft signs that Freudian-based psychoanalysis may be having a resurgence. See Bernstein (2023).
3 In the *Future of an Illusion* (1927b), Freud writes "the riddles of the universe and of reconciling us to the sufferings of life" (p. 27).
4 While the Ethics contains much wisdom, it is not technically part of the classical Jewish wisdom literature (e.g., Proverbs, Job, Ecclesiastes and the wisdom psalms) but a tractate of the Talmud.
5 Emmanuel Levinas believed that the Talmud was the most robust source of wisdom: "We begin with the idea that inspired thinking is a thought in which everything has been thought even industrial society and modern technocracy" (1990, p. 68). Citing another author, moral philosopher Bernard Williams (1993) noted, "To make the ancients [read Rabbis] speak, we must feed them with our own blood". In other words, when the Rabbis speak they do not just tell us about themselves. "They tell us about us. They do that in every case in which they can be made to speak". They can also tell us "who we are not"—that is, "they can denounce the falsity or the partiality or the limitations of ourselves" (pp. 20–21).
6 By good life I mean, following Freud, the capacity to love deeply and widely and to engage in creative and productive work, a life that is guided by reason and ethics and is aesthetically pleasing. This being said, Freud was well aware that "'Life is not easy'!" (1933b, p. 78). By flourishing life, I mean living "within an optimal range of human flourishing, one that connotes goodness, generativity, growth and resilience" (Fredrickson & Losada, 2005, p. 678).
7 I have used Bokser's (1983, pp. 231–257) translation of the Ethics of the Fathers throughout this book.
8 Freud defined education to reality as, "Men cannot remain children for ever; they must in the end go out into 'hostile life'" (1927b, p. 49). What constitutes reality is of course perspectival, and the so-called religious reality and the psychoanalytic reality differ in many ways (see Marcus, 2021).
9 Wikipedia (2022) provides a nifty thematic breakdown of the Ethics: Show kindness to others; Respect the other person's rights; Strive for greatness; Respect God; Seek peace; Take precaution to avoid transgressions; Be humble; Be intent in prayer; Combine Torah learning with labor; Do not exploit your learning; Be careful with speech; Do not seek reward; Do not judge another person; Be fair and deliberate in legal decision; The time for action is now; Patience; The punishment matches the sin.
10 As Adam Phillips notes, Ferenczi famously said "that the patient is not cured by free association, he is cured when he can free associate" (Phillips, 2021b, p. 33).
11 Most of the discussions among Jungians "of the transference/countertransference process in analysis allude strongly to the relation between healing and love" (Stein, 1998, p. 61). Loewald (1970) noted that the "scientific detachment in its genuine form, far from excluding love is based on it. In our work it can truly be said that in our best moments of dispassionate and objective analyzing we love our object, the patient, more than at any other time and are compassionate with his whole being" (p. 297). Other analysts, like Erich Fromm (1956) have made similar assertions.
12 Leo Strauss, the twentieth-century German Jewish scholar, is often credited with distinguishing the metaphors of Athens and Jerusalem (Smith, 2007).
13 Technically, there is no art of living but different arts of living depending on the historical situation one resides in. That is, what constitutes the art of living varies and is context-dependent and setting-specific.

14 Erich Fromm (1947) was probably the first psychoanalyst to use the concept of art of living, in his discussion of humanistic ethics, though Freud used the term "technique in the art of living" in *Civilization and its Discontents* (1930, p. 81). See also Hadot (1995), Nehamas (1998) and Ruti (2009). For example, Ruti says the following about the analysand living the good life: "To the extent that we hope to live our lives that allow us to actualize the nuances of our being, that feel dynamic and multidimensional, that contain flashes of inspiration and imaginative insight, and that are characterized by a level of psychic resourcefulness, the notion of living our lives as poetry can add tone and density to our existence. Furthermore, the idea that we can play with our identities can be a source of considerable pleasure" (Ruti, 2009, p. 25).
15 Sometimes the order of focus is reversed depending on the saying being considered; for example, the first saying.
16 Martin Buber (1878–1965) was a famous twentieth-century philosopher, religious thinker, political activist and educator. Austrian born, he lived most of his life in Germany and Israel, publishing in German and Hebrew. He is best known for his book *Ich und Du* (I and Thou), which differentiates between "I-Thou" and "I-It" modes of existence. Gabriel Marcel (1889–1973) was a prominent French philosopher, dramatist and critic who was associated with the phenomenological and existentialist movements in twentieth-century European philosophy and whose work and style are often described as Christian existentialism (Marcel preferred "neo-Socratic" because it suggested the dialogical, searching and sometimes inchoate character of his reflections). His main book was the two-volume *Mystery of Being* (the Gifford lectures). Both philosophers had their heyday when they were alive and have influenced many subsequent famous philosophers and others, such as Emmanuel Levinas and Paul Ricoeur. While Buber is better known, Marcel has recently been described as a "sorely neglected philosopher" (Treanor, 2006, p. 258). Emmanuel Levinas (1906–1995) was a French philosopher of Lithuanian Jewish lineage who is known for his work within phenomenology, existentialism and Jewish philosophy, concentrating on the relationship of ethics to metaphysics and ontology. He has influenced Derrida, Sartre and Ricoeur among other well-known scholars. His most famous books are *Totality and Infinity: An Essay on Exteriority* and *Otherwise than Being or Beyond Essence*. There has recently been an avalanche of scholarly work on Levinas.
17 Sacks (2023c) describes what he calls the "fallacy of translatability"—that is, the supposition that one language is completely translatable into another. Languages are only partly translatable into one another. "The key terms of one civilization are often not fully reproducible in another" (p. 1).
18 There have been literally hundreds of commentaries and editions on the Ethics (Greenberg, 2016).
19 These sixty-six Rabbis are viewed as role models of the good life by contemporary readers. Rabbis is capitalized to refer to these illustrious ancient sages.

Chapter 2

The Ethics of the Fathers

I will begin with the Ethic that I regard as being foundational.

1. Moral outlook

(1–2).[1] Simeon the Just [a Jewish High Priest during the Second Temple period] was of the last survivors of the Great Assembly.[2] He used to say: The world rests on three foundations: the Torah; the divine service; and the practice of lovingkindness between man and man [read: human to human].
(Bokser, 1983, p. 231)

In a certain sense, this passage summarizes in a nutshell the religious Jew's moral outlook (and by extension, to some extent, other "believers" from various religions). First, the emphasis on the Torah (teaching, direction, guidance, law, the commandments and behaviors it demands), the five books of Moses, Genesis, Exodus, Leviticus, Numbers and Deuteronomy traditionally viewed as written by Moses, and all the commentaries on the Hebrew Bible contained in the Talmud and elsewhere. For the religious Jew, Torah contains everything one needs to live a good or holy life, the latter being the superordinate goal of Jewish practice as it is in most other great religious traditions and spiritualities. According to Sacks (2023a), "The holy is where God is experienced as absolute Presence.... To enter holy space or time requires ontological humility, the total renunciation of human initiative and desire" (p. 2). Moreover, says Sacks, holiness can be achieved when one "acts like God" (2023c, p. 1). That is, the religious Jew's obligation is to engage in a life of divine service, of which lovingkindness between persons constitutes its main thrust. By lovingkindness is meant gentleness and consideration of others, and it can manifest itself in both big and small ways; for example, in smiling at a down-and-out stranger to helping a friend get a job so he no longer has to depend on charity.[3] What starts off as a moral obligation ends up being a heartfelt desire (Phillips & Taylor, 2009). As Soviet author and journalist Vasily Grossman noted, "This kindness, this stupid kindness, is what is most truly human in a human being" (Grossman, 2023, p. 17).

DOI: 10.4324/9781003453734-2

Psychoanalysis as I conceive it can be enhanced as a narrative of self-identity by better appreciating how the believer construes his reality (e.g., without pronounced reductionism), especially how spirit informs his everyday life. The idea of psychoanalysis as a spiritual discipline is not as far-fetched as some may think (Marcus, 2021). Indeed, it was Ludwig Binswanger who famously pointed out to Freud that a therapeutic failure they were conversing about could "only be understood as the result of something which could be called a deficiency of spirit" (1963, p. 1). Binswanger was surprised when Freud agreed, asserting, "Yes, spirit is everything" (ibid.). Freud further elaborated, "Man has always known he possessed spirit: I had to show him there is such a thing as instinct" (ibid.).[4] Neville Symington, a member of the Middle Group of the British psychoanalysts and an ex-Catholic priest, noted that psychoanalysis was "a mature natural religion" (accessible to reason without drawing from revelation)[5] and a "spiritual method relevant to the modern world" (1994, pp. 192, 137). Moreover, as Symington notes, "moral development through the course of a person's life is only possible through the stewardship of a dedicated spirituality" (ibid., p. 47).[6] Following in the tradition of the great sages and religious leaders of the Axial period (Marcus, 2019; Symington, 2012), Symington believes that it is unbridled narcissism that is the main psychopathology animating all others, mirroring Christopher Lasch (1991) and other social critics. While one can certainly question the veracity of Symington's claims, he does put into sharp focus the fact that psychoanalysis can be reasonably conceptualized as a spiritual/moral venture—that is, it is concerned with "right" (e.g., "healthy", "adaptive", "normal") and "wrong" (e.g., "unhealthy", "maladaptive" and "abnormal") behavior and the "goodness" (e.g., other-directed, other-regarding, other-serving) and "badness" (e.g., inordinate narcissism, self-centricity and selfishness) of character. Admittedly, these are intellectually, emotionally and situationally lodged value judgments based on knowledge and critical discrimination made by the analyst and analysand. This being said, all analysts maintain that the psychoanalyst must be ever mindful of not becoming moralistic—that is, making reflexive, pre-fabricated judgments about an analysand's morality (i.e., "superego moralism" (Wallwork, 1991)). Of course, reasonably distinguishing in a particular clinical context what constitutes psychoanalysis operating as a spiritual/moral venture versus a moralizing one, let alone distinguishing what instantiates these differences in the subtle registers of thinking, feeling and acting, is a hugely difficult value judgment to make. While psychoanalysis shuns moralizing, psychoanalyst Adam Phillips approvingly quotes Nina Coltart, who said that it "may be defined as a moral activity",[7] one in which symptoms are "disabling painful moral puzzles" (1994, pp. 138, 139).[8] For example, in psychoanalytic theory, truth-telling is at best undertheorized and at worst has no means of effectively making a distinction between acts which are true and false to the self or sincere and insincere (especially if an analysand's "yes" can mean "no" and "no" can mean "yes", and "yes" may not mean this specific "yes" (Forester, 2000, p. 318)), even though psychoanalytic practice largely depends on the analyst being able to do so (Rycroft, 1995, p. 10).[9] In other words, how can you discern a real change from a false one? (Phillips, 2021c). Thus, it is the analysand who ultimately determines what is true and sincere, just as it is the analysand who decides what kind of person to become (e.g., what constitutes a good life).

Returning to the question of what psychoanalysis can further clarify in the aforementioned passage from the Ethics. As Sacks and Angel point out in their commentary on the Ethics, Torah personifies an individual's efforts at self-perfection (perhaps more accurately, betterment).[10] It involves study, introspection and a commitment to educate and train oneself in the paths of righteousness. Divine worship personifies a person's desire for a connection to God—that is, it is through worship that one views life in terms of the Godly, "one transcends the limited and limiting boundaries of the mundane". Likewise, deeds of lovingkindness personify a person's relationship with fellow human beings. "The goal of life is not to be a recluse, but to participate generously in the well-being of others" (Sacks & Angel, 2015, p. 4). Sacks and Angel continue,

> Just as the world rests on spiritual foundations, so each individual's integrity depends on commitment to Torah (self-perfection through thought and study), divine worship (spiritual strivings), and acts of lovingkindness (authentic relationships with all human beings).
>
> (Ibid., p. 7)

The Ethics has as one of its main goals the quest for the most robust foundation "for harmony and cooperation" among our fellow human beings (Berkson, 2010, p. 18). This is easier said than done, for the typical person has many conscious and unconscious forces that propel him to self-referentially, selfishness and the like. Such a narcissistic commitment to self-interest often flies in the face of collective harmony and cooperation. Indeed, one of the shortcomings of the Ethics is that it assumes that most people are, for the most part, guided by consciously held rational or reasonable considerations. As Bokser points out, "Rabbinic Judaism also emphasized the importance of the conscious expression of human will" (1989, p. 8). However, what psychoanalysis has brought to consciousness is that, for the most part, people are unconscious about what goes into their decision-making (especially moral decision-making). Moreover, there are many context-dependent and setting-specific considerations, often not in awareness, that move against a person's efforts at living in the spirit of collective harmony and cooperation. Put straightforwardly, the typical individual is animated by irrational, unreasonable and often infantile ways of feeling, thinking and acting that the Ethics gives little attention to. As Freud wrote in *Civilization and its Discontents*, "the inclination to aggression is an original, self-subsisting instinctual disposition in man ... that it constitutes the greatest impediment to civilization" (1930, p. 122). This is not to say that the Rabbis were not aware of the darker forces at work in the human soul, the *yetzer ha-ra* (the evil urge) for example, but the emphasis is on promoting consciously rational and reasonable thought, which the Rabbis of the Ethics believe will quite likely lead to moral behavior, behavior that is guided by lovingkindness and other ethical considerations. As Yanklowitz (2018) points out in his commentary on the Ethics,

> Judaism requires the development of one's intellectual capacity through Torah study, emotional capacity through cultivating the service of God, and performative capacity through kind deeds. These constitute the cognitive, affective and behavioral aspects of one's whole being; indeed, Torah asks for the *whole self*.
>
> (pp. 7–8)[11]

Thus, what psychoanalysis puts into sharp focus are the many ways that an individual puts his own self-interest before that of others, often unconsciously, which opposes his more wholesome altruistic tendencies such as acts of lovingkindness. In a word, playing off Freud's famous comment regarding the goals of psychoanalysis, "where id was, there ego shall be", we can say, for the holy Jew (and ideally any religious believer), where narcissism was, there altruism shall be. In this context, altruism can be thought of in terms of the psychoanalytic definition of "generative altruism"—that is, the non-conflictual gratification in promoting the accomplishments and successes of other people (Selig & Rosof, 2001; Akhtar, 2009).[12] As Akhtar points out, drawing from Selig and Rosof (2001), this altruism is different than the other four categories of altruism: (1) Proto-altruism, which is mainly biological and instinctive, "is 'hardwired' in the human brain and contributes to the ordinary maternal protectiveness towards her infant", though such an attitude has other determinants too. (2) Conflicted altruism, which includes Anna Freud's notion of "altruistic surrender" (e.g., neurotically sacrificing one's own development for the advancement of another), in addition to generative altruism, which has become linked to emotional conflict. (3) Pseudo-altruism, which includes pleasureless compulsive generosity that acts as a defense for unconscious sadomasochism. (4) Finally, there is psychotic altruism, where delusionally motivated self-sacrifice for others' best interests and messianic acts of saving the world comprise the clinical presentation (Akhtar, 2009, pp. 11–12). Thus, generative altruism, "the nonconflictual pleasure in fostering the success and/or welfare of another", is probably the kind of altruism that the Ethics is pointing to (Selig & Rosof, 2001, p. 933). As Selig and Rosof note, all forms of altruism include a relationship with a significant other and are a complex amalgamation of direct satisfaction and tension reduction emanating from both internal and external sources. That is, "mature altruism like mature love requires mature, integrated object relationships and is [not] interfered with by superego [roughly the conscience] pathology" (ibid., p. 955).[13] It is also worth remembering that satisfaction of altruistic urges requires a response from the other person. However, sometimes a fantasized response can be adequate. For instance, when a person donates charity to a worthwhile cause, he or she may envision a response that is satisfying: "This response is not necessarily an expression of gratitude for the gift. Often the inner certainty of having facilitated the accomplishment of some good for others is what is sought" (ibid.). Adams Phillips has put the matter succinctly: "The only thing worth doing, ultimately, is being kind to each other" (Phillips, 2021b, p. 104; Phillips & Taylor, 2009).

2. Wisdom

> (I–6). Joshua ben Perahya [president of the Sanhedrin in the latter half of the second century BCE] and Nittai the Arbelite [vice-president of the Sanhedrin] received the tradition from them. Joshua ben Perahya said: Get yourself a teacher [a rabbi];[14] and acquire for yourself a companion; and judge all people favorably.
>
> (Bokser, 1983, p. 232)

This saying speaks to aspects of living that dovetail with the psychoanalytic oeuvre. First, to increase your wisdom, it is essential to find a teacher, often one teacher, someone who knows more than you do, to learn from. In the case of psychoanalysis, the teacher is the analyst, the person who has by dint of his training and experience (e.g., the analyst has allegedly "faced himself"; the analysand hasn't) knows more than you do and is better able to view your behavior from a more impartial point of view.[15] Paraphrasing Jesus, it is easier to see the spec in another person's eye than your own. As Greenberg points out in his commentary on the Ethics, "Rather than drift from teacher to teacher, find a primary teacher who can serve as an authority and consistent source of wisdom for you" (2016, p. 26). The ideal teacher promotes the student's independence and autonomy, the same goal as in a successful analysis. What constitutes a great teacher is hardly an easy question to answer.[16]

This being said, when it comes to choosing an analyst, Freud, Jung, Bion and Winnicott have given us some intriguing leads. For example, it is well known that the five empirically researched essential elements of psychotherapeutic support—presence, holding, caring, challenging and confirming—are what matter most in terms of engaged interaction between analyst and analysand (Heery & Bugental, 2005, p. 257). As Freud noted, "What turns the scale is not intellectual insight, but the relationship to the doctor" (1916–17, p. 445), while Jung claimed, "Every psychotherapist not only has his own method—he himself is that method ... The great healing factor in psychotherapy is the doctor's personality ... theories are to be avoided, except as mere auxiliaries" (Jung, 1966, p. 88). Bion quipped, "I would [rely on theory only] ... if I were tired and had no idea what was going on … the analyst you become is you and you alone—that is what you use" (Ogden, 2016, pp. 109, 111). Finally, Winnicott noted, "It is not what the analyst says that matters, it is how the analyst behaves" (Phillips, 2021b, p. 54). Thus, the analyst's "personal psychology", his beliefs and values etcetera, is deeply implicated in all aspects of his clinical engagement (Renik, 1993, p. 553). The personal and the technical are inextricably linked (Kuchuck, 2021). This can be problematic when we consider the fact that Jacques Lacan, "arguably the most original and influential psychoanalyst since Freud", was also an "arrogant, narcissistic, and deeply divisive figure", according to Lacan's biographer (Homer, 2016, p. 97).[17] The "trick" is to intuitively choose someone you feel comfortable with, someone you "click" with, so you can effectively work together over the long stretch of time. Research findings suggest this is what matters most in terms of a successful outcome of treatment.

As for the recommendation "acquire for yourself a companion", this is another way of recommending that one find a good friend (Olyan, 2017). Actually, the traditional meaning of this recommendation is that one should find a good study partner (who is, or becomes, a good friend). The sages believed strongly "that peers are a critical ingredient in true education. The concept here is that the goal of learning is not a matter of just memorizing facts, but also of observing a tradition and learning a way of thinking" (Berkson, 2010, p. 26).[18] As the Buddha said, "What we think we become". Such a form of education which ideally shapes the student into "a master of tradition" involves having not just a master of tradition who guides you but many apprentices that intellectually and emotionally interact with one another and enhance you (ibid.). While friendship is an incredibly complex subject, what the Rabbis are putting forth is a certain version of friendship, what can be called "biblical friendship", something which psychoanalysis hardly thinks about. Biblical friendship involves not just trying to potentiate a friend's highest good, but as Levinas noted, putting the friend's best interests before one's own (or at least as much as one's own). As Sacks and Angel note,

> Friendship is achieved when one invests time, effort, and kindness in another person. Friendship is the result of mutual understanding and respect. It does not simply happen of itself: one must acquire a friend through loyalty and ongoing empathy. A friend is important not merely to provide sociability or other utilitarian functions. Rather, a friend is primarily important as a fellow human being with whom to share the adventure of life. A friend is important not merely for what he/she can do, but for who he/she is. Until one learns the value of friendship, one lacks a fundamental ingredient in understanding life.
>
> (2015, p. 10)

The Rabbis appear to have in mind the aforementioned generative altruism, a manifestation of so-called mature altruism. While Sacks and Angel do not emphasize the other-directed, other-regarding and other-serving aspects of friendship, probably the two greatest contemporary Jewish theoreticians on interpersonal relationships, Martin Buber and Emmanuel Levinas (both steeped in the Bible), believed that responsibility toward the other before oneself (or at least as much as oneself) is the essential ingredient of friendships and, for that matter, all significant relationships at their best. For Levinas, such a relational ethic is serviceable (i.e., moral principles) with becoming "good" (i.e., responsible for the other). The latter way of being-in-the-world, responsible subjectivity, points to transcendence. As Levinas pointed out, the love commandment, which Freud also extensively commented on ("Thou shalt love thy neighbor as thyself"), "still assumes the prototype of love to be love of oneself"—that is, "self-love is accepted as the very definition of the person". However, Levinas's conception of the ethical subject also asserts, "Be responsible for the other as you are responsible for yourself" (Levinas, 1987, p. 225). Biblical friendship, the kind of friendship that the Ethics puts forth at its best, is characterized by a Levinasian gloss.

It was the psychoanalyst Leo Rangell who discussed friendship the most in depth. While I will not review in detail his fifty-one-paged paper (1963), the gist of it is important as it applies to the Ethic's notion of friendship. According to Rangell, "friendship is a deep, kind, enduring affection founded on mutual respect and esteem. Friendship is always mutual" (p. 11) (Levinas would disagree, asserting that friendship is ideally asymmetrical). Moreover, Rangell distinguishes the categories of friendly, friend and friendship:

> Friendly: propitious; favorable. Does not reach the significance of the noun's "friend" and "friendship". One may be friendly to those who are not his friends. To be in friendly relations often signifies little more than not to be hostile.
>
> Friend: One attached to another by extreme respect and non-erotic affection.
>
> Friendliness is the quality of friendly feeling without the deep and settled attachment implied in the state of friendship. Affection may be purely natural; friendship is a growth. Friendship is more intellectual and less emotional than love. Friendship is more calm and quiet, love more fervent, often rising to intensest passion. Friendship implies some degree of equality, while love does not.
>
> (Ibid.)

As Akhtar noted, Rangell generated a developmental line (roughly a developmental theory that emphasizes the continuous and cumulative quality of childhood development) for friendship and details the epigenetic progression of such relationships, from early childhood, adolescence to adulthood. Says Akhtar:

He [Rangell] also tackled the tricky matter of man-woman friendships, suggesting three possible dynamics underlying them (1) aim-inhibited heterosexual love, (2) 'aim-inhibited homosexual interest or link, deriving from the bisexuality of each' [Akhtar is quoting from Rangell] ... (3) continuation of aim-inhibited and desexualized love of a mother sister prototype.

(Akhtar, 2009, p. 116)

Quoting Freud, what Akhtar is putting into sharp focus is that "friendship or friendliness [regardless of the sex of the people] is aim-inhibited sexuality or aim-inhibited love" (ibid.). That is, by aim-inhibited is meant that the person has no conscious erotic desire in relation to the object (i.e., the other person), such as in friendships or affectionate relations toward cousins. As Rycroft further points out, "the concept assumes that, in the absence of inhibition, friendships would be overt homosexual relationships, platonic love would be consummated and incest would occur" (1995, pp. 5–6). While this Freudian glossed theory is debatable, drawing from Melanie Klein, Akhtar alleges that it does suggest that unconscious homosexual tendencies may motivate the main thrust of friendships though affection and sex are disconnected ("de-linkage"). Moreover, in childhood, homosexual affectionate linkage can act as a defensive regime against heterosexual anxieties. In other contexts, the affection that people feel in friendships may be a way of defending against their mutually unconsciously felt aggression. In fact, aggression and envy need to be clarified and reckoned with in most relationships. Still, in other contexts, says Akhtar, the role models of mother-daughter, father-son and relations with siblings (real or imagined) motivate the trajectory of friendships (Akhtar, 2009, p. 116). Thus, it is for these possible psychoanalytic reasons that people differ in their willingness and ability to have friendships, and the aforementioned reasons suggest why this may be the case. The Ethics can be enhanced by considering the huge psychological complexity and difficulty of friendship-making from a psychoanalytic point of view. As William James noted, "A man's relationship to his friends is a sphere where important aspects of his personality are revealed" (Rangell, 1963, p. 41).[19]

The Ethics concludes in this saying with the recommendation "to judge all people favorably".[20] Another way of translating this recommendation is to "be one who judges everyone by giving them the benefit of the doubt" (Greenberg, 2016, p. 25). What the Rabbis are getting at has been summarized by Yanklowitz, who quotes S'forno, an Italian rabbi who lived in the sixteenth century:

We are to judge everyone favorably because without this trait friendship will not endure. For the majority of statements, the listener can judge a speaker in a negative light. And this [attitude] will unquestionably annul all friendships.

(2018, p. 25)

The idea here is that one is better off accepting someone in terms of their presentation to you as if they are honest and worthy of trust even if there are questions about the person's integrity. It is true that the person may be hoodwinking you, but in general one is better off embracing what the person is positively saying in the present, at least to the degree that one is not hurt in the process (nor is someone else). As Sacks and Angel note, "this advice is appropriate in most situations, it need not be applied to people who are known to be hypocritical, dishonest, or violent" (2015, p. 13). It should be noted that the Rabbis believed that if one judges others by giving them the benefit of the doubt, God and others will judge you similarly. Likewise, it is a well-known empirical fact that in general people who give others the benefit of the doubt tend to be more content and happier compared to those who are prone to blame others or not trust them. People who only occasionally give others the benefit of the doubt are also more content and happier, providing they assign considerable psychological significance to the relationship. As Greenberg points out, the benefit of "giving people the benefit of the doubt creates an atmosphere of trust and safety. This encourages more honesty and openness, and more adventurous exploration, as people know they will not be put down or scorned for entertaining new possibilities" (Greenberg, 2016, p. 26).

What psychoanalysis focuses on in terms of giving people the benefit of the doubt is how difficult it actually is to implement. This is mainly because such advice goes against the existential mistrust and systematic doubt which is so much part of everyday life (and psychoanalysis tends to promote)—that is, the tendency to view others suspiciously as motivated by unsavory wishes. This is, in part, because we are all prone to distrust of others who are not the same as us (which is everyone technically speaking), and in other instances we have difficulty giving ourselves the benefit of the doubt. That is, we are not easily self-forgiving of our shortcomings (there are exceptions of course). In fact, perhaps the main issue pertaining to being critical of others is that one is self-critical. This is where the vicious cycle begins. That is, if one can become more kind to oneself and less demanding and critical, then one will have less high expectations of others and hence be less critical of them. This enhanced tolerance of others' deficiencies will have a ripple effect, leading to an increasingly benign self-concept.

Indeed, as the well-known saying goes, there is no love without forgiveness and no forgiveness without love. Forgiveness, the pardoning of the other's misdeeds when one feels mistreated, expresses the renewal of hope that is essential to any workable love relation. In a love relation, we all periodically feel hard done by—that is, narcissistically assaulted, or at least disrespected in terms of what we think we should be getting from our significant other—greater care, more accurate empathy, willingness to sacrifice and the like. Such narcissistic assaults tend to foster micro-dosed resentment, anger, revenge and other forms of aggression that are common in intimate relationships in some form. However, the capacity to forgive, the compassionate reconfiguration of thought and feeling about the other that forgiveness requires, generates a new moral context for the interpretation of the other's perceived hurtful behavior. When the aggrieved person chooses to give up his resentment, even hatred of the perpetrator for his misdeed, it signifies that he is, in effect, willing to deal with the pain that underlies the narcissistic rage evoked by his significant other's misdeed. Forgiveness increases one's range of alternatives just as it enhances one's freedom to grow and develop. It is the basis for the healing process that needs to occur to keep a love relation from disintegrating as a result of our all too human capacity to be destructive to our loved other. As Voltaire said, "every man is guilty of all the good he didn't do" (Klosterman, 2006, p. 263). Moreover, researchers have found that "forgiveness can be a boon to mental health, helping to do things like lower stress and improve sleep" (Pearson, 2023, p. D7).

Put succinctly, if you have a harsh superego, you are more likely to be critical of others and for sure more critical of yourself. Thus, from a psychoanalytic point of view, giving people the benefit of the doubt requires accurate empathy, the capacity to put oneself in the other's shoes. It also requires a compassionate moment ("to suffer with"). By compassion, I mean five aspects: recognizing suffering, comprehending the universality of human suffering, empathizing, enduring distressing feelings, and having the will and ability to alleviate the suffering (Strauss et. al., 2016).[21] One final aspect of giving people the benefit of the doubt is that it requires a generosity of spirit and benevolence to self. By generosity of spirit, I mean to behave with kindness and compassion, to be ready and willing to share with others without expecting them to return what you gave in kind. Such a capacity assumes that there has been a downward modification of narcissism to make "space" as it were to give with the fullness of one's whole being to the other.

3. Work

> (I–10). Shemaya and Abtalyon [two Rabbis whose parents were probably converts, of the early pre-Mishnaic period] received the tradition from them. Shemaya said: love work; hate domineering over others; and do not seek the intimacy of public officials.
>
> (Bokser, 1983, p. 233)

Yanklowitz summarizes the meaning of the phrase "love work":

> The goal of Jewish life is *not* to find nirvana in solitude [as some Buddhists tend to do, monastic seclusion], nor is it to return to recreational pursuits. No, the essential elements for a good life include working to support family and community, performing physical labor, and making contributions to society. By being productive, we contribute to society, grow in character, and support our communities. While we should make

the most of our professional lives, we should do so neither from avarice nor from the lust for power.

(2018, p. 34)

Freud famously told Erikson that "love and work" were the central therapeutic goals of psychoanalysis, the twin pillars of a sound mind for living a good life (Erikson, 1959, p. 96).[22] In fact, Freud opined on the meaning of work in his life: "A man like me cannot live without a hobby-horse, without a consuming passion, without—in Schiller's words—a tyrant. I have found one ['working well, writing well']. In its service I know no limits" (1895, p. 129). What is true about finding a satisfying life partner is also true about choosing a satisfying career. As Freud famously said, "all love is a re-finding": it tends to replicate emotional aspects of infantile templates, those impacting early experiences of satisfaction and frustration between parents and children. Psychoanalytic theory assumes that a person's choice of career is based on conscious and, most importantly, unconscious factors, and this is one of the reasons that choosing a suitable career and flourishing in it is so difficult.

The gist of the psychoanalytic perspective on career choice has been aptly summarized by Malach-Pines and Yafe-Yanai:

> Childhood experiences (both positive and negative) and familial heritage have a major influence on vocational choices. People choose an occupation that enables them to replicate significant childhood experiences, satisfy needs that were unfulfilled in their childhood, and actualize dreams passed on to them by their familial heritage.
>
> (2001, p. 171)

What the aforementioned means is that the chances of loving your work in part depends on what you have internalized from your parents in childhood. To love work it usually must be experienced as a "calling".

The capacity to love work begins with taking heed of Freud's wise counsel that when it comes to deciding on a career direction, one should be guided by the "deep inner needs of our nature" (i.e., the unconscious) (Reik, 1983, p. vii). As Freud noted, "But she [Nature] endowed me with a dauntless love of truth, the keen eye of an investigator, a rightful sense of the values of life, and the gift of working hard and finding pleasure in doing so" (Jones, 1953–1957, p. 118). Drawing from the vocational and organizational psychology literatures, a very useful way of applying Freud's advice is to conceive of choosing a career direction in terms of a "calling", as opposed to a "job" or "career". As sociologists Bellah and colleagues (1986) first pointed out in their bestselling book, *Habits of the Heart: Individualism and Commitment in American Life*, a person with a "job" orientation to work is geared toward earning a living for him and his family to prosper and to maximize their amount of leisure time. In other words, work is viewed strictly as a practical means to a financial end. Moreover, his sense of self is mainly defined by financial success, security "and all that money can buy" (p. 66). A "career" is a way to advance oneself in terms of accomplishment, status and prestige. Such people mainly work in order to move up the hierarchical ladder, to be promoted, a competitive process they very much enjoy. The sense of self that is associated with a career is characterized by a broader kind of success than a job, in that by attaining a degree of expanding power and competency, work itself becomes a way of sustaining self-esteem (ibid.). Individuals who have a "job" and "career" orientation toward work tend to have personal identities that do not significantly overlap with the actual work they do; to a large extent, they view what they do at work as distinct from the rest of their life (Berg, Grant, & Johnson, 2010, p. 974). They narrate their lives in terms of having a "work self" and a "non-work self", and rarely do they feel they are a "whole" or "complete self".

In contrast, a "calling" is a work orientation in which a person views their work as deeply satisfying and socially beneficial. That is, an individual chooses an occupation that he "feels drawn to pursue", often powerfully. He anticipates it to be "intrinsically enjoyable and meaningful", especially as a socially useful endeavor, and he views it "as a central part of his identity" (ibid., p. 973). As Bellah and colleagues noted, such work "constitutes a practical ideal of activity and character that makes a person's work morally inseparable from his or her life", and it links the person not only more intensely to his co-workers but to the larger community (ibid.).

Freud further elaborated the benefits of work:

> [N]o other technique for the conduct of life attaches the individual so firmly to reality as laying emphasis on work; for his work at least gives him a secure place in a portion of reality, in the human community.
> (1930, p. 80)

What Freud is getting at appears to be straightforward. Psychoanalytically, work has some of the following benefits to the individual. As Akhtar points out, work is not the same thing as maintaining a job, or earning money, though it may include them; it requires physical or mental activity designed to bring about a preferred outcome; it tends to bring about "narcissistic, object related, sexualized, and aggressive pleasure but these are secondary, since work has its own rewards for the ego", such as work being pleasurable for its own sake and a context for forgetting oneself (Phillips, 2021b); work helps regulate self-esteem and contributes to identity maintenance; "it follows a developmental line from infancy to old age with the phases of latency and young adulthood being the most important to its consolidation" (Akhtar, 2009, p. 308).

The phrase "hate domineering over others" encompasses some wise advice, for it speaks to both the one who dominates and the one who is dominated. The assumption here is that there is something pleasurable about domination in whatever form it takes. Domination assumes a particular kind of object relationship, and the Rabbis were repudiating this outlook and behavior in a similar way as psychoanalysis does. We should not dominate others—that is, exert toxic control or influence over someone or allow ourselves to be similarly controlled. That is, the Ethics is against all forms of "sadomasochism" as a way of being-in-the-world. By sadomasochism, I mean the form it often takes in everyday life, an alternating, see-saw, master-slave dynamic in which the protagonists exchange positions. Sadomasochism is not only seen in the bedroom,[23] but it can be enacted in everyday life with, say, a boss. Domination, in other words, is fundamentally a kind of social power, power over others, and this is best rejected as a way of being in everyday life (McCammon, 2018). But how does one hate domination?

The answer is to create a subjectivity that is respectful and humble when interacting with people in everyday contexts, at least generally speaking. It is the opposite of the so-called domineering personality. A domineering personality is typically driven by thoughts of winning over others, by competition and by reaching desired outcomes. They can also become obstinate, aggressive and overly direct in their dealing with others. Psychoanalysis is mindful of the difference between people who are commanding, confident and assertive and those who are dominating— admittedly a difficult clinical distinction to make. Perhaps the main difference is that the domineering personality takes pleasure in subjugating the other, a kind of sexual satisfaction even though it is not in the bedroom.

The phrase "do not seek the intimacy of public officials" puts into sharp focus the shabby side of political engagement. That is, there are those people who "fawn over those in power", gaining the reflective glory of being a satellite in their orbit (Sacks & Angel, 2015, p. 16). Politicians are notoriously self-centered and narcissistic and fair-weather friends, if not corrupt, and one is safest when one keeps a low profile in relationship to them, at least in certain circumstances. Such a way of being can be conceptualized as the masochistic side of the "don't dominate others" approach in that you are putting yourself in a position to be dominated, albeit with the hope of reflected power. Thus, this phrase of the Ethics is covertly emphasizing the developed capacity for autonomy, integration and humanity.

The Rabbis bunch these three phrases, "love work; hate domineering over others; and do not seek the intimacy of public officials", perhaps in part to underscore a desired form of self. That is, to love work is ego driven at best (it is not egotistical but lodged in reasonable thought and behavior). Hating domination suggests the possibility of transforming domination into assertive behavior without hurting anyone. It is against the quest for raw power, which is sexually and aggressively desired. Likewise, do not seek intimacy of public officials suggests that one should not need and want the reflected glory of intermingling with the institutionally powerful nor the demeaning of the self of the sycophant. Self-esteem and self-respect, rooted in a positive self-concept, can be best maintained by internalizing these three notions.

4. Self-interest

> (I–14). He [Hillel] also said: If I am not for myself who will be? But if I am for myself only, what am I? And if not now, when?
>
> (Bokser, 1983, p. 233)

This is one of the most famous sayings from the Ethics, emanating from the great biblical commentator Hillel.[24] The opening phrase "if I am not for myself who will be?" speaks to the fact that there are occasions where one should put self-interest above other considerations, such as the well-being of one's family and friends compared to strangers. Likewise, depending on others can be a questionable undertaking, at least in certain situations, such as people not coming through for you. To be willing and able to accomplish this psychic aim of looking out for one's self-interest requires a robust, "healthy" narcissism. According to Kohut (1971), the qualities of a robust, healthy narcissism are comprised of the capacity to embrace the admiration of others, a secure sense of self-esteem, self-worth and self-respect, and a wholesome sense of pride in oneself and one's achievements. From a psychoanalytic point of view then, Hillel's saying speaks to the need for a positive self and self-confidence.

Indeed, healthy narcissism means the reasonable capacity for assertive behavior and self-esteem maintenance not only without harming another but actually promoting the other's well-being. That is, Hillel is embracing what Buber, Marcel and Levinas put forth as the holy person: responsible subjectivity, being-for-the-other before oneself (or at least as much as oneself). As Levinas noted, "responsibility is the essential, primary and fundamental structure of subjectivity.... Ethics, here, does not supplement a preceding existential base; the very node of the subjective is knotted in ethics understood as responsibility" (Levinas, 1985, p. 95). The self, liberated of its self-enslavement, free to be responsible for the other, this is what Levinas means by "original goodness" (Freyer, 2004, p. 69).

Thus, "But if I am for myself only, what am I" speaks to considering other people's needs and desires when making decisions. That is, merely looking out only for oneself reflects self-centricity if it is not balanced by concern for the other. Sacks and Angel point out that

> a healthy well-balanced personality seeks to blend self-respect and respect for others. It is praiseworthy—not shameful—to stand up for one's self-interest.... Those lacking in self-respect can hardly depend on others to respect them and defend their interests.
>
> (2015, p. 20)

"And if not now, when?" speaks to the fact that a person must be willing and able to act in the here and now, in the present, and not procrastinate or put off making important decisions and engaging in assertive action. This requires a degree of situational awareness, knowing where you are and what is going on around you—that is, contouring one's decisions and actions in a manner that skillfully reflects their context-dependent and setting-specific character.

In summary, as Berkson notes, today, Hillel's well-known three questions are most often interpreted in a succinctly rhetorical manner, "meaning: look out for yourself and stick up for yourself, or no one else will; if you are only concerned for your own selfish interests, you are unworthy; and now is the time to act" (2010, p. 41). "Self-interest, yes; self-centeredness, no" (Greenberg, 2016, p. 46). It is not thinking less of yourself; it's thinking of yourself less. It's not becoming a shrinking violet and disappearing; it's about showing up by knowing how much space you should rightfully take up.

5. Hearing and listening

> (I–17). Simeon his son said: All my life I was raised among scholars and I found that no virtue becomes a man more than silence; what is more essential is not study but practice; and in the wake of many words is sin.
> (Bokser, 1983, p. 233)

Where psychoanalysis tends to view silence in the consultation room as a form of resistance to the analysis, the Ethics is suggesting just the opposite; namely, that silence can be, and maybe should be, mainly viewed as a unique form of listening (to the other and/or to one's inner voice). While silence can have many meanings, the Rabbis are suggesting that it can be an expression of a surety and self-confidence in which saying nothing is the right thing to do. In the rabbinic imagination, God is to be found in the "still small voice", the silence that envelops us. The *Shma*, the Jews most important prayer, is all about hearing and listening not talking. That is, "revelation is not a visible phenomenon of forms and images but about auditory experience" (Rotenstreich, 1968, p. 200). As the rabbis taught, we have two ears, one mouth because we're supposed to listen twice as much as we speak.

Indeed, because in psychoanalysis there is the notion of psychological multiple determination, silence can have a variety of functions/meanings, and there is no certain way of determining the function/meaning of the particular silence enacted by the particular analysand at a particular point in time in the analytic dialogue. What is therefore required of the analyst is greater empathy and attunement to the context-dependent, setting-specific function/meaning of the analysand's silence, and even then, this is an educated guess that can only be confirmed or disconfirmed by how the analysand views what the analyst says. As the meaning of all language is processive, emergent and situational, a methodology of checking out what was said and heard between the analysand and analyst becomes the bedrock of bringing a degree of clearance, clarification and intelligibility to their dialogue. This includes the analyst's "listening with the third ear", Theodore Reik's 1948 title of his book, in which, says Bruna Martinuzzi, the analyst "listens for the deeper layers of meaning in order to glean what has not been said outright. It means perceiving the emotional underpinnings conveyed when someone is speaking to you" (2013).

What are some of the positive aspects of silence from a psychoanalytic point of view? First, silence can be a kind of communication, as in "his silence was deafening". Silence can "restock" the ego by allowing quiet, preconscious amalgamation of subclinical conflicts. It can act as a form of discharge of, say, fantasy, and it can be a period of contemplation (Akhtar, 2009). Bollas has suggested that silence can be a vehicle for intermediate experience, "inner experiencing and inner processing of existence", as well as an opportunity for constructive "regressive experiences" (1987, pp. 264, 265). Silence also has many health benefits, according to researchers: "lowering blood pressure; improving concentration and focus; calming racing thoughts; stimulating brain growth; reducing cortisol; stimulating creativity; improving insomnia; encouraging mindfulness" (Garone, 2021).

As the great Stoic philosopher Epictetus noted, "Keep silence for the most part, and speak only when you must, and then briefly said".[25] The fact is that most people have great difficulty implementing Epictetus' wise words, words that the Rabbis of the Ethics would quite likely support. Rather, they are habituated to empty chatter and/or hearing themselves speak in search of self-validation. Such a compulsive or compulsive-like talking is much more common than most people admit, and the act of over-speaking often underlies the speaker's wish to dominate the listener ("in the wake of many words is sin"). While psychoanalysis is the talking cure, as Anna O. famously called it, it also involves high-level listening skills on the part of the analyst and analysand. Being a skillful listener requires a lot of hard work, especially controlling one's desire to talk too much, often a subtle form of domination, as I have suggested. As Alvarez noted, "Listening is nevertheless a complex art" (2012, p. 163).

What in part psychoanalysis offers the Ethics is a depiction of the "dark" side of silence. Indeed, as I said, silence can be used to resist authentic dialogue; it can be a form of resistance to analytic treatment. As Akhtar notes, silence in the analytic context, and by extension elsewhere (at least to some extent), can signify, as I have said, unconscious resistance, intentional withholding, enactment of fantasies such as identifying with a persistently silent parent, a sadistic attack on the analyst and/or the analytic process, and blank or empty contentless states of mind (Akhtar, 2009, p. 266). Take, for example, a "real-life" moment, the person who does not speak up when there is some injustice or abuse taking place. Such a person relinquishes agency and control and promotes the existing state of affairs. Silence can also be used in a manipulative manner such as in giving a significant other the "silent treatment". In these instances, silence is hardly the virtue that the Rabbis of the Ethics probably had in mind.

"What is more essential is not study but practice", reads the middle part of the aforementioned saying. Psychoanalysis is here useful in understanding the typical analysand who is intellectually self-aware; he understands the "why" of his behavior but is still not willing and able to change his behavior, which is what ultimately counts in terms of the art of living a good life. Much of the time, this inhibition of reasonable behavior is a way of maintaining the gratification associated with, say, the neurotic childish issue originally at play. The Rabbis, at least in this proverb, are not commenting on what are the difficulties of putting one's insights (e.g., one's learning) into practice. As Greenberg notes,

> Naturally, the sages advanced and praised the study of Torah. Still, they concluded that doing good, i.e., acting on the Torah's instructions, not studying about what to do, is the essence of Torah. Talk is cheap [not in analysis!]; action costs and counts.
>
> (2016, p. 54)

Carl Jung put this point just right when he said, "You are what you do, not what you say you'll do" (Stux, 2022).

Finally, the phrase "and in the wake of many words is sin" speaks to the fact that quite often people use language in sadistic (e.g., mean and nasty) and unethical ways (e.g., dishonestly). As Sartre said, sometimes words are like loaded pistols. However, psychoanalysis is familiar with those analysands who talk too much, nearly overwhelming the analyst with information that he can hardly process. The purpose of such compulsive speaking is usually to fashion an avenue of flight from themselves. That is, the analysand learns how to avoid being comprehended by the analyst. Outside the consultation room, such over-talking is often engaged in for defensive purposes, to push people away and overwhelm them with fundamentally meaningless words.

6. Community

> (II–5). Hillel said: Do not separate yourself from the community, and do not be sure of yourself until the day you die; do not judge your fellow-man until you have been in his position; do not make pronouncements which cannot be understood at once in the confident thought that they will be understood later on; and do not say you will study when you will have leisure, for you may never attain to leisure.
>
> (Bokser, 1983, p. 235)

The phrase "do not separate yourself from the community" speaks, of course, to the benefits of being part of a community and the responsibilities to others that it demands. As Greenberg (2016) notes, being part of a community is essential for a proper and healthy life. If one becomes so self-centered as to cut loose from community in order to live only for himself, quality of life will be lost. Our very humanness shrinks when we lose our connections to a group beyond ourselves.

(p. 75)[26]

The aforementioned is in sync with research findings. For example, Robert Waldinger, a Harvard psychiatrist, and director of the longest-range study of human contentment ever conducted, the Harvard Study of Adult Development,[27] found that the central factor that determines life satisfaction is not money or even achievement. Rather, it's "warm connections with other people". Moreover, "the big surprising take away from the study", he says, is the extent to which your interactions with other human beings affect not just your outlook on life but "how long you stay healthy, how long your brain will stay sharp. Having these good connections makes you less likely to get coronary heart disease. You are even less likely to get arthritis". It is not necessary to have "a life partner or an intimate partner", Waldinger says, you can have strong connections with friends, family members, work colleagues, "many different kinds of relationships". Even casual connections can have real benefits: with the coffee-shop barista you banter with, or the grocery cashier who greets you by name. "Those more casual ties turn out to give us little hits of well-being as well", he said. "We evolved to be social animals" (The Week, 2023a, p. 10).[28]

Moreover, some have claimed that there is a "loneliness epidemic" in Western nations (Kristoff, 2023, p. A27). As Kristoff notes, a majority of Americans, for example, now report experiencing loneliness, based on a frequently used scale that asks questions such as whether people lack companionship or feel excluded. According to an American Perspectives Survey between 1990 and 2021, the percentage of Americans reporting that they had no close friends at all quadrupled (French, 2023, p. A25). In addition, says Kristoff, loneliness is connected to strokes, heart attacks, dementia, inflammation and suicide. Loneliness—that is, social isolation—kills many more people each year than terrorists and murderers and costs the public huge amounts of money in preventable health costs (Kristoff, 2023, p. A27). The antidote to loneliness, at least in part, is as the Rabbis emphasized being a part of a vibrant community.

It is hard to argue with the gist of what Greenberg is saying. However, what the Ethics does not emphasize is the "dark" side of the individual-large group psychology. That is, groups have a destructive side to them; for example, the pressure toward conformity at the expense of individual difference, the phenomena of group-think and certain forms of nationalism. Volkan discusses the large group in its own right (not only what the large group means for the individual), and he provides formulations about the conscious and unconscious shared past and present historical psychological experiences that exist within a large group. Making such formulations enlarges our understanding of the emergence of present-day, societal-political-religious events and leader-follower relationships and allows us to look at the interaction between opposing large groups in depth (Volkan, 2020, p. xiv).

Freud coined the term "narcissism of minor differences" (1930, p. 114) to describe the tendency of groups that are similar to each other to nevertheless focus on their unimportant differences as the basis of intergroup hostility ("constant feuds and in ridiculing each other").

Thus, intergroup (and sometimes intragroup) conflict emanates, in part, from these aforementioned considerations. It is thus important to understand the duality of structure of the individual large group relationships, their positive and negative dimensions.

The phrase "and do not be sure of yourself until the day you die", refers to the need not to judge oneself until one is on one's "death bed" as it were, whether one has lived a life that is justified or not. Sophocles (2009) understood this too when he wrote "Let no mortal be called happy until the final fated day" (p. 171). This requires a superego that is gentle and forgiving rather than harsh and unforgiving. The fact is that "the game is not over until it is over"—that is, even late in one's life one can modify oneself in a profound manner and make decisive changes for the better (or worse) in how one lives one's everyday life. In a certain sense, the last quarter of one's life matters most. This Ethic is urging the person to be humble, hesitant and provisional in judging oneself and for that matter others, in part because the person is always evolving for better or worse. It also argues for living one's life as if it is the day before one dies, putting into sharp focus the existential importance of having the will and ability to live life intensely and fully each day. One should live each day with transcendent purpose, for one never knows when the end will come. Such living requires not being bogged down by neurotic and other conflicts which blunt spontaneity and aliveness and the like. Quoting Rilke, psychiatrist/Holocaust survivor Viktor Frankl noted that every human being should be "able to die his own death", in other words, to meaningfully incorporate death into the gestalt of life, even to fulfill the meaning of life in death (2019, p. 63).[29]

"Do not judge your fellow-man until you have been in his position" refers to the capacity for accurate empathy. By empathy, I mean "the imagining of another's subjective experience through the use of one's own subjective experience. Empathy has been posited by self-psychologists as the defining means by which the data of psychoanalysis are gathered" (Person Cooper, & Gabbard 2005, p. 551). Empathy should be distinguished from what Martin Buber calls "experiencing the other side", which may be more in line with what the Rabbis had in mind.

Experiencing the other side, says Friedman, "means to feel an event from the side of the person one meets as well as from one's own side" (Friedman, 2002, p. 102). Most importantly, it involves what Buber calls "inclusiveness", which realizes the other person in the actuality and "presentness" of his being

(Buber, 1965, p. 97). "Confirmation", the affirmation, acceptance and support of the other in his uniqueness, including challenging the other when required, is the main consequence of inclusion (Kramer & Gawlick, 2003, p. 202). Empathy, say Buber and Friedman, implies the capacity to "transpose oneself over there and in there", into the dynamic structure of an object, to "the exclusion of one's own concreteness, the extinguishing of the actual situation of life, the absorption in pure aestheticism of the reality in which one participates" (Buber, 1965, p. 97; Friedman, 2002, p. 102). Inclusion, says Buber, is the opposite of this: "It is the extension of one's own concreteness, the fulfillment of the actual situation in life, the complete presence of the reality in which one participates" (Buber, 1965, p. 97). Put in more conventional psychological language, we can roughly say that such a recast notion of empathy involves both being able to put your self inside the other without losing your self and at the same time being able to put the other in your self without eradicating the other's difference and otherness. How a self's ego is supple enough to incorporate or, more aptly, embrace the other into its experience without having to project anything upon or into the other is not clear, nor is it agreed upon by most psychoanalytic and social psychological theoreticians on empathy (Todd, 2003).[30] This being said, Winnicott noted,

> The sign of health in the mind is the ability of one individual to enter imaginatively and accurately into the thoughts and feelings and hopes and fears of another person; also to allow the other person to do the same to us.
>
> (Phillips & Taylor, 2009, p. 95)

The fact is that we are inclined to make judgments of ourselves and other people based on empathic immersion in the other, and this can sometimes be a good thing. For example, "rebuking to prevent wrong...; avoiding association with the wicked...; protecting ourselves from harm; and doing our duty as a judge or juror in a court of law" (Berkson, 2010, p. 67).

"Do not make pronouncements which cannot be understood at once in the confident thought that they will be understood later on" speaks to the need for speaking in a manner that is clear, concise and truthful, the opposite being a sign that one does not really know what one is talking about or one is possibly being dishonest and the like. Indeed, psychoanalysis is all too aware of those analysands who speak in a manner that reflects a lack of clarity and precision, this often being a defense against being comprehended as a full human being by the analyst. Unclear, imprecise and dishonest speech can surely be used for defensive purposes, including as an attack on the analyst. Disciplined thought is a sign of having superior knowledge of a particular subject matter without being impeded by neurotic and other conflicts. As Frances Tustin noted of the enigmatic Bion, "I have often been asked whether Dr. Bion talked in a somewhat inscrutable, oracular way in which he sometimes wrote. I can say firmly that that was not so.

He was always brief, to the point and extremely simple and clear" (Tustin, 1981, p. 175).[31] More generally, analysts give great thought to when to speak and when to be silent, and when they do speak what to speak about and in what manner to speak to the analysand about it (Polmear, 2016, p. 226).

"And do not say you will study when you will have leisure, for you may never attain to leisure".

This saying appears to be referring to the problem of procrastination, the act of delaying or postponing something. Procrastination is often related to perfectionism, the refusal to accept any standard short of perfection. People often hesitate because they are afraid that they will be imperfect regarding some activity like studying for an exam. Procrastination can similarly be a form of aggression against the self, an expression of self-punishment.

Finally, people get so engaged in their everyday activities and routines that they do not allow for time off from, say, work, to study and/or engage in intellectual pursuits etcetera. What this often boils down to is the fact that people never make such pursuits a priority; they simply don't make the time to do these other activities. I am reminded of a workaholic patient of mine, a man in his late 60s who wanted to retire from his job in the financial world. When I asked him what he would do if he retired, he told me he would read the books he never got around to reading and go to the museums and theatre performances he missed. When I gently pointed out to him that he had not read anything but the sports pages of the daily rag newspaper most of his adult life, and rarely made time for museums or theatre, that his retirement plan was ill-conceived, ill-advised and ill-fated, nevertheless, my patient retired, and he fell into a depression because he did not know what to do with himself. He lacked any vehicle to feel affirmed as a vital person.

7. Compassion

> (II–13). Said Rabban Yohanan to his disciples: Go and reflect on the highest good which a person ought to cultivate. Rabbi Eliezer said: A generous eye; Rabbi Joshua said: A good friend; Rabbi Jose said: A good neighbor; Rabbi Simeon said: Considering the circumstances of one's actions. Rabbi Elazar said: A kindly heart. Said he to them: I prefer the opinion of Rabbi Elazar because your views are embodied in his.
>
> (Bokser, 1983, p. 236)

While the Rabbis regarded generosity, friendship, neighborliness and consequential thinking as important in living a good life, it is a "kindly heart" which is given the greatest significance. Having a kindly heart is possibly another way of speaking about what may be the greatest passion, namely compassion.

Compassion, often referred to as empathy and/or altruism in the analytic and psychological literatures (not to be confused with Buber's "experiencing the other side"),³² involves the willingness and ability to engage another person's personal experience, in particular their suffering, which often leads to an upsurge to help make things better. Indeed, researchers have found a correlation between compassion and altruism that is decidedly operative in a love relation, in that one feels summoned to reduce one's partner's suffering through concrete ameliorative actions (Compton & Hoffman, 2012, p. 320). The Latin root for the word *compassion* means "suffering with" the beloved, calling to mind the great Biblical narratives in the Hebrew and Christian Bibles in which, for example, God had compassion on Israel and Christ's God forgave you. Both Martin Buber and Gabriel Marcel, Jewish and Catholic religious philosophers respectively, would agree with Elie Wiesel, who described man's ethical outlook as it is instantiated in a love relationship, in which a person chooses to take on the burden of another's suffering in compassion-infused fidelity and hope: "I suffer, therefore you are" (Berenbaum, 1994, p. 139).

Psychoanalysis rarely talks about the development of dispositional compassion as a worthwhile overarching goal for treatment (among other goals). However, it is aware of some of the typical signs of compassion. As Kendra Cherry notes, compassion is present when a person believes and feels that she has a great deal in common with other people, while knowing that she is unique too; it means being willing and able to comprehend what others are experiencing and feeling their distress; it means having the will and ability to take action when you come across someone else who is suffering; it means having a developed capacity for emotional intelligence such that you are willing and able to comprehend, manage and act on your own emotions as well as the emotions of others. Finally, says Cherry, it means feeling a sense of gratitude when other people manifest compassion for your own difficulties (Cherry, 2022).

Psychoanalytically speaking, an art of living a good life involves the willingness and ability for compassion to be the hallmark of one's behavior. This usually requires a downward modification of one's narcissism toward more "mature" object relations. As the aforementioned Rabban Yohanan deduces, a kindly heart includes a number of qualities: An individual with a kind heart "is generous, a loyal friend, a good neighbor, and aware of the consequences of one's words and deeds" (Sacks & Angel, 2015, p. 44). The development of sustained compassion as, say, a character trait requires not only the transformation of one's narcissism toward more mature object relations, but it also requires that one is not burdened by neurotic conflicts (and other problems in living). For neurosis, by definition, is self-directed, self-referential and self-centric, which is the opposite of compassion—which is other-directed, other-regarding and other-serving.

Neurosis assumes its most profound meaning when we comprehend it as a failed attempt to reach a new (i.e., a better) psychic condition (Zoja, 2007).

8. Loving your neighbor as yourself

> (II–15). They said three things. Rabbi Eleizer said: Let your friend's honor be as precious to you as your own; be not easily provoked to anger; and repent one day before you die. He also said: Warm yourself before the fire of scholars, but be careful not to be burnt by their glowing coals. The bite of scholars may be as sharp as that of a fox; their sting as that of a scorpion; their hiss as that of a serpent. Their words must all be treated as carefully as coals of fire.
>
> (Bokser, 1983, p. 237)

"Let your friend's honor be as precious to you as your own"[33] is another way of emphasizing the importance of mature object relations, and in particular the Golden Rule. Treat others the way one would want to be treated, an ethic that points toward the norm of reciprocity. Nearly every religion and spirituality emphasize the goal of loving your neighbor as yourself, doing unto others what you would have others do unto you, and the need to empathize and sympathize with the other. While this notion is a common one in our society, psychoanalysis suggests that it is a lot easier said than done. For to empathize with another person requires the willingness and ability to listen to others, acknowledge their feelings and comprehend them from their point of view (somewhat similar to Buber's experiencing the other side, see entry #6).[34] Such a mode of comportment involves a downward modification of one's inordinate narcissism. It should be noted that Freud commented on the Love Commandment in *Civilization and its Discontents* and elsewhere, claiming that it was a grandiose defense against man's intrinsic aggressiveness. Moreover, as Wallwork points out

> Freud criticizes the love commandment along five psychological and normative lines.... These are: first, that it cannot be kept; second, that its call for treating 'neighbors' with equal love is unjust to those to whom we are tied by special relations; third, that it ignores the evidence that not all persons are equally worthy of love; fourth, that it handles aggression so poorly that it actually encourages hostility towards outsiders; and fifth, that it is a source of considerable unhappiness to those who attempt to obey its grandiose requirements.
>
> (Wallwork, 1991, p. 199)[35]

This being said, Freud also wrote in *Why War* (1933a) that "Anything that encourages the growth of emotional ties between men must operate against war ... There is no need for psycho-analysis to be ashamed to speak of love in this connection, for religion itself uses the same words 'Thou shalt love they neighbor as thyself'" (ibid., p. 212).[36] Thus, Freud displayed a complexity and ambivalence with regard to the Love Commandment.

"Be not easily provoked to anger" speaks to the fact that anger is one of the most toxic emotions. In fact, the Buddha included it as one of three poisons: greed, hatred (aka anger) and delusion. From a psychoanalytic point of view, anger is typically provoked by frustration. It can be conceptualized as somewhat different to hatred in that anger tends to be of shorter duration than hatred and is frequently manifested in love relations. Most often anger is a consequence of some kind of narcissistic wound, another way of describing an injury to the ego or self-esteem, producing narcissistic rage (Rycroft, 1995, pp. 8, 71). Narcissistic rage is "love outraged", said the late Holocaust survivor analyst Henry Krystal. That is, where the expectation is to be loved, for example, to have a sense of self-worth and pride, one gets the opposite, traumatic assaults on one's self-esteem and self-concept (Krystal, 1988, p. 82). As Greenberg notes, "a bad temper repulses and/or beats down others in your life" (2016, p. 92). One of the common problems about anger is that people often do not know they are angry; their anger is unconscious, often leading to a toxic inner condition. Moreover, because anger is so unwieldly, people erect elaborate defenses against consciously feeling angry, often putting on a fake demeanor to cover up as it were the conscious or unconscious anger.

"Repent one day before you die" is another way of saying that one should be continuously trying to perfect oneself (repent, improving/repairing the state of the world), since one does not know when one is going to die. Likewise, if one is living as if it is the day before one's death,[37] then one will try and avoid ill-conceived, ill-advised and ill-fated actions, actions that are harmful to others. Finally, in general, greater mortality saliency tends to induce greater caring and compassion toward others. As Freud wrote, "If you want to endure life, prepare yourself for death" (1915a, p. 300).

"Warm yourself before the fire of scholars, but be careful not to be burnt by their glowing coals" suggests that there is much to be learned from scholars; however, one should not necessarily take in what is being said. A healthy skepticism emanating from autonomous strivings is the best way to avoid being swept away by the seductive views of those in a position of scholarly authority, this includes the analyst. In addition, there is an important difference between intellectual and emotional understanding (i.e., emotional truths, personal truths that may not be governed by logic or sequential thinking). The Rabbis tended to overvalue the intellectual and underplay the underlying emotions.[38] Sometimes a person is seduced into appropriating an intellectual idea, but they lack the emotional understanding that really matters. Analysands can grasp an insight intellectually but not the emotional underpinnings of what was said by the analyst.[39] Ultimately, the latter is what is most important, for it tends to facilitate change and reduce suffering.

9 and 10. Time and passivity

(II–20). Rabbi Tarfon said: The day is short; the task is great; the workmen are lazy; the reward is abundant; and the Master is pressing.

(Bokser, 1983, p. 237)

(II–21). He also said: It is not your duty to finish the work, but neither are you free to desist from it. If you have studied much Torah, you will receive much reward. Your Employer may be trusted to compensate you for your labor. And remember that the true reward of the righteous is in the world to come.

(Ibid.)

This first aphorism speaks to the topic of temporality, how a person relates to time in his everyday life, to the constructs of past, present and the future. In this context, time should ideally be experienced as a propulsive force in one's life, a way of "leaning" into the future. This aphorism has been explicated rather succinctly by Sacks and Angel:

Too often, people live passively; they drift through life rather than steer their way through it. They fritter away time, they make excuses for laxity and carelessness. They have no direction, sense of purpose, no feeling of urgency. Rabbi Tarfon teaches the need to stay vigilant. Life is short; much needs to be accomplished in the limited time of the human life-span.

(2015, p. 54)

Indeed, there are people who live their lives in a too passive manner. Too much passivity can lead to inertia, a lack of productivity, and in the extreme, psychic death as in the "walking dead" of the concentration or death camp (Akhtar, 2009). This being said, there are occasions where passivity is the fitting response to the external and/or internal worlds. For example, quiet states of mature solitude and introspection can benefit the individual (ibid). In this context, the passivity is external while internally they are actively engaged.

The aforementioned calls to mind the Taoist concept of *wu-wei*, inaction. Wu-wei, says Watson, "is not forced quietude, but rather the renunciation of any action that is occasioned by conventional concepts of purpose or achievement, or aimed at the realization of conventional goals" (1968, p. 161). As Xiaogan notes, there are several gradations and meanings of wu-wei in Taoist thought: wu wei as doing nothing; wu-wei as taking as little action as possible; wu-wei as patiently waiting for the spontaneous transformation of things; and wu wei as acting naturally (Xiaogan, 1993).

What is passive communication? As McNutty (2018, n.p.) pointed out,

> Passive communication is not expressing your honest feelings, thoughts or beliefs, allowing others to violate your rights, or violating your own rights in the way you communicate with others. It is also assuming responsibility for how others may feel or react.

McNutty also suggests some of the likely benefits of passive communication, such as you avoid or postpone conflict in the short term; you reduce anxiety in the short term; you are often admired for being selfless; others attempt to look out for you; you are infrequently blamed if things go wrong because you have not put yourself out there or taken control of the circumstances (ibid.). However, the costs of such communication are substantial: Others take advantage of you; your image is limited to being a lovable, good person in the eyes of others; repressing your anger or frustration can lead to ill-conceived and ill-fated anger outbursts and feelings of sadness; your self-esteem can be negatively impacted (ibid.). Moreover, repressed anger can limit the range of emotions a person can experience, and sometimes it leads to the person feeling as if he is a victim to circumstances.

Compare this to active communication, also referred to as assertive communication. As McNutty further notes, assertive communication comprises communicating your thoughts, feelings and beliefs in an honest and direct manner without violating the rights of others. It is the balanced "middle ground" between violating other people's rights and interests when being aggressive and violating our own rights and interests when being passive. Indications that you communicate assertively include: You implement direct, non-threatening eye contact; you communicate emotions appropriately e.g., smiling when satisfied and glowering when angry; you use 'I' statements when you speak; you don't permit others to take advantage of you; you don't criticize or in other ways attack others for their thoughts, feelings or beliefs; you actively listen to what others say; you make the division between fact and your opinion; you actively seek out the view points and suggestions of others; you are willing and able to explore numerous options; your speech tends to be steady, direct, relaxed and appropriate in how loud it is. The benefits of assertive communication, says McNutty, include: Your self-esteem will be enhanced as you act more in sync with your "true self"; others become knowledgeable about your authentic thoughts, feelings and beliefs; frustration and anger will be less likely to accumulate and build up; you will get to know others more deeply as you are less preoccupied with their potential for negative judgment of you (ibid.).

"It is not your duty to finish the work, but neither are you free to desist from it" refers to the fact that one should not look to the end product as the measure of all things, but in addition to reflecting on reaching one's goals, there ought to be the sense that there is always more to do, more to give of yourself. In fact, what matters most is the struggle to reach a goal, knowing that perfection is not, should not, be the desired goal. Put differently, it is the process of self-exploration that matters most and less so the end result, since the process is where the important learning takes place. The fact that one grows old and ideally wishes to pass on the wisdom one has attained to the next generation suggests the fact that each generation is obligated as it were to press on in making the world a better place. Erikson calls this generativity, a deep concern for establishing and helpfully guiding the generation that follows.

"If you have studied much Torah, you will receive much reward. Your Employer may be trusted to compensate you for your labor. And remember that the true reward of the righteous is in the world to come" directly speaks to the Jewish believer's way of being-in-the-world. That is, a typical believer profoundly believes that there is a God in heaven that is fair and just and that we live in an ethically caring universe in which ultimately all that is wrong is put right in the world to come. Having such an ideo-affective belief is, of course, deeply awe-inspiring and comforting because it means that this world is merely an antechamber to the world to come.[40] Karmic consequences are operative in the universe.[41] However, the typical secular analysand does not hold to such beliefs; rather, he tends to feel that we live in a post-metaphysical world, an ethically indifferent universe, in which there is no cosmic judge or the like that one is accountable to now or in the alleged world to come. The job of the analyst is to help the analysand come to terms with the assumed indifference of the universe; sometimes things appear to be radically unfair, and one can develop an outlook that can be characterized as resignation without despair (the opposite of nihilistic or hopeless despair). In *The Future of an Illusion*, Freud too spoke of resignation. "And, as for the great necessities of Fate, against which there is no help, they will learn to endure them with resignation" (1927b, p. 50). The fact is in many instances all does not work out well, and learning to live without consolation is part of the art of living, at least to the secular analysand. In a different context, a spiritual one, Levinas calls this quality of mind and heart "religion for adults" (1990, p. 11).

11. The "rules of engagement"

> (III–2). Rabbi Hanina, the deputy High Priest, said: Pray for the welfare of the government. Were it not for the fear of it [its awesome power], men would swallow each other alive.
>
> (Bokser, 1983, p. 238)

Yanklowitz summarizes one of the meanings of this aforementioned statement to the Jewish community and by extension to the life of other minority groups.

> Why, then, should Jews "pray for the welfare" of governments we know are corrupt, violent and filled with evil people? Because the alternative to government is anarchy. Anarchy is something that the Sages were loath to accept. Nonetheless, sometimes regimes are too unjust or even evil to be

prayed for. Rather, our response should be resistance and civil disobedience. One prays in vain if it is for the welfare of the Nazi regime, for Stalin, or for contemporary dictators who murder the innocent.

(2018, p. 127)

From a psychoanalytic point of view, this Hobbesian outlook (Greenberg, 2016) dovetails with Freud's view of society. As Hobbes famously put it, the "natural" state of humankind is a state of war in which life is "solitary, poor, nasty, brutish, and short", mainly because individuals are in a "war of all against all". Indeed, Freud believed that unless there were external controls individuals would be in a protracted state of conflict among themselves and with society. Freud thus comprehended culture, as he did dreams and symptoms, as a manifestation of desires in serious conflict with one another but also with society. While he maintained that religion, art and science could be significantly satisfying and purposeful, he stressed that culture is the consequence of impulses denied a more direct sexual or aggressive gratification. For the individual, it is his superego functioning that matters most, for it represents the internalization of the "rules of engagement" in our culture, evading chaos and objectionable behavior. Others have elaborated, if not disputed, Freud's gloomy view in terms of the "master narrative" they are lodged in (see entry #32). For example, Kohut's distinction between Freud's Guilty Man, the individual in conflict with his forbidden sexual and aggressive drives, and Tragic Man, the individual laboring to sustain cohesion of his feeble and fragmented self (Ornstein, 1998).

What needs to be emphasized about this aphorism is that one needs to have a reasonable superego function, one that is not too lax nor too severe so that one can live according to the reasonable rules of the nation one resides in. This involves negotiating the issues that are involved in large group identity (Volkan, 2020). Psychoanalysis emphasizes that collectively speaking there are major stumbling blocks that prompt inadequate or destructive large group identity. For example, knowing how much of yourself you can give to the state without losing yourself in the process or becoming entangled in morally compromising situations. By praying "for the welfare of the government", one is acknowledging that unless there are governmentally-sponsored reasonable rules law and order will collapse into anarchy, and preventing this involves having a superego that entails internalizing the best of what a government provides. It also means opposing society when it turns nasty. No doubt these are judgments each person has to implement in a context-dependent, setting-specific manner.

12. Humility

(IV–3). He [Ben Azzai] used to say: Do not despise any man, and do not disparage any object. For there is not a man that has not his hour, and there is not an object that has not its place.

(Bokser, 1983, p. 243)

"Do not despise any man.... For there is not a man that has not his hour" refers to the fact that "any and every person can and will make a contribution through his life and actions" (Greenberg, 2016, p. 175).[42] Put differently, the saying claims that it is a mistake to dismiss anyone as immaterial, for one never knows depending on the circumstances whether that person will assert his significance and even greatness (ibid.). Therefore, one should relate to others with respect and dignity for one never knows who will behave as a prince of a person.

The aforementioned calls to mind the legend of the "Lamed-Vavniks". It has its origins in the Talmud. Lamed-vavnik, a Yiddish term, actually comes from the Hebrew word for 30—lamed—and the word for six—vav.[43] Combined they make 36, the number of righteous individuals said to allegedly greet the Divine Presence, and without whom the world would not exist (PJ Library, n.d). That one does not know who is a lamed-vavnik means that one should relate to every man, including the beggar and other downtrodden and disenfranchised, with compassion and honor, for the world may exist because of their alleged righteousness. Interestingly, and perhaps most importantly, "the righteous ones do not know it themselves" (Fackenheim, 1987, p. 252).

Psychoanalytically speaking, such a viewpoint speaks to an existential comportment in which there is a downward modification of one's ill-conceived, ill-advised and ill-fated narcissism, such that one relates to others with a high degree of humility. Humility, having a modest or reduced view of one's own significance,[44] is not a quality of mind and heart that most people have, nor is it a common notion in psychoanalysis. Humility is one of the qualities that an analyst ideally personifies, especially when he offers an interpretation which at its best is an informed conjecture, hopefully a useful one. In essence, humility requires a liberation from pride and arrogance. In this view, as Maimonides noted, "humility is the midpoint between pride and self-aggrandizement" (Kravitz & Olitzky, 1993, p. 58). As Saint Augustine noted, pride is a particularly malignant form of self-love or narcissism. The main thrust of a prideful being is that he or she is not satisfied with the universe as fashioned but seeks more, to reconfigure it, and thus to establish him or herself as God (or God-like), as the Creator. Such a reconfiguring or reordering is based on a false claim to self-sufficiency, to falsely believing that one is self-created, self-sustained and self-dependent rather than interrelated, interdependent and interconnected. However, as Saint Augustine pointed out, we are not self-sufficient, not physically, psychologically or spiritually. Rather, we need to be connected to the infinite God (or its secular equivalent), the source of being, goodness, justice and absolute reality.[45] It is precisely this prideful turning away from God that leads us to a state of narcissistic entitlement, to the seeking of various forms of self-destructiveness, overindulgence and ultimately, to unhappiness. While this God-talk may not reverberate in the secular analysand, the secular equivalent may be a form of Humanism in which all people deserve being treated in the spirit of liberty, equality and fraternity, as the French say.

"There is not an object that has not its place" is an extension of the aforementioned. As Greenberg notes,

> there is a profound order in the cosmos and meaning for its constituents. That which you dismiss as trivial may yet have tremendous importance when the right circumstances come together. There is an ecology between living things and their environment. One change, omission, or disruption can turn into a cascade of loss.
>
> (Greenberg, 2016, p. 177)

Put differently, an object may have unforeseen importance at some time or in some place, and this is often beyond our control.[46] Therefore, one should treat an object as if it has a potential to be important in the larger scheme of things. Again, such an attitude speaks to a high degree of humility in which "everything matters, and everything is connected" (Yanklowitz, 2018, p. 200), even though we can't control the most important matters. Humility is thus a type of modesty that is brought about by comprehending our limited place in the order of things.[47] Moreover, it would appear that everything has its purpose, and this becomes apparent if one is patient, arguing for a high degree of frustration tolerance. As another ethical saying (the next one) in the Ethics puts it, "Let a person be exceedingly humble, for the end of moral man is but worms" (Bokser, 1983, p. 243, IV-4).[48] Humility, as I see it, to quote novelist/philosopher Iris Murdoch, is "a selfless respect for reality" (Szalai, 2023, p. 10). Freud would probably agree with the gist of this definition.

13. Repentance and good deeds

> (IV–13). Rabbi Eliezer ben Jacob said: He who performs a commandment has acquired a champion to protect him; and he who commits a transgression has acquired an adversary against himself. Repentance and good deeds are a shield against adversity.
>
> (Bokser, 1983, p. 244)

Twersky (1999) provides a succinct religious interpretation of this mishna:

> It is indeed true that for each mitzvah [commandment] a person does he acquires an advocate and for each transgression he acquires an accuser. These are thought of as "benign angels" or "hostile angels" who defend or accuse a person who is being judged by the heavenly tribunal.
>
> (p. 229)

Greenberg (2016) provides an elaboration on Twersky:

> Every human action, good or bad, will testify for or against the person in the final judgment. No action is wasted or ephemeral. There is a

> permanent record of every action, which plays a role in determining one's ultimate fate.
>
> (p. 198)

As for the antidote to such a severely judgmental perspective, for "the good person is the one who recognizes and admits having done wrong, then repents and undertakes good deeds to make up for the past" (ibid.). That is, continues Greenberg, "repentance and good deeds stop and reverse the sequence of evil set in motion by bad behavior [again, karmic consequences are at play]. Thus, they avert an extension of one's sin that could have, if unchecked, lead to calamity" (ibid.). Sacks and Angel (2015) note that

> perhaps this teaching is pointing to a lesson relating to human life. Each individual has strengths, virtues, and accomplishments. These reflect a person at his/her best, when he/she is "whole". But each person has weaknesses, moral blemishes, and failures.
>
> (p. 103)

The "trick", as it were, is not to overly concentrate on one's "good" proclivity (e.g., perhaps leading to egocentricity and conceit), or one's "bad" proclivity (e.g., perhaps leading to guilt and self-hatred), but rather to work out a kind of balance that acknowledges the bad side but does not dwell on it and tries to cultivate the good proclivity which ideally overwhelms the bad proclivity (ibid.). Repentance and good deeds appear to be an action of making reparations, calling to mind Klein's notion of the same name. For Klein love originates from the infant's feeling of gratitude toward the "good" mother, toward the gratifying "good breast" as Kleinians characterize it. This feeling is the foundation for the infant's and later the adult's "appreciation of all goodness in the self and in others" (Bergmann, 1987, p. 248). Thus, as Rycroft notes, reparation is a defense that diminishes guilt by action meant "to make good the harm imagined to have been done to an ambivalently invested object". This is a "process of re-creating an internal object which has in phantasy been destroyed" (e.g., psychological violence toward the other), a form of creative reparation (Rycroft, 1995, p. 156).

Notwithstanding the Ethic's claim that there exists some kind of fair system of reward and punishment in the world, or the world to come, a perspective that psychoanalysis in general regards as at least questionable, if not an illusion, this aphorism speaks to what constitutes good superego functioning. The superego has been defined as

> the seat of the individual's system of ideas and values, moral principles, prohibitions, and moral injunctions. It observes and evaluates the self and may either criticize, reproach, and punish, or praise and reward. It is thus an important modulator of self-esteem.
>
> (Person, Cooper, & Gabbard, 2005, p. 560)

The superego, roughly the conscience, needs to be gentle and kind rather than harsh and unkind. This is not to say one does not acknowledge one's dark side, including making judgments about objectionable behavior, but the overarching goal is to have a "reasonable" superego that scolds and rewards as necessary.

In theory, the source of harshness of the superego is from internalization of external judges, such as harsh or cruel parents etcetera, but also from one's own aggression. As Freud wrote,

> the evidence of psychoanalysis shows that almost every intimate emotional relation between two people which lasts for some time—marriage, friendship, the relations between parents and children—contains a sediment of feelings of aversion and hostility, which only escapes perception as a result of repression.
>
> (Freud, 1921, p. 101)

That is, the turning of the aggression against the self. One of the main aims of analytic treatment is to ameliorate this by analyzing and understanding the external forces at work and helping the analysand separate from the harsh parental and other authoritative figures rather than identifying with the aggression and behaving in the same harsh way to others as one was treated. It also involves giving a place for the expression of the anger in a safe, containing environment where the analyst's more benign superego can be eventually identified with and internalized. To the extent that one lives according to one's heartfelt beliefs and values, assuming they are life-affirming, one is likely to have a gentle and kind relation with one's superego.

14. Evil and suffering

> (IV–19). Rabbi Yannai said: We cannot wholly account for the ease of the wicked, nor for the affliction of the righteous.
>
> (Bokser, 1983, p. 245)

This observation is at the heart of the matter for the believing person, namely the problem of theodicy, the vindication of divine goodness and providence in light of the existence of evil. There are various theodicies that have been put forth by religious thinkers, though in my view (and those of many scholars) none of them are ultimately satisfying in terms of justifying evil. Levinas calls this "useless suffering". He claimed that evil and suffering are useless, by arguing that nothing, especially theodicy, conveys justice to the lives of the Jews and others who suffered during the Holocaust. Freud too cites theodicy as one of the arguments against believing in an all-powerful and all-good God (1930, p. 120). It is worth remembering that the "problem of evil" only exists for those individuals who expect the world to be good (Williams, 1993, p. 68).

What is interesting in terms of the believer is how he rationalizes his religious belief and lifestyle despite there being no satisfying theodicy available. Indeed, when such cognitive dissonance is in play, the typical believer tries very hard to rationalize his seemingly undeserved suffering, Job being the paradigmatic example. What this saying is asserting is that despite one's efforts there is no compelling theodicy available, and the best response to such suffering is to try to relieve it, whether it is personal or that of a suffering other. As Yanklowitz notes, "we can address human suffering by alleviating the pain and iniquity in the societies and bringing about peace" (2018, p. 242). In a certain sense, the issue is less why bad things are happening and more what interventions a particular person or group will make in the face of adversity. In a manner of speaking, God is "off the hook" as it were.

Rabbi Yannai is emphasizing that despite our best efforts we simply lack the intellectual acumen to explain when bad things happen to good people and why bad people seem to prosper. As Greenberg notes, "Rabbi Yannai neither offers the reassurance that reward in the future life will restore justice nor insists that all experiences in this world are providential and match up with one's behavior (i.e., measure-for-measure)" (2016, p. 211). From my therapeutic experience with believing patients, the problem of theodicy is hardly addressed; often relying in some variation on Rabbi Yannai's observation, we simply lack the power to understand God's inscrutable role in his relationship to the righteous and the evil people among us. Moral reckoning is the only reasonable response to human suffering, many believe.

From a psychoanalytic point of view, the typical analysand does not have a religious sensibility, such that the question of theodicy is hardly addressed. For them, suffering is a consequence of one's neurotic and other conflicts, or the real world bearing down on them, which leads them to respond to their suffering from a personal point of view. This being said, it is near impossible for an analysand to contemplate why he has been struck down by, say, anxiety and depression and/or other forms of mental anguish, except to say that this is how the ethically indifferent universe tends to unfold in real time. Again, resignation without despair appears to be the best psychoanalytically informed response to such situations. As Winnicott (2015) noted, "Probably the greatest suffering in the human world is the suffering of the normal or healthy or mature person" (p. 80).

15. Making oneself available

> (IV–20). Rabbi Mattithyah ben Heresh said: Be the first to extend greetings to every man; and choose to be a tail to lions rather than a head to foxes.
>
> (Bokser, 1983, p. 245)

"Be the first to extend greetings to every man" is seemingly an obvious expression of respect, kindness and friendship toward the other. In this conventional gesture of saying hello, we are in effect affirming the other's unique self and his equality as a person like us. As Greenberg further notes, "'Hello' means: I know you are there and I acknowledge you" (Greenberg, 2016, p. 212), opening the field to the possibility of having an I-Thou relationship, or converting an I-It relationship into an I-Thou one. Levinas says "that access to the face", a metaphor for meeting the other, "is straightaway ethical"—that is, it is "the best way of encountering the Other" (Levinas, 1985, pp. 87, 85). The Rabbis call this *pitchut lev*, an opening of the heart, a generous spirit.

Psychoanalysis points to the range of difficulties of making oneself available to the other in this simple straightforward manner. Being radically emotionally and intellectually open, to be ready, receptive, responsive and responsible to what a person encounters, the other, is no easy task. That is, there a wide range of neurotic and other conflicts and problems in living that interfere with and in other ways truncate a person's ability to comport himself in this goodhearted manner. This includes, for example, being afraid of such engagement with a strange other, an expression of a lack of trust that the outcome will be satisfactory. Or, the anxiety of not being good enough is related to the fear of being judged poorly by others. Most of the time, however, people are just so self-involved that they don't see the other as other or, for that matter, at all. As Eigen notes, "the ego is caught in the grip of a relentless rigidity and is bent on sealing itself off. It neither trusts itself nor the psyche as a whole" (Eigen, 2018, p. 347).

"And choose to be a tail to lions rather than a head to foxes" is a famous recommendation that connotes the following. As Joshua Kulp pointed out,

> It is better to attach oneself to a group of people who are above you, in wisdom and goodness and to be accounted the least among them, than to be the head of a group of people who are below you, in wisdom and goodness, and to be the first among them.
>
> (Kulp, 2023).

As psychoanalysts note, people often prefer to be the head of foxes rather than the tail of lions. They mainly are motivated by egoistic needs for affirmation; however, most often their self-respect is diminished over time, as is the respect from others. This aphorism also raises the important issue of leadership, for to be a leader of a questionable if not corrupt organization appeals to many people, for at least the person is in a leadership role, which is affirming of his egotistical needs. In contrast, to be a tail to lions suggests that one is taking a leadership role of a sort in an ethically robust organization, rooted in a realistic sense of self. Sometimes, a person needs to be seen as the head of lions, for it gives him a feeling of winning, as he lacks an adequate sense of self-regard rather than actually having a solid sense of self and self-confidence. In a word, he lacks a robust self-esteem.

16. Submissiveness

(III–16). Rabbi Ishmael said: Be submissive toward a great person; be gentle toward the young; and receive all people with a cheerful manner.

(Bokser, 1983, p. 241)

"Be submissive toward a great person". This Ethic is focusing on power relations. For example, when one is faced with a "great person", or even a person who is more self-actualized, like one's analyst, the proper way of comporting oneself outside the consultation room is, in general, one of "equanimity and harmony…. One should avoid conflict to the extent possible. Instead of being contentious with superiors, e.g., elders, teachers, those in power, it is preferable to defer to them" (Sacks & Angel, 2015, p. 76). As Greenberg quips, "Do not start up with a lion" (2016, p. 142).

The fact is, however, that to assume a submissive way of comporting oneself requires that the person not experience the submissiveness as a personal defeat, especially an Oedipal defeat. Indeed, many people relate to superiors as if they were Oedipally-tinged parents who they get into power struggles with and feel subjugated by. For example, the person who is in conflict with his boss as he unconsciously calls to mind his relationship with his dictatorial father. To avoid such conflict, the person has to have resolved his ambivalence toward his father or he will repeat the childhood pattern of conflict in his relationship with his boss. One of the main stumbling blocks to such an adult outlook is the fear of having an Oedipal victory or Oedipal triumph. Briefly, an Oedipal triumph in its simplest formation refers to: "The experience of a child whose rival parent of the same sex has buckled under and appeared as defeated, removed from his or her position of authority, and vanquished. This can happen due to the same sex parent's death" or say from divorce or desertion (Akhtar, 2009, p. 196). As a result of feeling that one has defeated the Oedipal father, the child and later young adult experiences strong feelings of guilt which might lead to a submissiveness that is tinged with a disrespect stemming from a view of the boss/father as weak and ineffective. Thus, to relate to a superior in a respectful, submissive manner requires that the person not be bogged down by residual Oedipal issues that make such submissiveness feel like they are being pounded into the ground the way an autumn rain pounds a flower into the mud.

"Be gentle toward the young" is the converse of the aforementioned saying. That is, to be willing and able to relate to the young in the spirit of "generativity", as Erikson calls it (vs. stagnation, Erikson's seventh psychosocial stage), requires that one have the will and ability to transcend personal interests to give care and concern for younger (and older generations). One can only be gentle toward the young when one does not view them as threatening to one's existence, especially to one's accomplishments. In other words, generativity involves the intrapsychic capacity to be kind to young people, to encourage their independence and autonomy, to promote their development and growth and to encourage them in their undertakings. This is best illustrated by the two kinds of parents (often fathers). Those that want their children to outdo them academically or financially and those that feel threatened by their children's success.

"Receive all people with a cheerful manner", a view that calls to mind Shammai's[49] words, "greet every person with a cheerful countenance" (Ethics, I:15, in Bokser, 1983, p. 233). This saying speaks to the fact that honoring the other (especially his otherness), regardless of who it is, is vital to live a good life. Such a view is implicitly optimistic and hopeful (Greenberg, 2016).

But what does it take to have an optimistic and hopeful way of being-in-the-world? An optimistic person is someone who believes in his or her agency—that is, that depending on how one frames a situation one can see the silver lining in any difficult situation. Hope is different than optimism: the latter connoting confidence about the future or the successful outcome of something. Rather, as philosopher Gabriel Marcel, the great theoretician of hope noted,

> hope consists in asserting that there is at the heart of being, beyond all data, beyond all inventories and all calculations, a mysterious principle [the Absolute Thou, i.e., God?] which is in convivence with me which cannot but will that which I will, if I will deserves to be willed and is, in fact, willed by the whole of my being.
> (Marcel, 1995, p. 28)

Hope, in other words, is always embedded in patience and humility, just as it is embedded in trust and love—that is, hope is communion. For Marcel, hope is not merely subjective/psychological experience, but rather it reflects a person's spiritual life, which can at best be faintly apprehended as with any abiding mystery of being, like fidelity, faith and love. This is very different than the hope that is rooted in, say, the overindulged oral phase that leads to hyper-optimism as analysts construe it; hope as a defense against anxiety and sadness connected to castration fantasies; and hope as a manifestation of character armor that maintains reality testing (Akhtar, 2009).

17. Hospitality

> (I–5). Yose ben Yohanan of Jerusalem said: Let your home be a place of hospitality to strangers; and make the poor welcome in your household; and do not indulge in gossip with women. This applies even with one's own wife, and surely so with another man's wife. The sages generalized from this: He who engages in profuse gossiping with women causes evil for himself and neglects the study of the Torah, and he will bring upon himself retributions in the hereafter.
> (Bokser, 1983, p. 232)

This ethical saying is probably one of the worst examples of male sexism in the Jewish oeuvre. In fact, Berkson notes, "this Mishnah is the most prominent of wrong-headed statements about women in the Talmudic literature" (Berkson, 2010, p. 24). Indeed, as Tamar Rudavsky has noted, "Most Jewish feminist scholars agree that halakhah [Jewish law] is a document written by men for men, one in which women are conceived as 'other'" (Rudavsky, 2007, p. 338). Jewish philosopher Emil Fackenheim also notes, "To deny it ... the existence of male chauvinism within rabbinic Judaism ... is impossible" (1987, p. 151). Greenberg puts the aforementioned passage about women in historical context:

> In a society where men and women were socially isolated from each other (and women were often segregated in their own homes), excessive socializing and talk between men and women could lead to improper thoughts and actions. This passage is a reminder of the extraordinary entrance of women into contemporary society and their rise to the dignity of public activity in the past century.
>
> (Greenberg, 2016, p. 24)

Sacks and Angel offer a second interpretation:

> The Rabbis assumed, based on the reality of their time, that most women were not versed in Torah. Thus, a man conversed with a woman was invariably wasting time that should have been spent on Torah study. (This objection also implies that one should not converse too much with a man who is ignorant of Torah.)
>
> (Sacks & Angel, 2015, p. 11).

Rather than defend the indefensible sexism and gender bias of this ethic, or elaborate the corrective contemporary literature on women's prominent role in Jewish life (and religious life in general), I want to focus on two points emphasized in the first three sentences of this ethic: "Let your home be a place of hospitality to strangers; and make the poor welcome in your household; and do not indulge in gossip with women" (read: other people).

All religions and spiritualities emphasize the importance of hospitality, the belief that strangers, especially the poor, should be helped and protected during their travels. The gist of hospitality is having the will and ability to serve others—strangers, guests and friends—not for self-aggrandizing reasons like self-pride or social climbing but for its own sake (Sacks & Angel, 2015). But what is the main psychological thrust of such hospitality? In hospitality,[50] conceptualized as an instance of intersubjective creativity, the division of giving and receiving is overcome. As believing, Catholic philosopher Gabriel Marcel notes:

> If we devote our attention to the act of hospitality, we will see at once that to receive is not to fill up a void with an alien presence but to make the other person participate in a certain plenitude [a palpable sense of "fullness" or completion]. Thus the ambiguous term, "receptivity", has a wide range of meanings extending from suffering or undergoing to the gift of self; for hospitality is a gift of what is one's own, i.e., of oneself. ... To provide hospitality is truly to communicate something of oneself to the other.
>
> (1964, pp. 28, 90)

Thus, to "receive" someone is to open oneself to the other, to let the other into one's inner reality, to literally and symbolically let the other into one's "home", a place of refuge and safety. To "receive" a visitor, I must unlock the door and allow him in, clutch his hand and openly and responsively give myself to him (Cain, 1979, p. 27). Feelings of vitality and generosity spontaneously emerge. Hospitality is both a moment of receiving and giving, of being receptive and responsive, but also of being responsible to, and for, the other. At this juncture, receiving and giving are impossible to tell apart. Marcel puts this point succinctly:

> I can only grasp myself as being—on condition that I feel; and it can also be conceded that to feel is to receive; but it must be pointed out at once that to receive in this context is to open myself to, hence to give myself, rather than undergo an external action.
>
> (Marcel, 1964, p. 91)

It is a psychological paradox that to give the best of oneself is the surest way one can receive. For example, research inspired by Frederickson's "broaden and build" theory has found that, in the workplace, institutionalized caregiving and supportive attachments and other pro-social behaviors that are rooted in heartfelt collective values that reflect "organizational virtuousness" generate upward emotion spirals, so compassion begets compassion among employees (Lilius et al., 2012, pp. 276, 278).

Thus, as in hospitality, the most receptive and responsive person, the one who is able to engage life openly with the fullness of his whole being, is also the most creative. It is within this context that the creator enters the realm of what Marcel calls "creative testimony" or "creative attestation", an existential place "where the human person bears witness to the presence of being" (Cain, 1979, p. 75).[51] "Creative generosity", as Marcel calls it, being ready, receptive, responsive and responsible toward the other, is the opposite of self-centeredness. It is the capacity for "openness to others" and "to welcome them without being effaced by them" (Marcel, 1973, p. 39) that matters most in terms of hospitality when understood as an ethical moment.

Gossiping is decried in every major religion and spirituality. While there is no agreed upon definition of gossiping in the scholarly literature, a serviceable one could be casual or unconstrained conversation or reports about other people, typically involving negative details that are not determined as being true. Gossip, sociologists tell us, is "universal in time and social space, occurring always and everywhere" (Heilman, 1973, p. 161). Gossip can be positive or negative; it is a continuum concept, though I am most interested in malignant gossip that is meant to put another person down in some form.[52] As the great rabbinic theoretician of gossip Rabbi Yisrael Meir Kagan (d. 1933), "The Chofetz Chaim", noted in his famous *Guard Your Tongue* (1975), "One who speaks or listens to gossip deserves to be thrown to the dogs" (Marcus, 2010, p. 81).

Following Heilman (1973), we can say that the collectively oriented psychological significance of gossip lies in the support it gives for the group's so-called ego needs—what a group needs to survive and flourish. Gossip is a way of exercising, asserting and reinforcing communal values and feelings, consolidating and solidifying group identification, sustaining group cohesion and emotionally regulating the group and the individuals that give it its very character and life. Gossip may also be a means of classifying the group membership, differentiating intragroup cliques (e.g., gossip circles, those "in the know" from those who are outsiders) and validating various kinds of relationship from the most fleeting and impersonal to the most long-standing and intimate. In other words, "in its content and patterns gossip reflects" (Heilman, 1973, p. 162) what Erving Goffman called "the relational structure of the individual's social world" (ibid., p. 153)—that is, how people are interconnected. In this sense, gossip is an extremely important way in which individuals use their "moral imagination" (Stewart & Strathern, 2004, p. 4) to find their way and better manage their social world, a world that is often experienced as confusing, anxiety-provoking and threatening.

As to the individual significance of malignant gossip, which is always treacherous, since it's spoken behind the gossipee's back, manifests itself in, for example, saying something to a co-gossiper that is deliberately hurtful or hostile about a colleague, friend or family member; circulating a negative rumor about someone else; telling a secret, especially an awkward or embarrassing secret that a person promised to keep; distorting or lying about something at the gossiper's expense, and "raining on someone else's parade". Most importantly, in all of these instances, the gossiper, often motivated by meanness, vengeance or spitefulness, wants the gossipee to be hurt, and that his trust should be compromised and relationship radically subverted, if not broken up (Marcus, 2010).

As I have indicated elsewhere (ibid.), gossip is motivated by at least three factors: gossip as truncated ties to empathy; a deficit in the self-regulation of aggression; and gossip as a form self-esteem maintenance. Clearly someone who chronically gossips has an insufficiently developed ability to identify with and understand another person's feelings or difficulties, suggesting that the gossiper also has narcissistic problems. Disrespecting the other for the sake of self-affirmation and self-aggrandizement is the governing principle of such gossipers, and for that matter all ethically disabled persons. Gossip is also a way of reducing perceived severe threat and anxiety to the self, a way of shoring up and shielding an enfeebled self. Moreover, as a self-protective and self-enhancing expression of power, it allows the discharge of aggression (e.g., anger, envy, revenge) while avoiding dangerous confrontation, open conflict and additional injury to the self. Finally, we can say that the gossiper often suffers from reduced self-worth and self-respect, social anxiety and an inordinate need for regard, attention and admiration from others. Malevolent gossip mainly helps to maintain and bolster self-esteem by enhancing the gossiper's sense of status and power; however, this is always achieved by denying the worthiness, respect and honor of the other that is the gossipee.

What makes gossip so destructive is that it is a "triple murder". As the Chofetz Chaim notes, gossip "kills three people: the speaker, the listener, and the subject" (1975, p. 183). Indeed, gossiping can destroy the gossipee's reputation, it can obliterate relationships and it can cut deeply into a person's self-concept and self-esteem. In a word, malignant gossip, which often grows out of the fertile breeding ground of more benign habitual gossiping, can be soul-murdering to the gossipee. Gossip can also cut deeply into the co-gossiper, in that it can profoundly negatively change how one sees the gossipee. Finally, gossip also in some sense murders the gossiper; over time it warps his outlook and diminishes his social effectiveness. The gossiper uses and hurts others to gain increased status, power and admiration and by doing so is corrupted, sacrificing his soul in his quest for self-aggrandizement. The malignant gossiper, in other words, ultimately murders himself. It is probably for these and other moral reasons that the Ethics, and for that matter all major religions and spiritualities, are so against all forms of gossip.[53]

18. Truth, justice and peace

> (I–18). Rabban Simeon ben Gamaliel said: The world rests on three foundations: truth, justice, and peace. As it is written (Zechariah 8:16): "You shall administer truth, justice and peace within your gates."
>
> (Bokser, 1983, p. 234)

The aforementioned Ethic is focused on the existential basis of the believing Jew's raison d'être, the underpinnings of his sense of reality: he must strive for truth, justice and peace, in himself, in relation to others and in terms of the "proper conduct of human society" (Greenberg, 2016, p. 158). For the believing Jew, truth as a metaphysical entity is an objective notion; it refers to something "out there" as delineated by religious tradition (it is not viewed as a social construction of reality). Exactly what is objective truth or metaphysically based absolute truth is not easily discernible (if at all) by the rabbinic mind of the Talmud, hence justice is the method that mortals use to arbitrate absolute truth within the vicissitudes of practical reality (Sacks & Angel, 2015). Thus, truth in the biblical sense was not simply being accurate in one's utterances; in addition, it was mainly a moral notion of truth-telling and included "honesty, keeping promises and avoiding deceit" (Berkson, 2010, p. 50). As Sacks and Angel further note,

> Absolute truth is objective—and generally unattainable [in theory there is no "immaculate perception" as Nietzsche called it]. Justice is the process by which humans attempt to mediate abstract truth with the exigencies of concrete reality. Peace is the desired goals of maintaining society based on truth and justice.
> (Sacks & Angel, 2015, p. 26)

Berkson, citing the Talmud, makes the important distinction between an earlier Ethic (entry #1), "The world rests on three foundations: the Torah; the divine service; and the practice of lovingkindness between man and man" [read: human to human]. The way to reconcile this saying with the current one is to claim

> that those three [the Torah, divine service and lovingkindness] are the purposes of which God created the world, whereas justice, truth, and peace are the principles that sustain the world, and prevent it from collapsing. The three values in this mishnah can be seen to promote the welfare of humanity on two levels: the interpersonal and the social.
> (Berkson, 2010 p. 50)

Our focus is on the interpersonal or intersubjective level. Truth is necessary for trust and adequate communication between people, while lies subvert relationships from within. For instance, infidelity subverts a marriage as it is a betrayal, but lying about it may do considerably more damage than the unfaithfulness itself (Greenberg, 2016). As Zoja notes, "the core aim of" psychoanalysis "is ethical: analysis aims at doing battle with lies—first and foremost, of course, the lies that we tell ourselves" (2007, p, 33).

The Rabbis were well aware that truth, justice and peace don't always smoothly coordinate or correlate with each other. For example, sometimes telling the truth causes more harm than good, such as when one doesn't lie to build someone up in an hour of vulnerability and need (e.g., telling someone who is self-destructive that they are better than this). Or, as it says in the Talmud, to tell an ugly woman on her wedding day that she is beautiful. In these instances, the lying is meant to enhance the person's existence and would appear to be acceptable (though Augustine, Aquinas and Kant absolutely prohibit lying, under any circumstance, including to save a life

(Berkson, 2010)). In other instances, truth and peace can collide until one understands that bending the truth a little for the sake of familial peace is a superordinate value. Greenberg aptly summarizes the dynamics between truth, justice and peace:

> Truth is not always identical to justice, and it is often incompatible with peace. Think of the daily white lies and unspoken criticism which protect peace in the family or the workplace. The ideal society will reconcile all three principles. For the sake of peace one may yield some aspect of justice or, for the sake of justice one may override some aspect of peace. The key to a just and harmonious society lies in balance and limits. If an individual or group pursues one principle to the exclusion of the others, then there will be serious trouble.

Moreover,

> "Peace above all" leads to appeasement and loss of peace. Justice, when pursued relentlessly while sweeping aside compromise or the established interests of others may well lead to conflict, tyranny or worse. The wisdom of democracy is that it distributes power and puts limits on the pursuit of any one of these principles.
>
> (Greenberg, 2016, pp. 58–59)

Psychoanalysis has a somewhat different interpretation of the aforementioned values of truth, justice and peace, largely because its main focus is on the individual's way of being-in-the- world.

In general, psychoanalysis does not believe in any form of originalism, the belief that a text like the US Constitution or the Talmud (or a person) should be interpreted in the present in a way consistent with how it would have been understood or was intended to be understood at the time it was written (or in the case of a person, generated or produced). Truth is regarded as socially constructed and therefore radically perspectival. Truth in psychoanalysis is generally regarded as narrative truth, to quote Donald Spence (1982)—that is, the truthfulness of how a story or narrative is told by a person (e.g., its coherence and accuracy).[54] Loewald made a similar point when he wrote "that a piece of good analytic work is an artistic creation fashioned by patient and analyst in collaboration" (1991, p. 149). As Spence notes, he believes that a coherence view of truth is the operative criterion of truth in psychoanalysis as opposed to a correspondence theory (Hanly, 1990, p. 377).[55] As Hanly further claims, in this context the analyst functions mainly as a pattern-maker, capable of creating artistic masterpieces, rather than a pattern-finder (ibid., p. 376). As Akhtar notes, narrative truth "was constructed in the clinical encounter and the need for coherence and significance added to both embellish and discard various objective realities of the patient's experience as they existed before the psychoanalytic exploration" (Akhtar, 2009, p. 183). Historical truth pertained to the "objective realities of the analysand's experience" as they were in play before the psychoanalytic exploration (ibid.). This is because any alleged objective realities are socially constructed—that is, it is impossible to discern with absolute certainty what objectively occurred in a person's childhood history (there is no definitive historical accuracy). Memory of so-called objective truths change for the better or worse as one evolves as a person. In other words, the past is a function of the present and the future outlook. Such a viewpoint of narrative truth was supported by emphasizing that the language in which the analysand records and reports his experience is highly personal and carries a specific associative context which is hardly possible for the analyst to share or communicate on an accurately empathic level (ibid.). Analytic theory is not a set of laws but rather "a set of metaphors" used to describe (not explain) the events that occur in the consultation room (Ogden, 2022, p. 98). In other words, a "good" interpretation implies a good "fit" or correlation between the analyst's and the analysand's co-produced narrative (Modell, 1999).

This being said, where the rabbinic outlook and the psychoanalytic one are in sync is that they both believe that speaking the truth in love is what matters most. Decisions or statements "must not only be right—they must also be good. The commandment to truth must be accompanied by an overwhelming commitment to compassion" (Sacks & Angel, 2015, p. 26). The analyst must speak in such a manner that truth as he views it is spoken with a compassionate or loving intention. Indeed, as I have said earlier, Freud described psychoanalytic treatment as the "scientific cure by love" (McGuire, 1974, pp. 12–13).[56] Elsewhere, Freud wrote in a letter to Ferenczi, "Truth is only the absolute goal of science, but love is the goal of life, which is totally independent of science" (Phillips, 2021a, p. 75). Likewise, in a successful analysis, the analysand can learn how to speak the truth in a similar manner to himself and to others.

Thus, psychoanalysis argues for a more benign take on what constitutes the truth of a person's history, especially childhood history, in that judgments should not be too severe. Once one has a better grasp of what probably happened then and there, in the past, this should lead to a degree of peace of mind, since the traumatic history has been understood in a manner that is gentler and kinder. In this context, truth, justice and peace are the overarching goals of analysis. Put differently, the analysand must wrestle with the emotionally driven lies (truth), injustices (justice) and unrest (peace) that are part of his way of being-in-the-world (Yanklowitz, 2018).

As I have earlier pointed out, truth-telling in psychoanalysis has no adequate way of effectively making a distinction between acts which are true and false to the self or sincere and insincere, even though psychoanalytic practice mainly relies on the analyst being able to do so (Rycroft, 1995). Interestingly, for example, in Winnicott's twin notions of "True" and "False" selves, the true self is never defined; it probably referred to living authentically, a judgment which is exceedingly hard to make (Akhtar, 2009).Winnicott believed that the goal of psychoanalysis was to provide the analysand "with an opportunity to find out what, if anything, for them makes their life worth living", a complex and ambiguous determination (Phillips, 2021b, p. 20). Thus, it is the analysand who ultimately determines what is true and sincere, just as it is the analysand who decides what kind of person to become (e.g., what constitutes a good life).

Finally, the conflict between truth, justice and peace is most evident in psychoanalytically oriented couple's therapy. Indeed, what a wife, husband or partner believes is true and just, and leading to peace between the warring couple, often varies in the extreme. For example, one party may feel that their partner tends to bend the truth in self-serving ways or does not do their fair share of domestic obligations, leading to conflict. In this context, the analyst tries to find common ground, sites where arbitration and compromise are likely to have traction. A similar approach is useful in large group psychology where there is conflict between groups or intragroup conflict.

19. Greed and envy

> (II–16). Rabbi Joshua said: An evil eye, and evil passion, and hate for one's fellow man—these undermine a man's life in this world.
>
> (Bokser, 1983, p. 237)

An evil eye refers to "greed, envy, and looking down on people" (Greenberg, 2016, p. 94).

It is important to distinguish between *an* evil eye and *the* evil eye. As Kravitz and Olitzky note in their commentary on the Ethics, "*an* evil eye is simply the dissatisfaction with what one has, envious of the possessions of others". *The* evil eye connotes a considerably more menacing meaning. It implies envy textured with malice, an envy that doesn't only resent the other his possessions but in addition wishes evil upon that individual for partaking in them (Kravitz & Olitzky, 1993, p. 27).

An evil passion refers to the "evil urge", "the urge to do evil to others" (Greenberg, 2016, p. 94). In rabbinic psychology, the individual tries to expand and deepen the urge to do good and control the urge to do evil to others. This internal struggle of contradictory impulses is what constitutes human nature. This calls to mind the psychoanalytic metaphor, a struggle between Eros (the life force and the sexual instincts) and Thanatos (the death instinct). As the Rabbis noted, the evil urge also has a positive aspect to it, for it can be constructively channeled, "For were it not for the *yetzer hara* [the evil urge], no one would build a house, marry, start a business" (Kravitz & Olitzky, 1993, p. 27). The evil urge can thus be sublimated and channeled into more life-affirming aspects, this being the overarching goal of rabbinic and psychoanalytic psychology.

"Hate for one's fellow man ... undermine[s] a man's life in this world" states the truism that a person who is consumed by hatred of others/groups and/or humanity in general is destined to have a disastrous life of social isolation and the like as well as subvert society. As Sacks and Angel note,

> The art of living the good life depends on the ability to follow the good impulse and to harness the evil impulse. A person who readily gives in to harmful and immoral temptations is a person without self-control, without a strong moral conscience. Giving free rein to one's evil inclinations is a recipe for disaster, destroying one's own life and undermining society.
> (Sacks & Angel, 2015, p. 48)[57]

The concepts implicit in an evil eye, evil passion and hate are foundational in the psychoanalytic oeuvre. It is the more precise formulation of these emotions, particularly envy, jealousy, greed and hatred, that psychoanalysis offers the Ethics, as well as spelling out the real-life consequences for human relations. All of these emotions have their origin in early childhood experience, and it is the work of Melanie Klein (d. 1960), a disciple of Freud, that has probably illuminated most the unconscious roots of the aforementioned emotions.

Envy has been defined psychoanalytically as "discontent over another's possession of what one would like for oneself" (Moore & Fine, 1990, p. 68). As Person et al. has noted, envy is a type of aggressive emotion that differs from jealousy,

> since it [envy] embodies a wish not only to have what the other person has but to deprive the person of what is valuable and make them suffer for having possessed it. Envy is often confused with jealousy [Neubauer, 1982] which involves three parties [as in a Oedipal conflict] and has the aim of winning the exclusive love of the object ["the person who is the focus of one's wishes and needs"] over a rival for love ... the wish to destroy the rival is secondary to the wish to become the person who is more loved.
> (Person, Cooper, & Gabbard, 2005, pp. 551, 555, 554)

Envy has been specifically defined by Klein as

> a destructive attack on the sources of life [originally the breast, a part-object], on the *good* object [the good of the main parental caregiver], not on the bad object [the bad of the main parental caregiver], and it is to be distinguished from ambivalence and frustration.

Moreover, such envy is viewed as innate in origin as a component of the instinctual endowment and necessitates the mechanism of splitting as the first defense in play at the onset (Hinshelwood, 1991, p. 167).

Splitting, an ambiguous term, has been defined in various ways. As Person et al. have noted, perhaps the clearest way of understanding splitting is to view it as the division of positive emotions and perceptions, directed either at the self or toward other people, from negative emotions and perceptions in order that the self or object is viewed as either "all good" or "all bad"; for example, a husband who views his wife as "all good" or "all bad" depending on whether she satisfies all of his needs and wishes on demand. Freud regarded splitting as a defense mechanism, while Klein alleged that it was a normal developmental phase in the perception of self and other and only later activated as a defense mechanism (Person, Cooper, & Gabbard, 2005, pp. 560, 555).

The destructive impulse that is part of envy is counterbalanced by its opposite, gratitude.

Gratitude, says Klein, is

> a full gratification at the breast [which] means that the infant feels that he has received from his love object a unique gift which he wants to keep. This is the basis of gratitude ... gratitude is closely bound with generosity. Inner wealth derives from having assimilated the good object so that the individual becomes able to share its gifts with others.
> (Klein 1957, pp. 188, 189 as cited by Akhtar, 2009)

Gratitude is intimately connected with trust in others and adds to the amalgamation of satisfying relations with them (Akhtar, 2009). The important point to bear in mind is that gratitude is potentiated toward an object by the satisfaction that the object gives, and it therefore is a form of object-love. Envy kills gratitude felt toward the object (Hinshelwood, 1991, p. 313).[58] As Erich Fromm notes (1947), "There is perhaps no phenomenon which contains so much destructive feeling as moral indignation, which permits envy or hate to be acted out under the guise of virtue" (p. 120).

Greed refers to the infant's insatiable hunger; it emanates from an ungratifying oral tie with the mother and, as Klein noted, has at least two purposes:

> (1) to get hold of good substances and objects (ultimately, "good" milk, "good" feces, "good" penis and "good" children) and with their help to paralyze the action of "bad" objects and substances inside the body, and (2) to amass sufficient reserves inside itself to be able to resist attacks made upon the external objects, and if, necessary, to restore to its mother's body, or rather to its objects what has been stolen from them.
> (1931, pp. 246–247 as cited by Akhtar, 2009)

The voraciousness of greed originates from the fact that internalization of "good" objects is usually followed by their destruction or in some instances functional diminishment by internalized aggression (Akhtar, 2009).

Hatred is a complex emotion that also impacts the hater's cognitive style. Hatred involves the relentless wish to injure, damage or annihilate the hated object (in reality and/or in fantasy).

Freud viewed hate as a threat to the ego's integrity, though in his later publications hate was conceptualized as an expression of the death instinct (its opposite is love) (Rycroft, 1995). Hate incorporates various unconscious fantasies, especially "the belief that one has been wronged, betrayed, and injured by others" (Akhtar, 2009, p. 128). Along with this fantasy is the rigid cognitive focus that alters the capacity to compassionately reason. In addition, the superego (roughly the conscience) is defective, allowing the hater to violate the rights of others as he manifests his hatred and destructiveness. As Akhtar notes, and is common knowledge, hatred can manifest itself in many ways in the one-to-one context, from literal murder or abuse to emotional domination, intellectual control and the insatiable need to demonstrate one's moral superiority over others (ibid.). Also worth mentioning is the fact that envy can morph into hatred and often does.[59] Finally, there are those people who are prone to engage in the paradox of "loving hatred" (Bollas, 1987, p. 117). Loving hate, says Bollas (1987), is "a situation where an individual preserves a relationship by sustaining a passionate negative cathexis of it" (read: investment of energy). Moreover, "the primary aim of loving hate is to get closer to the object" (ibid., pp. 118, 134). Some couples are into an erotic form of hate in which the goal is to cause harm to their partner (ibid., p. 133).

The brief psychoanalytic survey I have put forward describing envy, jealousy, greed and hatred only touches on the impact of these feelings on an individual's life, especially the truncated ties to empathy. I have not elaborated on the place these emotions have in personality disorders, particularly borderline personality disorder, and the extent to which they distort the ability to make and sustain relationships, in terms of giving and receiving love. In this sense, the Rabbis are right: A person consumed by envy, jealousy, greed and hatred rather than, say, gratitude is someone who will quite likely have a very troubled and troubling life—"these undermine a man's life in this world". They "shrink a person's life" (Greenberg, 2016, p. 93).

20. Death

> (III–1). Akavyah ben Mahalalel said: meditate on three things and you will be spared from the power of sin: Consider whence you came, and wither you are going, and before whom you are destined to give an accounting. *Whence you came*—from a putrid drop; *whither you are going*—to a place of dust, worms and maggots; and *before whom you are destined to give an accounting*—before the King of Kings, the Holy One, praised be He.
>
> (Bokser, 1983, p. 238)

This Ethic is indicating a strong correlation between sin and Thantophobia, fear of death or death anxiety. Sin in the rabbinic mind of the time could mean lots of things, but it is often correlated with the sin of pride, an inordinately high view of one's own ability or value coupled with an arrogant feeling of being better than others (e.g., teenagers often present themselves as having an exquisite blend of ignorance and arrogance). The idea here is that if the person critically reflects on where he comes from, a putrid drop,[60] where he is going, a place of dust, worms and maggots, he will be willing and able to avoid being drawn into lust, the desire for money (Kravitz & Olitzky, 1993), violations of trust, hurting another person and defying God, etcetera (Greenberg, 2016). Likewise, if one is a believer, one should reflect on the fact that ultimate judgment by God awaits one, so there is no escaping the negative consequences of sin. Sacks and Angel aptly summarize the meaning of this Ethic:

> Akavya advises humility as the basis of a righteous life. Since life is transient and since everyone ends in the grave, there is no point in being arrogant, jealous, or greedy. If one keeps in mind his/her life is answerable to God's judgment, one will avoid sin to the extent possible.
> (Sacks & Angel, 2015, p. 59)

Yanklowitz adds some real-life drama to what Sacks and Angel are saying:

> However, standing at a graveside, staring down into the black hole into which the body will be lowered, who is not humbled by the lowliness of the self? Virtually no one will remember our names after our deaths. Realizing our own relative insignificance can bring us to despair. Or to hedonism—*just eat, drink, and be merry, for tomorrow we die.*
> (Yanklowitz, 2018, p. 124)

Yanklowitz continues:

> But the religious response in this Mishnah is the exact opposite. Rather, we can do *t'suvah* [repentance] to engage in self-transformation to return to our fundamentally good selves, our inner divine spark. This return to God can inspire awe in us mere mortals and a desire to become our best selves.
> (Ibid.)

Though there is a lot of God-talk in the aforementioned Ethic, it is hard not to agree with most of what this Ethic is saying. The value of humility, for example, is a central one in the rabbinic mind and still has value in our time in terms of an art of living a good life. Likewise, focusing on one's individual behavior with an eye to changing ourselves for the better seems like sensible advice. If one is a believer, one has probably internalized a God notion, such that one's superego can be rather severe in terms of self-judgment and behaving in accordance with, or against, God's will as characterized by religious tradition. By sin I mean a re-casted version of "original sin":

> all of us are born with limited capacities to pursue the good, and that left to our own devices all of us will betray ourselves and our fellow man. Man's inhumanity to man is a reflection of the natural course of human affairs when unchecked by a context of moral force.
> (Patterson, 1984, p. 89)

Thus, sin as I define it is a common human quality. As the Augustian scholar Phillip Carry notes, there may not be original sin, and it possibly makes more sense to believe that we are born innocent. Yet apparently to most people it feels the other way, as if for as long as one can remember one has been sinning and impure. Moreover, from a psychological perspective, it seems a good thing to take account of that feeling (Marcus, 2003, p. 157).

What psychoanalysis adds to the aforementioned Ethic is a deeper and more expansive view of death anxiety, especially at it applies to a non-believer's outlook and behavior. The believer has the "world to come" belief to fall back on, where all will be put right, as well as that of being sent to hell, the more or less opposite of the world to come.

As Stolorow (1973, p. 473) noted in his review article, a psychoanalytic view of death anxiety indicates that it is a "multi-faceted phenomenon" which has been formulated at numerous levels of analysis, such as "the level of infantile conflict and intrapsychic structural tensions [e.g., superego versus the id], the level of primary instincts and the level of object relations" (and as the atheistic existentialists like Sartre and Camus note, on the level of ontological givens (ibid.)).

For example, in classical Freudian theory, anxiety about death is usually regarded as a compromise formation[61] or derivative which both masks and symbolically expresses other unconscious infantile complexes (ibid., p. 474). One formulation of death anxiety, says Stolorow, is that it is a derivative fantasy of castration fear. The fear of death is a fear of any type of libidinal lack and is thus closely entwined with the castration complex in the broadest sense. Another theory is that death anxiety originates as a derivative of the fear of separation or object loss (ibid., p. 477). Freud believed that death anxiety may be regarded as the conclusion

> of a developmental sequence of specific separation anxieties: such as the birth trauma, the fear of object-loss in early infancy, the fear of castration which would eliminate the possibility of Oedipal union with the mother, the fear of abandonment by the superego.
> (Ibid.)

The fear of death has also been thought of as originating from superego dynamics. Following Freud, says Stolorow, this view presupposes that living means the same thing as being loved by the superego and that this fear of death, such as in depression, may express the fear of abandonment and/or persecution by the superego. In other instances, some believe that death anxiety may emanate "from the fear of one's own introverted destructive impulses or from the fear of ego-loss associated with overwhelming sexual excitement, and from infantile fears of physical immobility or of the dark, or of suffocation" (ibid., p. 475). Common to all of these interpretations, says Stolorow, is the notion that death anxiety is largely a secondary phenomenon, a derivative of other unconscious processes (ibid.).

In summary, Stolorow believes that there are four fantasies that underlie the fear of death; they include the fear of castration (e.g., of bodily injury, losing one's relational potency) as Freud noted, the fear of separation and object loss (e.g., being separated from a parent in divorce or their sudden death), the fear of one's own overpowering masochism (i.e., to be self-destructive, the repetition compulsion), and the fear of talionic punishment by the superego for one's death wishes toward other people (an "eye for an eye" mentality) (Akhtar, 2009, p. 107).[62] It has also been found by empirical researchers that death anxiety seems to be a foundational fear at the center of a continuum of psychological disorders, including hypochondriasis, panic disorder and anxiety and depressive disorder (Iverach, Menzies, & Menzies, 2014).

Finally, the awareness or analysis of the roots of the death anxiety (the Ethics is suggesting the need is to face it head-on) would theoretically put one in the position of recognizing one's wish and need for others but also the possibility of internalizing the "mother" (i.e., the main parental caregiver) such that one is able to sustain oneself without their actual presence. Furthermore, the aggression and fear of losing the object can be modified by a recognition that those feelings can be "owned" and not seen as so destructive and final. Psychoanalysis also works toward a less severe or judgmental superego such that whether one views it as God's accounting or a secular equivalent it is a more benign judgment that is aimed for. While the amelioration and the role of religion may be operative in the promise of an afterlife, it does not detract from the exhortation of the Ethics to be more humble in recognition of the fleeting nature of man's time on earth.[63]

21. The Nighttime and idleness

(III–5). Rabbi Hanina ben Hahinai said: He who stays up nights and he who journeys alone upon the road at night, and he who likes to idle away his time—all these are guilty of undoing their own lives.

(Bokser, 1983, p. 239)

In the time of this mishna, those who stayed up late at night usually were up to no good. Rabbi Hanina ben Hahinai "warns of behaviors that disrupt religious serenity" (Sacks & Angel, 2015, p. 62). Sacks and Angel continue,

> If one stays awake at night (unless engaged in Torah study or religious meditation), one's mind is likely to be filled with frivolous thoughts. If one travels alone, one's mind is preoccupied with possible dangers. If one harbors idle thoughts, one thereby ejects thoughts of Torah and Godliness.
>
> (Ibid.)

As Greenberg noted, it was believed at the time that when everyone was sleeping, so to speak, the individual may be preparing to engage in a crime, or he may be making himself vulnerable to the lifestyle of a criminal and commit wicked deeds. So-called respectable people were asleep at night. Likewise, at the time it was believed that traveling alone on empty roads can be unsafe (it still can be). Given the dangerous character of roads, most people tended to travel in groups with guards. The lone traveler was likely engaged in questionable or worse behavior (Greenberg, 2016, pp. 19–20).

The person "who likes to idle away his time" of course speaks to the well-known notion that idleness often leads to engaging in ill-conceived, ill-advised and ill-fated behavior. If a person is not using his time constructively, in effect wasting time, he is likely to engage in "bad actions or illegitimate pleasures", according to Rabbi Hanina ben Hahinai (ibid., p. 120). Such a person is "guilty of undoing their own lives" or in another translation "bears guilt for one's soul" (Yanklowitz, 2018, p. 135).

Finally, quoting Rashi[64] and Bartinoro (a popular fifteenth-century commentator on the mishna), Kravitz and Olitzky (1993) point out that the first clause of this Ethic specifically relates to one who spends the hours "thinking the wrong kinds of thoughts". Likewise, Bartinoro links the last two clauses by alleging since the night tends to be a dangerous time in most people's minds "the lone traveler dare not distract his mind from Torah, which would be his only real defense against brigands and deadly accidents" (ibid., p. 39).

From a psychoanalytic point of view, what comes to mind is the fact that this Ethic describes three behaviors that are construed as "bad" and judged very harshly as an undoing of lives. It would seem that this particular Ethic is open to many different interpretations, e.g., traveling alone at night may not mean one is up to no good but could indicate that the traveler is putting herself in harm's way as a form of aggression turned on the self. Furthermore, these actions could even be seen as positive behaviors. For example, "He who stays up nights" may well be a desirable action such as studying for an exam or tending to a sick family member. Likewise, "he who journeys alone upon the road at night" may not be putting himself in harm's way nor being up to no good but in fact is engaging in positive behavior such as visiting a dying friend or clinching an important charitable business deal. Finally, "he who likes to idle away his time" may not simply be wasting his time. The fact is, for example, that a certain amount of idle time is necessary to incubate ideas in the creative process.

In other instances, being alone through the night or traveling alone at night requires the capacity to be alone, no easy achievement. Indeed, it was Donald Winnicott (1958) who famously wrote about the capacity to be alone as a good thing (he was not talking about social withdrawal, introversion or loneliness). Being alone in a recurrently serene experience like listening to music or reading a book calls to mind the experience of being alone in the background presence of the "good enough" main parental caregiver: "this experience is that of being alone, as an infant and small child, in the presence of mother" (ibid., p. 416). As Winnicott notes, there is a paradox at work; the pleasurable experience of feeling alone when in fact the main parental caregiver is also present. Separation without separation. Such an internalized experience of aloneness as an adult is desirable and constitutes "one of the most important signs of emotional maturity" (ibid.), including creative sublimations like in art and writing. While forms of social withdrawal, introversion and loneliness tend to deplete the ego, the capacity to be alone is usually ego-enhancing (an expression of "ego-relatedness" (ibid., p. 419)), mainly because it repeats an earlier period of being psychologically contained by a non-invasive, accurately empathic and loving main parental caregiver ("the ego-supportive environment is introjected" (ibid., p. 418)).

To make matters even more emotionally demanding, sometimes one has to be alone at the scariest time, when it is nighttime, which is dark or even pitch black. One thinks of the lonely soldier who has been ordered to stay put at night, waiting for the enemy to make the first move.

Or the young child who has to face a dark bedroom. Darkness acts as a void onto which the child (or adult) can project his most unacceptable thoughts and wishes. The projection of aggressive wishes leads to the fear of attacking ghosts, monsters, burglars and kidnappers etcetera. Handling darkness is a psychological achievement, for darkness is linked in most people's minds with chaos, death and the underworld, while light is linked with life and immortality. Moreover, "darkness, in all of its many forms, represents the infinite gap between the self and the other. There is no measurement for space or time in the dark—merely endless solitude and despair" (Yanklowitz, 2018, p. 135). Of course, not everyone experiences darkness as something frightening. I am reminded of my patient who enjoyed wandering the late-night streets of Manhattan thoroughly enjoying the darkness, as it meant he could lose his identity, fade into the night and just observe the nightlife. He also enjoyed frightening, or at least intimidating people as he wore all black. When he came home at dawn, he told me he always felt "fulfilled".

22–24. Sin and lovingkindness

> (III–11). Rabbi Hanina ben Dosa said: He to whom the fear of sin is more important than wisdom, his wisdom will endure; he to whom his wisdom is more important than the fear of sin, his wisdom will not endure.
>
> (Bokser, 1983, p. 240)
>
> (III–12). He used to say: He whose deeds exceed his wisdom, his wisdom will endure; he whose wisdom exceeds his deeds, his wisdom will not endure.
> (Ibid.)
>
> (III–13). He used to say also: He in whom people take pleasure, God will take pleasure in him also. And he in whom people have no pleasure, God has no pleasure in him either.
>
> (Ibid.)

The first two sayings are bunched together because the second one completes the first one. It stresses the relevance "not only of avoiding sin, but also of doing good deeds" (Berkson, 2010, p. 114). "The beginning of wisdom", it famously says in the Proverbs (1:7), "is reverence for God".

Reverence for God implies recognizing the awe-inspiring, holy nature of the Almighty. As the psalmist says in Psalm 111:10, "The beginning of wisdom is fear [i.e., reverence] of the Lord". But what is wisdom? Wisdom is to be distinguished from knowledge. As Sacks and Angel explain,

> One must study in order to attain knowledge. A component beyond the collection of facts and figures is the ability to see unities, to understand how the various branches of knowledge are interrelated. Another component is to be able to draw distinctions, to isolate individual facts and figures and see how each thing stands alone. Yet one might be intellectually competent and still lack genuine wisdom.
>
> (Sacks & Angel, 2015, p. 73)

Wisdom, however, is lodged in humility, in its extreme, viewing oneself as "nothingness" (it calls to mind Socrates's famous dictum, "The only true wisdom is in knowing you know nothing").

It is exactly, until such time that the person realizes that compared to God he is nothing, he knows nothing that he can be said to have attained wisdom. It is this fear of God and fear of sin that situates life in a proper moral context (ibid.). Also, the Rabbis were aware that while knowledge can be derived from reading books and going to lectures, wisdom is found in significant human experiences. A wise individual, is one who has a deep grasp of human psychology, who can offer proper guidance based on the special needs of those who turn to him/her. The essence of wisdom is humility; but this humility must be blended with profound empathy for human beings and keen awareness of human frailty.... Enduring wisdom is based on one's standing in the presence of Eternity; on one's interactions with human beings; on one's sympathetic involvement in the lives of others.

(Ibid., p. 72)

Finally, says Sacks elsewhere, "Wisdom is the ability to see God in Creation, in the intricate complexity of the natural universe and the human mind" (2023c, p. 2).

Psychoanalysis might view these aforementioned sayings as emphasizing the important distinction between intellectual understanding and emotional understanding (i.e., emotional truths). The former is called intellectualization while the latter is called insight. Psychoanalysis is "not about knowledge, it's about experience" (Phillips, 2021b, p. 45). Analysts are well aware of analysands who have an intellectual grasp of an important issue but lack emotional insight, leading to the absence of changed behavior. Intellectualizing has been defined as "the exaggerated use of intellectual measures such as abstract philosophizing, speculative thought, or pedantic logic as a defense against anxiety or other unwelcome affects. It is commonly mobilized in adolescence. It may be associated with obsessional or paranoid thinking" (Person, Cooper, & Gabbard, 2005, p. 553). Woody Allen in some of his films depicts something of this character; he knows a lot about himself psychologically speaking but not about the emotional stuff that leads to affective and behavioral change. The point is that the emotional weight impacts the kind of things we know, and what we think is true (Sagal, 2023, p. 13).

Insight has been defined as

> an understanding of some previously unrecognized truth about one's self, one's behavior, or the actions and motivations of others. It may actually accrue gradually or be experienced as a flash [a spontaneous seeing of relations], and may be associated with feelings of relief or pain.
>
> (Person, Cooper, & Gabbard, 2005, p. 553)

In this view, the wise person has considerable wisdom based on personal insight.

Fear of sin and doing good deeds is the key recommendation to attain wisdom in the aforementioned sayings. While Rabbi Hanina ben Dosa emphasizes the fear of sin, the fear of desecrating God and religious tradition, the psychoanalyst would regard such a valuative attachment as rather severe. In psychoanalysis, the superego, the repository of parental injunctions and prohibitions that emanate from the resolution of the Oedipus complex, should ideally be gentler and kinder. Fear of sin in psychoanalytic theory boils down to a fear of conscious or unconscious parental judgment. As one gets older, being less tough on others and oneself is a sign that the superego, as it were, is experienced as more benign. That is, there is less of a need and desire to rally ego defenses against instinctual wishes.

While wisdom is given considerable attention in the Ethics, the concept of wisdom does not appear in the five psychoanalytic dictionaries I looked at, suggesting that it is not part of "mainstream" psychoanalytic thought.[65] However, it was Erik Erikson who famously described eight stages of the life cycle. It is the last stage, old age, where the ego crisis is Ego Integrity versus Despair; that, says Erikson, is where the ego virtue or ego strength of wisdom ideally comes into play. As Monte (1980) notes, the adult in whom ego integrity has fully unfolded understands that his individual life is merely one life cycle in the movement of history. He is persuaded that what had to be was, and it was gratifying. In contrast, says Monte, despair of what has been suggests that what has been has been for nothing. "Despair is a protest of a person who is not yet satisfied with a life that has never been satisfying" (ibid., p. 258). The most significant bequest that parents can give their children is their inner strength, demonstrated in their own example, to confront ultimate concerns like death without the disintegration and disorganization effects of fear and/or anxiety. Thus, the ego virtue or ego strength that acts as the sign of the climactic stage of the life cycle is Wisdom. "Wisdom", says Erikson, "is detached concern with life itself, in the face of death itself" (1964, p. 133). As Monte says, adults who exemplify this kind of integrity Erikson describes as wise, in the manner that they judge their limited lives as a totality that transcends petty disgust at the feeling of "being finished" (Monte, 1980, p. 258). That is, they have the will and ability to transcend the despair "of facing the period of relative helplessness which marks the end as it marked the beginning" (Erikson, 1964, p. 134). Indeed, Erikson's notion of wisdom is compatible with the Ethics, which sees wisdom as essentially humility and standing in the presence of Eternity (Sacks & Angel, 2015).

The third aphorism claims that God desires from his religious devotees the display of lovingkindness toward others (e.g., doing both the negative and positive commandments). In this way, others will cherish being with them. As all humans are made in the image of God, they demand being treated respectfully and decently (Greenberg, 2016). It is worth noting that when religious people display what is judged as immoral behavior, they are disrespecting God, and this is particularly shoddy behavior as judged by one's fellow devotees. Many non-religious people display a fair amount of schadenfreude, malicious joy, at the religious person's fall from grace.

What is also of interest about this aphorism is that God seems to take his "cue" from the behavior of man, as if to say that when man treats others kindly and generously God is present or at least "comes to mind", as Levinas put it.

Psychoanalysis, conceived as a meaning-giving, affect-integrating and action-guiding activity, puts great stress on relationships with others, and like the Rabbis it emphasizes the fact that unless there is changed behavior all the intellectual and emotional understandings are not to be overvalued compared to treating people better (deep and expansive love and creative and productive work, said Freud). Put differently, following Levinas, Morgan notes

> the most primary or fundamental features of the world as human beings experience it are features of interpersonal relationships and actions; the world makes sense to human beings most fundamentally in terms of how human beings are related to one another as they live in the world together, rather than merely in terms of how they think.
> (Morgan, 2011, p. 238)

Psychoanalysis sees man as being fundamentally object-seeking not just pleasure-seeking. This is the difference between the object relational and classical Freudian view of the human condition. This issue, the connection between words and deeds, is in sharp focus in the termination phase, when the analysand has to say good-bye to the analyst and the formal analytic process (this can take a year). That is, after all the discussions about ending treatment have taken place, it is up to the analysand to stop talking and take the leap into faith that he or she can flourish without the help of the analyst. Just as learning Torah is not simply intellectual acumen but has deeper meaning in terms of transforming moral consciousness, so analysis has its deeper meaning, which is the application of one's insights and understandings in the real world in terms of changed behavior (i.e., emotionally, cognitively and interpersonally) as the analysand construes the matter.

25. Social learning, self-control and gratitude

> (IV–1). Ben Zoma said: Who is wise? He who learns from all men. As it is written (Psalm 119:99): From all who taught me have I gained understanding. Who is mighty? He who subdues his passions. As it is written (Proverbs 16:32): He that is slow to anger is better than the mighty, and he that rules over his own spirit than he that conquers a city. Who is rich? He who is happy with his portion. As it is written (Psalm 128:2): When you enjoy the labor of your hands, happy will you be, and all be well with you. *Happy will you be* refers to your state in this world; *and all will be well with you* refers to your state in the world to come. Who attains honor? He who confers honor upon other men. As it is written (I Samuel 2:30): Those who honor me will I honor, and those who disparage me, I will esteem lightly.
> (Bokser, 1983, p. 242)

This Ethic with its proof texts is actually four interrelated notions. I will discuss them one at a time. "Who is wise? He who learns from all men". The idea here, says Greenberg (2016), is that the wise person is he "who is learning all the time from everyone.... Remain open to learning from everyone you encounter" (p. 168). While the knowledgeable person may be wise, it is not a pre-requisite for wisdom, for as Sacks and Angel (2015) point out, "Wisdom is measured by quality, not merely by quantity" [of knowledge] (p. 89). For example, the intellectual situated in the "ivory tower" may not be wise (Yanklowitz, 2018). Moreover, "One who learns from everyone has the intellectual curiosity and humility which are the sine qua non of real wisdom" (Sacks & Angel, 2015, p. 89). That is, it is the lack of conceit that fosters in the wise person the will and ability to learn from someone who may not be as learned or wise (Kravitz & Olitzky, 1993). Berkson (2010) summarizes the likely meaning of the afore-mentioned saying:

> Most of us are willing to learn from teachers and those in power over us. It is more unusual to be willing to learn from those who have less schooling, are younger, or are in positions subordinate to us—and that is probably the point of this saying.
>
> (p. 134)

Psychoanalysis more than most forms of psychotherapy is in sync with the gist of the above saying. That is, every analysand is a "universe" as it were, and the analyst's goal is to learn as much about the person as he is able. But what does it mean to learn from a person in the analytic context? It is only in the transference that the analyst knows the "whole" person, especially his archaic and immature child self, which is not usually evident or in focus in ordinary human interchange outside the consultation room. Transference is a well-known term, but it is worth reminding the reader what it is in the ana-lytic conversation. Transference has been defined as "the patient's emotional experience of and fantasies about the analyst, which though they may be based in part on actual perceptions of the analyst, recapitulate experiences with and fantasies about objects in the patient's childhood" (Person, Cooper & Gabbard, 2005, p. 561). Transference neurosis is quite similar to transfer-ence, except the focus is on "the analysand's re-experiencing of his or her characteristic psychic conflicts and modes of defense, finding their expression in fantasies about the analyst" (ibid.). As Freud noted, "it is still true that the transference neurosis [is] the essential subject of psycho-analytic study" (1920, p. 52). It is through transference and transference neurosis that the analyst accesses the analysand's unconscious and is said to "know" the person and learns from him. This is actually an example of social learning—that is, we are receptive to learning from others, we are enhanced from their experience as well as our own, and we can internalize their knowledge and wisdom into our outlook and practice. Learning from one's patient is not a passive process but one that necessitates effort and dedication on the analyst's part. Analysts do this through techniques such as free association, free-flowing interchanges, dream analysis and interpretation, and transference exploration and interpretation. With these techniques, psychoanalytic therapists attempt to help their analysands gain insight into how their past experiences animate their present outlook and behavior. In this sense, the analysand is better known by the analyst; the analyst has learned from the analysand, and the analysand's relation to himself is more knowledgeable and insightful.

It is also important to recognize that in order to learn from the analysand, especially when he or she is in a transference or transference neurosis, it demands a certain kind of listening that is unique to the analyst, as far as I know. This "evenly suspended attention" (Freud), "free-floating responsiveness" (J. Sandler) or the "analyst's reverie" (W. Bion, T. Ogden)[66] creates the conditions of possibility for the analysand to free associate and ultimately to provoke an interpretation by the analyst (a "conjecture", what is "really" going on). The point is that to the extent a person can learn to analytically listen he will become exquisitely attuned to what the other person is saying and is more likely to be willing and able to, say, potentiate an I-Thou relation. In Judaism, "listening is a deeply spiritual act"; for example, "to listen to God is to be open to God" (Sacks, 2023d, p. 1).

"Who is mighty? He who subdues his passions" puts into sharp focus the importance of self-control and self-restraint in everyday life. As Greenberg (2016) notes, "it takes more internal strength to control one's temper and restrain himself than to lift weights [e.g., to siphon the anger] or to lash out verbally" (p. 168). Sacks and Angel (2015) have a similar view: "We see that a strong person has physical strength; [but] we realize that one with moral self-control may have much greater strength of character than the hero" (p. 89). For example, in Maimonides's rationalist philosophy "self-control is central to the good life" (Berkson, 2010, p. 136). Maimonides maintains that our central goal in living should be to reach our highest potential as a human being, which requires great self-control. "And this highest potential is, according to Maimonides, our real though limited ability to know God" (ibid.). In the context of rabbinic psychology, self-control is a matter of controlling the *yetzer-hara*, the inclination to do evil, rooted in, say, anger, envy, lust and hatred (Berkson, 2010) that is constantly in conflict with the inclination to do good (Kravitz & Olitzky, 1993).[67]

While there is no entry for self-control in the five psychoanalytic dictionaries I consulted, suggesting that self-control is not a "mainstream" concept,[68] the fact is that the notion speaks to the heart of psychoanalysis. As Freud said, "where id was, there ego shall be" (1933b, p. 80). In other words, to the extent that the ego can control one's anti-social impulses and the like, the better functioning a person is likely to be. In this context, strengthening the ego is the goal. Likewise, sublimation, one of the overarching goals of most versions of psychoanalysis, requires self-control. Sublimation has been clearly defined as the "resolution of intrapsychic conflict by changing the sexual and aggressive aim of an urge and finding a substitute gratification.

The term ... implies a constructive or socially admirable outcome that is satisfying and flexible" (Person, Cooper & Gabbard, 2005, p. 560).

Self-control is one of those words that nearly everyone bandies about, but it is difficult to define (as is the psychoanalytic notion of self-regulation).[69] Self-control, or what I prefer to call, following Nietzsche, "self-mastery"—an ethic of self-rule over one's emotions and passions and a striving for excellence—is best viewed as an important aspect of moral psychology, in part because one's freedom is truncated to the extent that one is not master of himself. Such a valuative attachment is entirely in sync with a psychoanalytic outlook, for as Freud noted, "Analysis does not set out to make pathological reactions impossible, but to give patients the freedom to decide one way or another" (1923, p. 50).[70]

While space limitations do not allow me to detail how the aforementioned moral beliefs and values can enhance self-control and potentiate morally praiseworthy, artful fashioning of a good life, I want to say something about this topic that is underappreciated and undertheorized in mainstream psychoanalytic thought, though less so in experimental social psychology (though implied in the Ethics). Indeed, as sociologists and criminologists have pointed out, "the incorporation of morality and self-control into a larger theoretical framework remains in its infancy, with empirical research slowly emerging but with mixed results" (Rocque, Posick & Piquero, 2016, p. 521).

For example, the role of how one "frames" one's frustrating situation, or more generally and profoundly how one conceptualizes one's extreme suffering, has bearing on to what extent one can exert patient self-control and persevere. Indeed, this capacity is lodged in deeply internalized transcendent-pointing beliefs and values that are both an expression and affirmation of one's autonomy, integration and humanity. Drawing from a limit-example of the human condition, Primo Levi described "the saving force" of the religious (e.g., devout Jews and Catholics, Jehovah Witnesses) and secular (e.g., devout Marxists) believers' faith in the Nazi concentration camps, in contrast to the secular intellectual lodged in a skeptic-humanistic category (e.g., psychoanalysts such as Bettelheim noted):

> Their universe was vaster than ours, more expanded in space and time, above all more comprehensible, they had a key and point of leverage, a millennial tomorrow so that there might be a sense to sacrificing themselves, a place in heaven or earth where justice and compassion had won, or would win in a perhaps remote but certain future: Moscow or the celestial or terrestrial Jerusalem. Their hunger was different from ours. It was a Divine punishment or expiation, or votive offering, or the fruit of capitalist putrefaction. Sorrow, in them or around them, was decipherable and therefore did not overflow into despair.
>
> (Levi, 1988, p. 146)

What Levi is getting at is that it was through the believers' strongly felt, flexibly and creatively applied, transcendent-pointing moral beliefs and values, specifically as they related to pressing on amidst the horror of the immediate future, that the devout religious and political camp inmate was able to transform their dehumanizing reality into something "more", something "otherwise". It is a gross understatement to say that this required self-control and other qualities associated with self-mastery. For it is documented that many camp inmates threw themselves into the electrified barbed wire, or allowed themselves to become a *muselmann*, slang for one of the "walking dead". As Auschwitz survivor Jean Améry put it, the believer was to some extent shielded from the worst of Nazi dehumanization in that he was paradoxically both more distant and closer to his horrifying reality:

> Further from reality because in his Finalistic attitude he ignores the given contents of material phenomenon and fixes his sight on nearer or more distant future; but he is also closer to reality because for just this reason he does not allow himself to be overwhelmed by the conditions around him and thus can strongly influence them.
>
> (Améry, 1980, p. 14)

The aforementioned observations of Levi and Améry have been supported by research-based psychologists of religion. They "have shown that religion as experienced and practiced by many people in the 21st century is associated with higher self-control and specific elements of self-regulation" (McCullough & Carter, 2013, p. 127). That is, "research suggests that religion and self-control are indeed related at the level of personality" (ibid., p. 128). In other words, at its best, religion can be a fertile breeding ground for the development and implementation of self-control, which can have positive outcomes in a wide range of behavioral and psychological domains. For example, many of the unruly impulses, emotions and desires that get people into trouble, making their existence and those they care about miserable, are reinforced by the highly valued self-control-oriented features of the world religions, such as moralizing gods, a belief in an afterlife and the self-monitoring/policing aspects of the sanctification of everyday life (ibid., pp. 124, 126, 129). Of course, this is not to say that religion at its worst can't promote self-control failures, like when religious fanatics have apocalyptic notions or engage in murder of innocents for the "sake of god". Religion can also facilitate over-control that inhibits and self-alienates a person, that, to quote one of my practicing Catholic analysands, made them "feel twisted up like a pretzel".

My point is that when self-control is understood within the context of self-mastery as a manifestation of a broad set of strongly felt, flexibly and creatively applied, transcendent-pointing moral beliefs and values that tend to be other-directed, instead of being understood in the short-term (e.g., resisting ice cream while dieting), chances are that one will be willing and able to exert reasonable self-control, especially in important matters and exceptional accomplishments. Such self-mastery resonates with what has been called "grit", which has been "defined as passion and perseverance for long-term goals despite setbacks, failures and competing pursuits" (Eskreis-Winkler, Gross & Duckworth, 2016, p. 380). Grit requires having a superordinate goal that, along with sound judgment and empathy, motivates a person to struggle toward a culminating point of actualization, sometimes for a lifetime (ibid., p. 390). Such self-mastery includes resisting foolish or dangerous temptation and summoning the courage to act in the face of challenge or assault. In both of these contexts, one's behavior is perceived as an affirmation of one's autonomy, integration and humanity that is rooted in one's identity-congruent, life-promoting moral beliefs and values. Indeed, "one of the recent shifts in self-regulation theory has been to propose that effective self-regulation operates through habits or habitual avoidance of conflict" (Maranges & Baumeister, 2016, p. 55). That is, "People with good self-control do not necessarily resist temptation and desires, more often or more effectively than others. Rather they seem to set up their lives to be less exposed to temptations" (ibid.). This shift in self-regulation and self-control theory clearly suggests that certain moral beliefs and values and their associated other-directed, other-regarding and other-serving enactments in "real life", such as those of aforementioned religious/political believers, potentiate high levels of habitual self-control that can be a significant factor in living a morally praiseworthy, good life.

"Who is rich? He who is happy with his portion" is an assertion of the ill-conceived nature of envying what others have compared to what one has acquired: "No matter how wealthy one is, the desire for more (or envying others who have more) can make a person feel poor or deprived" (Greenberg, 2016, p. 169). Sacks and Angel (2015) note, "We understand that real wealth is embodied in an attitude of satisfaction and gratitude for what one has" (p. 89). As Berkson (2010) claims, Ben Zoma's statement about the nature of happiness may have been influenced by Greek and Roman Stoic philosophers. However, where the goal in Stoic philosophy was to be free of distress (suggesting indifference to pleasure and pain was aimed for), Ben Zoma's ideal of being happy with one's portion does not suggest such indifference to pleasure or pain, "but rather enjoyment of life and freedom from envy, based on gratitude to God" (p. 138).

What does it mean psychoanalytically speaking to be happy with one's portion, to be satisfied with what one has? Surely, such satisfaction is correlated with what one expects. That is, the greater the correlation between one's expectations and one's fate, the greater the likelihood that one will be more content with one's life circumstances. Some people, however, are extreme consumers, and they care mainly about amassing more and more of a thing, a kind of insatiable hunger for things, including psychic income like accolades. Briefly, for Freud, happiness was the human goal, and this could best be obtained, at least to some degree, through the deep and wide capacity to love and the capacity for creative and productive work.[71]

Following Melanie Klein, I have already mentioned the role of envy and gratitude in human experience (see entry #19), though in terms of this saying, a bit more should be said about gratitude. The gist of envy is not only wanting what the other has, a kind of jealousy, but also not wanting the other person to have the desired quality, to in effect steal it from him. Envy is thus considerably more aggressive than jealousy, and it is the opposite of gratitude. As I have said, for Klein love emanates from the infant's sense of gratitude toward the "good" mother, in Kleinian language, toward the satisfying "good breast". This feeling is the basis for the infant's and later the adult's "appreciation of all goodness in the self and in others" (Bergmann, 1987, p. 248).

Gratitude, the willingness and ability to be thankful that evokes the wish to return kindness, has a central role in all the great ancient religious and spiritual wisdom traditions; it also has been regarded as important in contemporary secular contexts. For example, as early as the 1960s American psychologist Abraham Maslow emphasized that what he believed was the innate drive for self-actualization in part culminated in a person embracing a "count your blessings" outlook (Compton & Hoffman, 2012, p. 316). Likewise, Winnicott believed that the infant (and later the adult), if provided with the facilitating environment, has an "inherent potential to care about the (m)other" and that "goodness and morality and forward movement don't have to be taught, rather it is *there* waiting to be found and met" (Slochower, 2018, pp. 99, 100). Gratitude is an expression of this "goodness and morality", as Melanie Klein noted in her formulations of the infantile basis of gratitude: "A full gratification at the breast means that the infant feels that he has received from his love object a unique gift which he wants to keep. This is the basis of gratitude", an experience that is entwined with trust and generosity (Klein, 1957, p. 189).

Another way of thinking of gratitude plays off the ancient "count your blessings" notion that Maslow believed was part of self-actualization. For contemporary philosophers Martin Buber and Gabriel Marcel, such a saying is headed in the right direction when it comes to love but needs to be expanded by using a modern saying like: "When I count my blessings, I count you twice". The "you" denotes a person who acts as a blessing in someone's life, an acknowledgment that there is something miraculous-like that the person evokes by virtue of being in the person's life that deserves, if not demands, cherishment, a manifestation of the "mystery of being", as Marcel calls it. The capacity to experience and express gratitude personified the spiritual sensibility that Marcel advocated, just as Maslow, Winnicott and Klein believed that experiencing and expressing gratitude were important manifestations of a "mentally healthy" person. Indeed, empirical researchers have found that gratitude can function to sustain and improve romantic attachments and friendships (Algoe, Gable & Maisel, 2010). Moreover, gratitude has been correlated with greater life satisfaction, optimism and more positive and less negative emotional experience (Emmons & Mishra, 2011). Such findings suggest the impressive role gratitude has in enhancing closeness and intimacy, along the lines of Buberian/Marcelian love (Compton & Hoffman, 2012, p. 317). Thus, what Buber and Marcel add to our understanding of gratitude is that when the significant other is viewed as "good", as deserving of our affirmation and cherishment, we are in fact allowing them to view themselves in the reflection of our high regard, which means that we assist them in becoming the best they are capable of being. This is an expression of the other-directed, other-regarding and other-serving thrust of gratitude.

"Who attains honor? He who confers honor upon other men". The idea here is that honor is not about seeking out tributes or forced recognition (which often backfires, leading others to judge you as inauthentic or worse), but rather it is an "internal process. If you honor others, they will reciprocate. Respect for others evokes respect for you" (Greenberg, 2016, p. 169). As Sacks and Angel (2015) point out, an honored person is not one relentlessly questing after public honors or awards, for they are superficial acquisitions that are ultimately pointless. "Real honor derives from honoring others, from living in a respectful relationship with others" (pp. 88–89). Giving this saying a theological gloss, one could say, following Rashi, that "if God will honor those who honor God, how much more fitting is it that we who are merely flesh and blood honor those who honor us" (Kravitz & Olitzky, 1993, p. 57).

There is little doubt that the sociologically explicated norm of reciprocity typically applies to the dynamic of honoring others and them honoring you in return. But one can imagine that what separates the ordinary "decent" person from the righteous person is that the latter honors another person even if they do not return the favor. Such a Levinasian perspective on honoring others no doubt sets a very high moral bar. What fosters such willingness and ability to honor the other irrespective of him honoring you in return is the remarkable capacity to downwardly modify one's narcissism, that form of self-love that Christopher Lasch (1991) and others have claimed embodies the "culture of narcissism". That is, the self-regarding selfishness, the normalization of pathological narcissism in our Western society.

I said in the beginning of this Ethic that they are interrelated notions. Indeed, who is wise? Who is mighty? Who is rich? Who attains honor? All describe the ideal way the Rabbis thought a person should treat another person. The wise person learns from everyone, the mighty person controls his self-centric cravings and wish to control and dominate, the rich person controls his envy, insatiable hungers and other such anti-social emotions, and one should honor other people even if it is not reciprocated. In a word, "Ben Zoma is teaching the ethics of relationships" (Yanklowitz, 2018, p. 189).

26. Verbal communication

> (V–9). There are seven[72] characteristics of the uncultured man, and seven of the wise man. A wise man does not speak before one who is greater that he in wisdom;[73] he does not interrupt another man's speech; he is not hasty to answer; his answers are on the subject of the discussion, and his replies are to the point of the inquiry; he deals with first things first and last things last; he acknowledges what he does not know; and he affirms the truth. The opposite of these are the characteristics of the uncultured man.
>
> (Bokser, 1983, p. 248)

The subject of this mishna is, in part, effective verbal communication (even though some human communication is non-verbal in nature). The idea here is that the wise person

> is aware of his or her limits, and thus listens to and refrains from interrupting others. A wise person focuses on the core issues and sticks to the topic. A wise person admits when he or she has not heard some piece of information or does not know something, and acknowledges the truth even if it turns out to be the opposing viewpoint.
>
> (Greenberg, 2016, p. 254)

Sacks and Angel (2015) elaborate on what constitutes the wise person in terms of verbal communication:

> Respectfulness, patience, thoughtfulness, clarity of thought, orderliness, intellectual honesty, modesty. The uncultured person lacks these virtues. A wise person seeks truth [regardless of whether it is Truths or usable truths]. It is no embarrassment to admit that one does not know something; but it is shameful to pretend that one has knowledge that one in fact does not have. It is no embarrassment to change one's mind if one has been proven wrong; but it is shameful to egotistically persist in holding a false opinion even when having been shown its falsity.
>
> (p. 126)

Psychoanalytic conversation affirms the aforementioned but operates along somewhat different coordinates. Much of the communication is unconsciously transmitted through free association, free-flowing interchanges, dream analysis and interpretation, and transference exploration and interpretation. However, this Ethic does depict rather well how the analyst should consciously approach the analysand, as a wise person. I have earlier described the analyst, qua listener (entries #5 & #24), but there is something important that needs to be said about how the analyst speaks to the analysand so that his words can be embraced as important and maybe even perception-altering.

The analyst, qua wise person, should speak with "knowledge, understanding and insight; in other words, wisdom" (Greenberg, 2016, p. 254). An analyst should be aware of his or her limits, and therefore should be a careful listener who does not interrupt the analysand until he has finished talking. Likewise, an analyst concentrates on the main issue in sharp focus and sticks to the topic without getting distracted by his or the analysand's extraneous thoughts and verbalizations (not withstanding that the analysand is free associating) (ibid.). The aforementioned boils down to the analyst not assuming an arrogant way of being-in-the-world. For arrogance blinds the analyst to important information and discerning the usable truths that may contradict his own point of view (ibid.). For example, giving an interpretation that has emotional significance—that is, with an eye toward deepening and expanding insight and integration—requires that the analysand's transference and real relationship be more or less positive.

What is also worth mentioning about this Ethic is that in psychoanalysis it is not only the meaning of the manifest content of what is said that matters (as in the Ethic's recommendation), but in addition, the analyst and analysand focus on the process of verbal communication. That is, it is not only what is said but how it is said, and it is not only how it is said but also the likely unconscious meaning of a specific communication that "really" matters, particularly the emotional response to the jointly constructed narrative truth. Such truths, such shared understandings and two-way processes, are context-dependent and setting-specific to the analytic situation, and it is up to the analysand to ultimately decide what is true or false, authentic or inauthentic to the self. As Ogden noted, assisting the analysand to dream dreams that he is incapable of dreaming on his own is the main goal of psychoanalysis (Ferro & Civitarese, 2018, p. 35). That is, dreaming our experiences, including the destructive ones, "by imaginatively engaging them" (Bagai, 2023, p. 162).

27. Generosity

> (V–13). There are four types of character among people. He who says: What is mine is mine and what is yours is yours, is a medium type [the average person], and some say that his type is of the wicked city of Sodom; he that says: What is mine is yours and what is yours is mine, is an ignoramus; he that says: What is mine is yours and what is yours is yours, is a saintly man; he that says: What is yours is mine and what is mine is mine, is a wicked man.
>
> (Bokser, 1983, p. 249)

This Ethic is a quick study of what it means to be generous toward others. "What is mine is mine and what is yours is yours" connotes the fact that in the rabbinic way of moral thinking an individual has a right to his or her own money-making and acquisitions. This is how the average person thinks; it is a live-and-let-live outlook.[74] It perpetuates neither self-control nor generosity (Greenberg, 2016). However, such a view also goes against the fact that in Judaism there is no absolute ownership (i.e., we are caretakers of possessions), since all that exists is actually property that belongs to God. To be uncharitable, inhospitable and unkind is to be like a person from Sodom, at least that is how the Rabbis viewed it, based on Scripture. As is well known, in the Hebrew Bible, Sodom was a very sinful, corrupt, vice-ridden city (Sacks & Angel, 2015).

"What is mine is yours and what is yours is mine" is an ignoramus. That is, the ignoramus is the opposite of the wise person, and he too embraces a live-and-let-live outlook, but it lacks discipline, and it mixes up in a confusing manner everybody's possessions (Greenberg, 2016). The ignoramus is a rustic boor who lacks education and engages in absurd interchanges (Kravitz & Olitzky, 1993). For in this saying the give-and-take exchange of a possession amounts to ending where one began.

"What is mine is yours and what is yours is yours" is what a saintly man desires. Living according to this calculus connotes a sacrificial outlook in which what the other needs and wants takes precedence over oneself (at least when it is reasonable). This is a Levinasian optic. It is the view of a completely unselfish person, a pious, saintly genre who gives without expecting anything in return (Greenberg, 2016). Finally, what is yours is mine and what is mine is mine is a wicked man and connotes the negative qualities of a narcissistic and selfish man who wants everything for him or herself.

Psychoanalysis, in my view, tends to embrace the average man's perspective, "what is mine is mine and what is yours is yours". That is, the person's autonomy, integration and humanity lead him to an ethic of symmetrical fairness. Or to put it another way, it emphasizes mainly looking out for oneself in this every-man-for-himself philosophy (ibid.). Such a view respects the other's needs and wishes but from the perspective of one self; the other is entitled to have what he has as am I. You have what you have and I have what I have. It also calls to mind Freud's words from the Introductory Lectures, that "a rogue [is someone] who gives more than he has". In other words, to try and give what one does not have will inevitably fail the other person, and in this sense the rogue is stealing the psychic income from the recipient, since what he gives, if at all, is not authentic and may not be desired or appreciated.[75]

It is the Levinasian optic that most subverts the ethic of symmetrical fairness of the average person in favor of putting the other's needs and wishes before one's own ("what's mine is yours and what is yours is yours"). As I earlier indicated, Levinas claimed, "responsibility is the essential, primary and fundamental structure of subjectivity". Moreover, "ethics, here, does not supplement a preceding existential base; the very node of the subjective is knotted in ethics understood as responsibility" (Levinas, 1985, p. 95). Indeed, Freud at times tilted in this direction as did Erich Fromm when he noted that the majority of individuals do not really want freedom, in part because freedom includes responsibility, and the majority of people are scared of responsibility. Psychoanalysis could possibly be enhanced by adopting a Levinasian ethic such that the image of the person is one who cares about the other more than oneself (or at least as much as oneself), for this can generate a psychoanalysis that centrally has an ethical thrust to it. This resonates with analysts Selig and Rosof's (2001) "generative altruism" mentioned earlier (see entry #1).

Levinas's version of the human condition makes the ethical demand of the other as the ultimate affect-integrating, meaning-making, action-guiding hermeneutic horizon. In a Levinasian-inspired psychoanalysis we have a very different version of the human condition than that of "mainstream" psychoanalysis, one that makes ethics—that is, being-for-the-other, goodness, holiness, "otherwise than being"—its main focus and ideal mode of being-in-the-world. The self, in this context, is said to be "hostage" to the other, to the other's needs for love and justice (Levinas, 1987, pp. 112, 118). "Strictly speaking the other is the end; I am hostage, a responsibility and a substitution supporting the whole world in the passivity of assignation, even, in an accusing persecution, which is undeclinable" (ibid., p. 128). In other words, the self is not fundamentally and firstly for "oneself" and "by oneself" but rather, prior to freedom of choice and assertion of identity, it is the "for the other" of responsibility that ultimately defines the self. As Levinas says, "perhaps the possibility of a point in the universe where such an overflow of responsibility is produced ultimately defines the I" (Levinas, 1969, p. 244). I leave it to the reader to decide whether for psychoanalysis such a narrative of the human condition could be illuminating and useful in our theorizing and clinical work (Marcus, 2010). However, what seems clear is that the aforementioned Ethic regards the saintly type to be at the highest rung of the ethical ladder, a view that resonates with Levinas's perspective and my incorporation of his perspective into a re-casted view of psychoanalysis.

28. Charity

> (III–8). Rabbi Elazar of Bartota said: Give to God what is His, for you and all you possess are His. And thus did David express it (Chronicles 29:14): All things are from Thee, and we have given Thee only what is Thine.
>
> (Bokser, 1983, p. 239)

In Judaism, just as in Christianity and Islam, there is no absolute possession, for what one acquires is borrowed from God, or it is His type of gift-giving, sometimes called grace.

In his commentary on the Ethics, Twersky explains the meaning of this saying.

> This mishna is generally understood to mean that a person should not begrudge giving *tzedakah* [charity], because one is merely giving the poor

person that which is rightfully his, and had been provided by God to the donor in safekeeping until a needy individual would ask for it.

(Twersky, 1999, p. 155)[76]

Put differently, "this saying sums up the Jewish view that reverence for God requires a person to be charitable" (Berkson, 2010, p. 112); at least ten percent of one's earnings and no more than twenty percent (Yanklowitz, 2018). As Greenberg points out,

> Acts of charity and financial outlay for religious [and other] purposes should not be seen as taking money out of our pockets to give to another. Rather, God has given us all that we possess. We are only giving back a fraction of the goodness bestowed on us.
>
> (Greenberg, 2016, p. 126)

Psychoanalysis does not usually deal with giving charity as a subject to be theorized about. In general, most analysts probably approve of greater generosity compared to stinginess or almost stinginess, one of the hallmarks of an anal fixation or worse. To be generous materially and/or psychologically—that is, lovingly—is to have attained a high degree of autonomy, integration and humanity.

This being said, most secular analysands probably view their possessions as their own and not a heavenly gift from God that they are earthly caretakers of (they feel blessed). As a result of this belief, secular analysands may become emotionally tied to their objects in ways that have a particular intensity, even suggestive of the clinginess and attachment to things that the Buddhists say leads to terrible suffering. Whether it is physical objects that make a person feel complete or whole, or the psychic income that comes from receiving accolades, including, for example, receiving status, power and financial reward, the fact is that if these people viewed their objects from a Divine perspective as in the Ethics, they may not be as emotionally attached to short-lived things and fleeting experiences that they relentlessly pursue to increase their self-esteem and enhance their self-concept. They can become better, more generous givers than takers. Indeed, some people are more attached to their material things than they are to people. For example, I have three patients now who are by far more attached to their I-Phones and other devices than they are to cultivating human relationships (Btw, they are not on the spectrum). To some extent, the current societal "technomania" reinforces people being more attached to their devices than they are to other human beings, even more so with the advent of Artificial Intelligence. This is a pretty grim picture in my view, especially when we recall that the research on happiness points in a different direction.

For example, as I said in entry #6, the longest-range study of human contentment ever conducted is the Harvard Study of Adult Development.

Starting in 1938, the study followed more than 700 people throughout their lives, eventually including their offspring. The study found that the central element that determined satisfaction was not financial reward or achievement. Rather, it was "warm connections with other people", from casual to intimate (the other as "an anchor of connection") (The Week, 2023a, p. 10).

Returning to the question of what it is like to give charity when one views oneself as caretaker of the asset as opposed to feeling that the asset comes from one's pocket alone, could it be easier to give charity when one views one's assets as a gift from God rather than simply something that one has earned through one's hard work? From what I can clinically tell, to the extent that a person has this religious perspective he is more likely to be willing and able to give generously to the needy as the Ethics imply. In fact, researchers have found that individuals who are religiously affiliated are more inclined to make a charitable donation of any kind, whether to a religious congregation or to another type of charitable organization. Their research found that 62 percent of religious households give to charities of any kind, compared with 46 percent of households with no religious affiliation (Fowler, 2021, n.p.).

Likewise, no doubt a person can work hard and earn a lot of money and be generous in his giving because he has a secular equivalent to the religious person who references God; namely, the love of humanity, earth and the like. In this context, such a person may feel that he too is a caretaker of Mother Earth and the greater good, and therefore gives generously to those charities that support his beliefs and values.

The aforementioned puts into sharp focus the complex issue of why people give charity. As Evgeny Redjebov points out in his blog, research has demonstrated that the most important motivator for charitable giving is the desire for reward and social attachment. In other words, says Redjebov (2022),

> we give because it feels good and that good feeling connects us to others in ways that we find satisfying. While that might sound selfish, all it really means is that people are wired to feel happy when they're being kind.

That is, we have evolved over time to be social animals. Also worth mentioning in closing is the fact that in a study described in *Psychology Today*, 85 percent of respondents said the reason they gave was simply because someone asked them. In other words, "meeting your donors' needs for giving will help open their heart and wallet to supporting your work" (Rees, 2023).

Indeed, research has found that "people find it rewarding to spend money on others"; moreover, social scientists have devised numerous situations in which research subjects were given the chance to behave either selfishly or cooperatively, and they chose the latter (Brooks, 2023b, p. A19).

29. Belief/value structure

> (III–6). Rabbi Nehunia ben Hakeneh said: He who submits to the yoke of the Torah liberates himself from the yoke of circumstance. He rises above the pressures of the state, and above the fluctuations of worldly fortune. But he who rejects that yoke of the Torah submits to the yoke of circumstance. He falls prey to the pressures of the state and to the fluctuations of worldly fortune.
>
> (Bokser, 1983, p. 239)

The word "yoke" is a crucial one in this Ethic. In this context, by yoke is meant something that balances the load and makes it easier to deal with.[77] It is a form of linking. In this case, it is the Torah that one should be passionately yoked/linked to. Sacks and Angel give an illuminating interpretation of the aforementioned Ethic:

> One devoted to Torah has inner freedom and will not yield to the control of worldly matters. Such a person will not spend inordinate time and effort to gain ephemeral political or material advantages. On the other hand, one who casts off the yoke of Torah will thereby become engulfed in worldly concerns. Life will be frittered away worrying about mundane matters rather than focusing on spiritual elevation.
>
> (Sacks & Angel, 2015, p. 65)

What this Ethic is putting forth is the need for a person to have an "inner center of gravity", or as Yanklowitz says, "We must be firmly planted somewhere". That is,

> At times, this is in Torah and Jewish communal life. At times this means larger societal undertakings. We don't have to feel guilt when we prioritize where to focus our attention if we are fully committed to the vision of a more just society.
>
> (2018, p. 139)

Without an ideologically informed overarching universe of meaning, including strongly felt, flexibly and creatively applied, transcendent-pointing moral beliefs and values that are meant to guide a person and are believed by the individual to be absolute, a person tends to be impacted, often negatively, by the circumstances he is situated in. This dynamic was in play in an extreme form in the Nazi concentration camps. For example, Bruno Bettelheim, Primo Levi, Jean Améry and Eli Wiesel all testify to the fact that the believer fared better in the camps than the intellectuals, the liberals, the humanists (including psychoanalysts, according to Bettelheim)[78] etcetera.

Says Bettelheim, who was not in a death camp like the other survivors mentioned above but a concentration camp:

> It is a well-known fact of the concentration camps that those who had a strong religious and moral conviction managed life there much better than the rest. Their beliefs, including belief in an afterlife, gave them a strength to endure which was far above that of most others. Deeply religious persons often helped others, and some voluntarily sacrificed themselves—many more of them than of the average prisoners.
>
> (1979, p. 296)

Bettelheim's claim that transcending values and moral convictions was critically important to concentration camps inmates in their struggle to maintain their autonomy, integration and humanity has been supported by a number of Auschwitz survivors.

For example, Primo Levi has written,

> The believers in any belief whatsoever, better resisted the seduction of power ... they also endured the trials of the Lager and survived in proportionately higher numbers.... Not only during the crucial moments of selection or the aerial bombings but also in the grind of everyday life, the believers lived better.
>
> (Levi, 1988, pp. 145–146)

Jean Améry, also a celebrated survivor/author, has noted that those inmates with strong beliefs or ideology had a "firm foothold in the world from which they spiritually unhinged the Nazi state.... They survived better or died with more dignity that their irreligious or unpolitical intellectual comrades" (Améry, 1980, p. 13).

Elie Wiesel has made a similar assertion:

> Within the system of the concentration camp ... the first to give in, the first to collaborate—to save their lives—were the intellectuals, the liberals, the humanists, the professors of sociology, and the like ... Very few Communists gave in ... They were the resisters ... Even fewer to give in were the Catholic priests ... yet there were exceptions. But you could not have found one single rabbi—I dare you—among all the *kapos* or among any of the others who held positions of power in the camps.
>
> (1974, p. 273)[79]

Indeed, without such a transcendent belief/value structure, the person is more likely to "fall prey to the pressures of the state and to the fluctuations of worldly fortune" as the Ethic indicates. In other words, as Anna Pawelczynska has further noted, "models and values that are deeply internalized create the strength to resist every alien system which denies those values" (Pawelczynska, 1979, p. 137). The aforementioned observations of Bettelheim, Levi, Améry, Wiesel and Pawelczynska are in sync with the insights of social theorists like Erving Goffman, who wrote that "strong religious and political convictions have served to insulate the true believer against the assault of a total institution" (Goffman, 1961, p. 66).

In contrast to the above, psychoanalysts have no transcending concepts that can transport them to a different dimension of the spirit, or that can protect them from the extreme situation by radically altering the meaning of their suffering. To the psychoanalyst, religion and politics, at least the type that we are referring to as they relate to the camp inmates, are an "admirable and redeeming illusion, but an illusion nonetheless" (Hanly, 1993, p. 17). As psychoanalyst/philosopher Charles Hanly points out, "Psychoanalysis finds itself at odds with ideologies because they are governed by visionary ideas and values that are exempted from critical investigation" (ibid.).[80] From the point of view of, say, Martin Buber and Gabriel Marcel, this is a self-serving overstatement, for there are those that hold the aforementioned "illusions" and "visionary ideas and values", such as religious ones, but do so in a non-ideological manner, as typically understood, that continually demands rigorous analysis and reasoned argumentation on the way to a leap to faith and a way of life linked to sacred realms and forces. Moreover, an ideology can be judged as bad or good; it is "a set of cultural beliefs, values and attitudes that underlie and thereby to some degree justify and legitimate either the status quo or movements to change" (e.g., White racism and gender oppression versus the Green movement and radical feminism) (Johnson, 1995, p. 137). As Eigen notes, "The analyst works with the felt impact of the patient, and affective-ideological transformations of this impact" (Marcus & Rosenberg, 1998, p. 190). Finally, both Buber and Marcel would regard Hanly's comments as a questionable form of "psychologism", for he does not deal with the ontic realm of human existence (i.e., what a specific being, for example, Dasein, human existence, can or does do),[81] and therefore reduces cosmic phenomena to purely psychic ones. This is based on Hanly believing that his perspective has epistemic superiority on such matters.

There is one other important point relevant to psychoanalysis that emanates from the aforementioned comments and is worth considering. While Freud considered religious faith "a delusional remolding of reality" in *Civilization and its Discontents* (1930, p. 81), as "an idealized object of human consciousness, the outward projection of man's inner nature" (Rotenstreich, 1968, p. 124), psychoanalysis has, to some extent, progressed in its respect for the psychologically helpful function of religious faith for the individual and group. Moreover, the positive role of personal illusion in cultural experience, such as in religious phenomena, aesthetic creation, play and the like, has been widely accepted by most analysts, thanks to Donald Winnicott and others. That psychoanalysis has no transcending concepts that can transport them to a different dimension of the spirit, or that can shield them from the extreme situation by radically changing the meaning of their suffering, perhaps it can develop such concepts. This seems like a fruitful idea. To date, not even the Unconscious can operate in a comparably transcendent manner, or at least not like the believer's life-sustaining, identity-saving beliefs and values did as described earlier.

30. Jealousy

> (IV–28). Rabbi Elazar ha-Kapor said: Envy, lust, and seeking after honor, undermines a man's life in this world.
>
> (Bokser, 1983, p. 246)

We have already discussed envy in previous Ethics, so rather than repeat myself, I will go with Twersky's translation of what Bokser calls envy, as do other commentators (e.g., Greenberg, 2016; Sacks & Angel, 2015), and translate the Hebrew word to mean jealousy: "Jealousy, lust, and glory remove a man from the world" (Twersky, 1999, p. 263; Yanklowitz (2018) also translate the Hebrew word to mean jealousy).

Jealousy is regarded by the Rabbis as a detrimental emotion, for it can lead to forgetting his or her knowledge of the Torah (the same is true of lust and seeking after honor) (Kravitz & Olitzky, 1993). Along with lust and inordinate ambition ("seeking after honor"), these emotions often propel one into "irresponsible, sometimes reckless, sometimes highly dangerous behaviors" (Greenberg, 2016, p. 227), which might even put one's life or health at risk. Moreover, says Greenberg, such behavior is stressful in terms of the person's inner experience, which over time can possibly cut short a person's life. Yanklowitz succinctly makes a similar point:

> When one wants what another has [i.e., jealousy], one is no longer present in one's own situation. Instead one has veered off into envy in yearning for another's property or status. Similarly, lust is yearning for another person's body. Wishing for glory ["seeking after honor"] is yearning for recognition....
>
> (2018, p. 274)

I have already distinguished envy from jealousy by pointing out that psychoanalytically speaking jealousy involves three parties, as in an Oedipal conflict, and has the aim of winning the exclusive love of the object (e.g., a parent) over a rival for love (e.g., a sibling, father). However, unlike envy, in jealousy the wish to destroy the rival is secondary to the wish to become the person who is more loved (Person, Cooper & Gabbard, 2005).[82] What more can we say about the experience of jealousy that makes it such an undesirable emotion? This is a huge topic, but why jealousy is so toxic deserves some comment.

Jealousy "is the emotion associated with the idea that someone that you love is in love with someone else. The aim of the jealous person is to win the love of the beloved from the rival" (ibid., p. 554). As I said, jealousy emanates from the Oedipal situation, in which the goal is to have an "exclusive relationship to the primary object, which later in life is referred to other objects. Love [understood as say appropriation], not gratification of needs or attention alone is the objective" (Moore & Fine, 1990, p. 106). According to Akhtar (2009), an important aspect of jealousy is that whether it is rivalry with a sibling or a same-sexed parent, there is a triangle at play, leading the child (or adult) to feel a sense of vulnerability in feeling less affectionately considered compared to the rival. Moreover, says Akhtar, jealousy is a mixture of love of the desired other, like a mother, and hate for the rival for love, like a sibling or father. Jealousy, then, is so toxic because it is a mode of ill-conceived and ill-fated reaction to the fear of losing one's partner. Where there is authentic love, being-for-the-other before oneself (or as much as oneself), there is no jealousy, because the fear of betrayal is not a credible coordinate of the relationship.

Lust, a powerful sexual desire toward someone,[83] at least in the context of the Ethics, refers to sexual desire for an "inappropriate" (or forbidden) other, such as a neighbor, colleague or friend, when say one is married or in a long-standing partnership.[84] Lust seeks out variety and multiplicity, as Marquis de Sade noted. Such sexualization of the inappropriate other can lead to overt sexual contact, which in the context of a marriage or partnership often signals there are serious problems or the end of the primary relationship. Lust is often conceptualized as reflecting the desire for power and ego-gratification, in other words, it is highly narcissistic (Sacks & Angel, 2015). The "trick" here is to be able to sublimate one's libido into non-sexual activities. Sublimation is originally a "developmental process by which sexual energies are discharged in non-instinctual forms of behavior". "High-level" sublimations are socially acceptable ones (Rycroft, 1995, p. 176). As Balzac said, after a night making love to a woman, there always was a novel left between the sheets. In other words, as Theodore Reik (1949) famously wrote, "The sex urge hunts for lustful pleasure; love is in search of joy and happiness". This observation roughly corresponds with Ferenczi's "language of passion" and the "language of tenderness" (Dimen, 2016, p. 406).

"Seeking after honor" refers to inordinate ambition—that is, ambition that emanates from a sense of weakness where one needs the affirmation of others, thereby acknowledging to what extent one is dependent on the changeable, inconsistent and capricious outside world to feel good about oneself. Most often, inordinate ambition, admittedly a judgment call, often emanates from distressing experiences in childhood that evoke inferiority and shame (Akhtar, 2009) like having a cleft lip and being made fun of by peers. In this context, ambition becomes a way of undoing the sense of inferiority and shame, sometimes leading to great creative output and social accomplishments (ibid.). In other words, inordinate ambition may be a response to a narcissistic assault that has to be put right. This is not to say that there are no "good" reasons to be reasonably ambitious, but that is different than inordinate ambition, which often expresses itself in manipulative, power-hungry motives and behavior and in other questionable ways. Such inordinate ambition has a way of corrupting most other important relationships, like with one's life-partner and/or children.

What joins these three detrimental emotions—jealousy, lust and seeking after honor—is the fact that they all represent inordinate narcissistic desires that demand something from the other with little or no concern for the other's best interests. Whether it is the excessive wish to be loved by a mother or life-partner, or using another person as a mode of mere hedonic gratification, or clawing one's way to success, leading to fame, in all of these instances, the person is relating to the other as an object to be manipulated, as a part-object; in short, he or she is embedded in an I-It mode of relation (i.e., a relation of objectification and utility).

31. Love

> (V–19). A love for which is for an ulterior motive will end when the motive has ceased. But a love that is not for a transient motive will never end. What matter of love is for an ulterior motive? The love of Amnon for Tamar (II Samuel 13). What manner of love does not depend on a transient motive? The love of David and Jonathan (II Samuel 1: 26).
>
> (Bokser, 1983, p. 250)

This Ethic is a succinct statement about the nature of love as far as the Rabbis viewed it. A love that is dependent on an ulterior motive, or a specific quality in the beloved (Greenberg, 2016), like say physical beauty, wealth or notoriety, will last as long as the specific quality exists; however, once the quality wanes, then the love is diminished or ceases to be. Of course, one can argue that if the love has an ulterior motive or is based on a specific quality it is not authentic love in the first place but something more like an infatuation. The so-called love of Amnon for Tamar, his half-sister, was based on her physical attractiveness, her sexualized body; once Amnon raped her, he lost interest in her, or actually hated her. In contrast, David's love for Jonathan was based on the total or whole person; they were fellow warriors in battles against the Philistines and had a pact of friendship that ran deep and wide (Berkson, 2010). Greenberg (2016) summarizes the point of this Ethic rather well:

> Love may start with a particular attractive quality in the other: beauty, goodness, fame. As love matures, it relates to the total person beyond any one quality—even the quality that attracted the lover in the first place [i.e., the "love depends on something beyond itself" (Kravitz & Olitzky, 1993, p. 85)]. If the love remains fixed on a particular quality in

the beloved, it is immature. And if the particular quality is lost or loses its appeal, the love is vulnerable and liable to disappear also.... And as for David, he was also eventually attached to the whole person of Jonathan, not to the crown prince celebrity, the fellow warrior, the friendly, helpful co-conspirator.

(Ibid., pp. 271–272)

The love that this Ethic recommends is the love that has been beautifully described fairly recently by philosophers Martin Buber, Gabriel Marcel and Emmanuel Levinas (Marcus, 2021). Most importantly, Buber says, "Love is responsibility of an *I* for a *Thou*", and without such a conviction, it is nearly impossible to engage in those actions that are correlated with love, "helping, healing, educating, raising up, saving" (ibid., p. 34); Marcel described love as the "essential ontological datum". What Marcel means by love as "the essential ontological datum" is that it requires a commitment to, and a responsibility for, the other, one that can only be made when there is mindfulness "of the absolute value and eternity of the person loved" (Keen, 1967, p. 32). Levinas notes, "The responsibility for the other is the grounding moment of love. It is not really a state of mind; it is not a sentiment, but rather an obligation" (Robbins, 2001, p. 133). (Elsewhere, Levinas says, "to know God is to know what must be done", an obligation (1990, p. 17)). He also approvingly notes in his discussion of Buber and Marcel that, "Love means, before all else, the welcoming of the other as Thou" (Levinas, 1976, pp. 5–6).

What these three giants are getting at is that the goal of human relationships is to relate to the other as a whole person such that one acts in a manner that reflects the other's totality of circumstances as a Thou. As I said earlier, what comprises the "whole self" is difficult to clearly define; moreover, judging when the whole self (as opposed to part of the self) is allegedly in play is a complicated and tenuous activity. Says Sacks and Angel:

> A fellow human being can be treated as an It, an entity that provides a service. In an I-It relationship, the I is not interested in a deep human interaction [the center of the universe is the I]; rather, the I simply wants the It to perform a function that is useful to the I. In an I-Thou relationship [the center of the universe is the other] both parties relate as subjects, not objects. They appreciate each other's human qualities, they have mutual respect.
>
> (Sacks & Angel, 2015, p. 141)

Psychoanalysis views these two different ways of relating to an external other in terms of part and whole objects. As Melanie Klein noted, a part-object is when the individual experiences

> the object as only one aspect of the object rather than the entire object in its full complexity. This aspect may be a particular body part (e.g., the

breast) or an experience of the object dominated by one affect (e.g., the good or bad object) or of a function of the object (e.g., feeding containing).

(Person, Cooper & Gabbard, 2005, p. 555)

The point here is that when one relates to the alleged loved other as a part-object one does not acknowledge the other as a whole person with feelings and desires and the like, but rather the other is viewed as existing only or mainly to gratify one's narcissistic needs and desires. When one relates to a whole object, one recognizes the other as having feelings and desires that are unique to them. This distinction calls to mind the difference between an I-It relationship and I-Thou relationship.

For Klein, it is the working through of the paranoid-schizoid position, leading to the depressive position, that allows the adult person to relate to the other as a whole object. Briefly, the paranoid-schizoid position involves the person dealing with his hypothesized innate destructiveness by splitting both his ego and his object representation (the mental picture of the object) into good and bad parts and projecting his destructiveness on to and into the bad objects whom he then feels persecuted by (Rycroft, 1995). In the depressive position, the person (originally the infant) realizes that the object, like his parental caregiver (or analyst), is both loved and hated and is the same person. This leads to feelings of guilt directed at the other person or parental caregiver over his destructiveness, leading to the wish to make reparations to the aggrieved person (in real time and/or in phantasy). Moreover, in Kleinian theory it is from this matrix that the mature capacity to love the whole person emanates.

For Freud, all love relations are "the finding of an object" that "is in fact a refinding of it" (Freud, 1905, p. 222), roughly analogous to the emotional experience of symbiotic togetherness with the mother or primary caregiver (Moore & Fine, 1990, p. 113). Moreover, the quest for the Oedipal object is an enduring embedded quality of all love relationships. What this "finding/refinding" notion means in terms of establishing love relations is that to some extent the choice of our significant other repeats or calls to mind aspects of our childhood caregivers. Love, says Freud, "consists of new editions of old traits and it repeats infantile reactions", this being "the essential character of every state of being in love" (Freud, 1915b, p. 168). That is, all love is based on infantile templates, is fundamentally a fixation on the parents, what Freud calls transference love. According to Reuben Fine, transference love and ordinary love only differ in terms of degree (Fine, 1979, p. 48). The problem with this, of course, is that if we refind that which is "bad" from our childhood experiences, it usually leads to impoverished and/or destructive intimate relationships. The "trick", then, is to refind in the significant other that which is consciously and unconsciously "good" from our childhood caregivers, so that we have a better chance of being relatively happy in our love relation. Most often, this "refinding" involves a subtle "refining" of earlier caregiver experiences, suggesting that the significant other is apprehended as a corrective emotional experience of a sort. For example, a man who refinds his "good" mother in a woman who has the best maternal qualities but is also capable of being a focus of passionate desire on the rigorously sexual level has engaged in a refinding and refining (e.g., the fantasy that happily blends the "mother and whore" in the significant other). To attempt to refind the "impossible" significant other who will re-create the imagined perfection associated with the parent/child symbiosis is a doomed effort from the onset (Bergmann, 1987). This involves both an idealization of the original union and splitting, only searching for the perfect/the good and not being able to tolerate the imperfections and the bad. It is only when one has refound the original parental object and has also refined the object such that one can tolerate and embrace both the good and bad of the other that one relates to the whole object and accepts their essential humanness. This is the basis of mature love.

32. The good life

(II–1). Rabbi Judah ha-Nasi said: Which is the right course for a person to pursue in his life? That which is honorable in his own eyes, and which will bring him honor from his fellow-man. Be careful with the observance of a seemingly minor commandment as with a major one, for you do not know the true merit of each commandment. Learn to balance the loss incurred in the performance of a commandment against the reward thereof, and the gain by a transgression against the loss thereof. Contemplate three facts and you will be spared from the power of sin: Know what is above you—an Eye that sees, an Ear that hears, and a Book in which all your deeds are entered.

(Bokser, 1983, p. 234)

What is most striking about this Ethic is the important question it raises: Which is the right course for a person to pursue in his life? In other words, what constitutes the good life for the Rabbis? Undoubtedly, the path to the good life is one that personifies righteousness and compassion; in the famous words of the prophet Micah, do justice, love mercy and walk humbly with your God. It also includes being a God-fearing Torah Jew who observes all of the mitzvot, for these are the ways one can get near to God, to be intimate with Him.

In this Ethic, the Rabbis point to the importance of living a life that is regarded as praiseworthy by oneself and also by others. While having care about what others think can turn into mindless conformity, conventionality or worse, the fact is that the Rabbis believed that one should be mindful of how others judge your behavior, for sometimes what they think is more plausible and credible than one's self-judgment (e.g., in terms of what is judged as "right" or "wrong"). One of Judah ha-Nasi's (the second century CE redactor/editor of the mishna) most famous and illuminating statements about the importance of considering what others think is, "I learned a lot from my rabbis, even more from my colleagues, and most of all from my students" (Greenberg, 2016, p. 65).[85] The important point here is that the recommended path in life is one that is respected by others while also evoking a modicum of self-respect.

Sacks and Angel (2015) have an interesting take on the important question the Rabbis ask in the opening line of this Ethic:

> Life can be lived actively or passively. A passive approach is characterized by having one's decisions directed by other people or by external circumstances [notwithstanding that what others think can in some instances be more plausible and credible than what one thinks; balanced consideration is called for here]. Life is essentially reactive. An active approach entails taking personal responsibility for one's choices; it involves planning ahead, developing a philosophy to guide one's life.
>
> (p. 31)

Thus, Rabbi Judah ha-Nasi teaches us the significance of embracing the active approach. In other words, one should behave strongly and decisively; one should engage in effective consequential thinking; and one's life should be informed by a life-affirming worldview (ibid.).

"Be careful with the observance of a seemingly minor commandment as with a major one, for you do not know the true merit of each commandment". The point here is that since one does not know the significance of a "minor" mitzvah one can never be certain that it is truly minor, for it might have huge ramifications in the near or far future. In the believer's mind, only God knows a mitzvah's ultimate significance, so every mitzvah should be done with the right intention and attention to detail. For example, an unemployed person having financial problems can be enormously helped by getting him employment (Greenberg, 2016).

"Learn to balance the loss incurred in the performance of a commandment against the reward thereof, and the gain by a transgression against the loss thereof". This aphorism is claiming that consequential thinking really matters, not immediate gratification of one's desires, even one's heartfelt desires (ibid.). Moreover, given the fact that to the believer all mitzvot are God-given, they should therefore be observed with appropriate importance. That is, a person should "not weigh material gain or loss when it comes to mitzvah observance; rather one must keep in mind that the mitzvot are expressions of the infinite God and are the means He has provided for coming closer to Him" (Sacks & Angel, 2015, p. 30).

Finally, the last aphorism in this Ethic, "Contemplate three facts and you will be spared from the power of sin: Know what is above you—an Eye that sees, an Ear that hears, and a Book in which all your deeds are entered". This powerful metaphor depicts the rabbinic doctrine of individual providence, including the idea that God is watching over we humans, that he can intervene in our lives when he wishes to or not, and most importantly, he will judge our behavior in this life or the next one (Berkson, 2010). As Buber noted, a person "must understand himself as standing every moment under the judgment of God" (Wright, 2007, p. 112). Needless to say, this aphorism is pointing to the powerful role of the superego in the psychic life. In this context, the Rabbis seem to be implying that pleasure is like licking honey off a razor blade.[86]

What does psychoanalysis make of all of this? As I said, while the main thrust of this Ethic is an intense religious outlook and behavior, what is most important is the fact that the key question is being asked: Which is the right course for a person to pursue in his life? Indeed, this question is one that comes up in every analysis, for it suggests the direction in life that a person chooses to take. Obviously, there is no one right course for a person to choose, because it is context-dependent and setting-specific. Asking what the best course of life is, is like asking what the best chess move is; it clearly depends on the situation one is in. In psychoanalysis, this often depends on the theory one is lodged in. For example, psychoanalysis has a number of "master narratives" about what constitutes being-in-the-world (what might more aptly be called "morality plays" as Adam Phillips called them, including what denotes a good life), that guide its clinical practice, its way of conceptualizing psychopathology and doing treatment.

For example, analysts have very different narratives about the self: the self fashioned by its defenses against instincts (Freud), the self formed by its inner objects (Klein), the self shaped by its internalized relationships (Kohut) (Jones, 1991) and "the self as a narcissistic misrecognition, represented thorough the symbolic order of language" (Lacan) (Elliot, 1994, p. 113). Moreover, depending on which master narrative one is lodged in, the goals of psychoanalytic treatment tend to be conceptualized differently: We have, for instance, "the taming of the beast within" through reason and love (Freud), the "mad person within raging about" who becomes transformed through compensatory reparative activities (Klein), the "discovery of the self within" and the development of compensatory self-structures (Kohut), and "to speak what heretofore has been unspeakable", to reclaim the voice of one's desires (Lacan) (Roth, 1998, p. 327).[87]

Each of these master narratives becomes a guiding framework of a sort for the analysand to consciously or unconsciously choose his right course of living. In other words, each theory sets up certain coordinates that the analyst and analysand tend to develop their conversation around.

While all of the aforementioned master narratives have their plausibility and credibility in the hands of a skilled clinician, another way of viewing the analytic conversation that possibly jives with the Rabbi's philosophy of life emanates from the work of Martin Buber and Gabriel Marcel (Marcus, 2021).

Very briefly, for Buber and Marcel, their roughly similar concept of the person is that he is a *homo viator*, a spiritual wanderer or itinerant being who longs for the immanent, unique, unprecedented and singular Thou. He engages in a groping search toward the light. Moreover, every particular I-Thou encounter points to an all-embracing transcendence (a trans-subjective reality that is discovered/ encountered, not created), an ineffable, inexhaustible, glimpsed Presence (the eternal/Absolute Thou) apprehended and intuited with our being, not our mind's eye, which completes, consummates and existentially grounds the specific I-Thou encounter (Kaufman, 1992, p. 68). Thus, for Buber and Marcel, the most impressive instantiation of "Thou-ism" as dispositional, as a way of being-in-the-world, is holiness (i.e., the restoration of the sacred in everyday life in harmony with the lived Presence, in affinity with eternity). That is, an orientation toward life that is infused with a form of ethicality, an outlook and behavior that are centrally animated by other-directed, other-regarding and other-serving considerations as well as praiseworthy virtue ethics. As Marcel noted, "Philosophically, the road to the other leads through the depths within myself" (O'Malley, 1984, p. 281),[88] and amidst this self-exploration and lived existence much can go painfully astray. The first master narratives, as I have said, give a pathway to an art of living; the master narrative of Buber and Marcel probably more closely relates to the rabbinic outlook and behavior, as it emphasizes the spiritual and the importance of how one relates to the other (e.g., the mind has a spiritual caste).

33 and 34. Torah

> (V–25). Ben Bag-Bag said: Study the Torah again and again, for everything is in it; yea, contemplate it, grow old and gray over it, but do not swerve from it, for there is no greater virtue than this.
>
> (Bokser, 1983, p. 252)

> (V–26). Ben He-He said: The gain is in proportion to the pain.
>
> (Ibid.)[89]

For the Rabbis, the life-long study of Torah is the surest way to have a purposeful and contented life. The first Ethic speaks to the fact that in the mind of the religious person the Torah is the repository of all spiritual and other wisdom. The more one is embedded in the study and living of Torah, the more one can be said to have achieved a sense of "wholeness and satisfaction" (Sacks & Angel, 2015, p. 151). As Yanklowitz (2018) points out,

> All a person has to do is study Torah and grow in one's wisdom. This is the key to a healthy intellectual life ... the whole of Torah is dedicated to the radical notion that human beings are better than their physical selves, that we have the inherent ability to develop our potential and make it real in the world.
>
> (p. 362)

"The gain is in proportion to the pain" refers to the amount of effort it takes to master the religious texts. As Maimonides noted, what is learned easily is forgotten easily, and what is learned with great difficulty is forgotten with great difficulty (Kravitz & Olitzky, 1993). Of course, what is most important is whether what is learned can be implemented in real life, and there lies the rub. This Ethic is geared to a spiritual lesson. That is, without some pain in doing what God commands, one is unlikely to have attained a spiritual gain (there are exceptions of course).

"Study the Torah again and again, for everything is in it" speaks to the sacred quality of the Torah to the believing Jew. However, this kind of elevation of a sacred text calls to mind what most psychoanalysts believe about studying the Freudian oeuvre. For Freud's followers, there is a recurrent need to return to the textual study of what Freud wrote in his twenty-four volumes as well as the secondary literature. Psychoanalysis has gone in many interesting directions since Freud, as the post-Freudian literature demonstrates. Similar to the ancient sages' view of Torah study, there are many opinions and differences about nearly every aspect of what Freud wrote.

Indeed, Freud belongs to the group of authors that Foucault calls the "founders of discursivity" (1984, p. 114). Like Homer, Aristotle, the Church Fathers, Galileo and Marx, for example, Freud is unique in that he is not just an author of his own work. He has "produced the possibilities and the rules for the formation of other texts ... an endless possibility of discourse" (ibid.). That is, Freud is the point of departure for all psychoanalytic theorizing. He is the author of a theory, tradition and discipline in which all subsequent psychoanalysts must situate themselves one way or another. As Foucault further notes, Freud has "created a possibility for something other than his discourse, yet something belonging to what he founded" (ibid.).[90]

Psychoanalysis, of course, tends to agree with the notion that the gain is in proportion to the pain.

As I said earlier, psychoanalysis is a painful, deconstructive, demythologizing and defamiliarizing process for acquiring greater self-awareness and self-understanding, especially of one's destructive unconscious emotional activity, one that transforms moral consciousness by expanding and deepening one's capacity to love. Self-understanding leads to self-mastery, which leads to self-transcendence (this is exactly what the rabbinic idea of *teshuvah*, repentance, return to the "straight" path, is). Indeed, the analytic process is fraught with psychic pain as one begins to face oneself, especially one's limitations as a person as well as the childhood and other traumas one has lived through and relives in the transference. In a way, there is an operative assumption: With hard work there is a reward of a type, which is greater self-understanding into what makes one tick, self-mastery and self-transcendence. Elevated personal achievement or self-mastery tends to come only when one is willing and able to do the difficult analytic work of self-confrontation that psychoanalysis specializes in. Indeed, the process of analysis is a very painful endeavor that constantly harps on the need to explore the self, especially the dark side (e.g., the lies one tells oneself). While the Rabbis probably had the pain associated with mastering religious texts like the Talmud in mind, in analysis this painful process is most associated with a modicum of self-understanding, self-mastery and self-transcendence in terms of the art of living a good life.

35. Peace

> (I–12). Hillel and Shammai received the tradition from them. Hillel said: Be of the disciples of Aaron. Love peace and pursue peace; love your fellow creatures and bring them near to the Torah.
>
> (Bokser, 1983, p. 233)

Aaron, the brother of Moses, was the first High Priest and was regarded as a peacemaker between high-conflict parties. He had the tendency to judge other people's motives in a favorable manner. This mishna suggests that a person should love peace and actively pursue it by delving into the specifics of the conflict with an eye toward fair resolution. In fact, when one is aware of a conflict between people, one should not stand idly by but rather should helpfully intervene and try to reinstate a peaceful resolution (this of course requires great tact and skillfulness) (Greenberg, 2016). As Sacks and Angel (2015) further note

> Aaron was a peaceful and compassionate leader…. [He] was congenial and easily approachable. In highlighting Aaron as his religious model, Hillel underscores his conviction that religious leadership must reflect kindness. One should not merely love peace and harmony in the abstract, but must actively pursue the goal of bringing peace and harmony to others.
>
> (pp. 18, 21)

An example of Aaron's peaceful disposition was, says Rashi, the story of an irritable husband who refused to participate with his wife by not sleeping with her until and unless she would spit in Aaron's eye. When Aaron heard of this conflict between the husband and wife, he went to the wife and complained that he had an eye condition that needed saliva to cure it. In this manner, the poor-soul of a wife would be able to comply with her husband's disgraceful demand (Kravitz & Olitzky, 1993).[91]

The last line of this Ethic, "love your fellow creatures and bring them near to the Torah" actually refers to the problem of facilitating converts to Judaism. At the time of this mishna, rabbinic Judaism was somewhat of a missionary religion (ibid.). Loving your fellow creatures refers to the fact that in the eyes of God all people are equal and deserve respect and compassion (Greenberg, 2016).

Psychoanalysis has something to offer when it comes to conflict resolution, whether it is between two people (as in psychodynamic couple's work) or large groups like warring nations. It does this by focusing not only on the conscious reasons for the conflict but the shared unconscious ones that animate how a person or large group approaches their adversary. Volkan (2005), for example, has elegantly written about the concealed aspects of the national or international affairs that may bring about anxiety and other distressing emotions, and how they are in part the conditions of possibility for intergroup conflict. Recent formulations have considered less the large group and the leader (which Freud wrote about), to focusing on the "mental representation of the large group itself as seen by the individual" (ibid., p. 527). Volkan advocates analysts focusing mainly on large group identity in its own right, its formation and the group's need to protect itself, sometimes at all costs. For example, "chosen glories" are "the mental representations of a large group's past triumphs and the heroes and martyrs associated with them" and lead to an intensification of the feeling of "we-ness" and potential intergroup conflict (ibid., p. 530). Likewise, a "chosen trauma" is "the shared mental representation of a negative event in a large group's history in which the group suffered catastrophic loss, humiliation, and helplessness at the hand of another large group" (ibid.). Such mental representations are often transmitted to the next generation as in the offspring of Holocaust survivors, thus becoming a fertile breeding ground for the development of later conflict between, say, nations and other malignant outcomes. It does this in part through "time collapse"—that is, "when what is remembered from the past is felt in the present and is expected for the future, coming together in a time collapse" (ibid.). Volkan has developed many other concepts such as the role of mourning in large groups (it is different than individual mourning), but what is important for us is that his work represents a novel way of understanding and practically working with those ensconced in national or international conflicts (e.g., politics and diplomacy).

"Love peace and pursue peace" raises the very interesting question of how one achieves peace of mind from a psychoanalytic perspective. That is, how does one feel safe and protected, to reside in a calm and untroubled emotional state? Psychoanalysis sometimes uses the term homeostasis to describe this ideal state of mind:

> a state of stable psychic equilibrium, in which the different agencies of the mind [ego, superego, id] work together in harmony so as to achieve reasonable satisfaction of the individual's needs and adaptation to external reality, without being overwhelmed by affects or external stimuli.
> (Person, Cooper & Gabbard, 2005, p. 552)[92]

Easier said than done.

Some have claimed homeostasis as an outdated model in favor of allostasis, stability through change (Stulberg, 2023, p. 10). Homeostasis maintains that healthy systems return to the same starting point following change: X to Y to X. By comparison, in allostasis, healthy systems desire stability; however, the baseline of that can be somewhere new: X to Y to Z. In other words, continues Stulberg, "The way to stay stable through the process of change is by changing, at least to some extent" (ibid.). This requires being

> tough, determined and durable, to know your core values, what you stand for. To be flexible is to consciously respond to altered circumstances or conditions, to adapt and bend easily without breaking, to evolve, grow and change your mind. Put these qualities together, and the result is gritty endurance, one that helps you maintain your strong core even in fragile moments.
>
> (Ibid.)

In my view, the experience of peace of mind depends in part on one's object relations, one's relationships with other people, often shaped by one's early childhood experiences. As I mentioned earlier (see entry #32), psychoanalysis has a number of "master narratives" that recommend specific forms of treatment based on their assumptions about what constitutes the human condition. These, in effect, describe how one can achieve a modicum of peace of mind.

For example, we have the Freudian worldview and its view of treatment, "the taming of the beast within" through reason and love. If one wants to achieve a degree of peace of mind, one needs to modulate one's sexual and aggressive desires through greater self-awareness and rational control, and loving object relationships. As Freud famously told Erikson that "love and work" were the central therapeutic goals of psychoanalysis, the twin pillars of a sound mind for living a good life (Erikson, 1959, p. 96).

We have the Kleinian worldview and treatment recommendation, the "mad person within raging about" who becomes transformed through compensatory reparative activities. In this narrative, if one wants to acquire a little peace of mind one needs to moderate one's sexual but especially aggressive drives, by developing practical conscious strategies and unconscious dispositions that repair the real or imagined loved object, a consequence of one's real or imagined aggression.

Next, we have the Kohutian worldview and perspective on treatment, the "discovery of the self within" and the development of compensatory self-structures, which requires the finding/creating of satisfying selfobjects. The self within probably relates to the authentic or "true" self. A selfobject refers to the "individual's experience of another person as functioning as part of the self or necessary to fulfill a need of the self", usually unconsciously (Person, Cooper & Gabbard, 2005, p. 559). Compensatory selfobjects can range anywhere from archaic to mature, and they extend to the entire life cycle. In analysis, but also in real life, a selfobject may include a person's need for affirmation and idealization etcetera (ibid.), which allow the individual to experience a more fulfilled and peaceful self state.

Finally, we have the Lacanian worldview and treatment recommendation "to speak what heretofore has been unspeakable", in other words, to reclaim the voice of one's desires. In this view, says Lacanian analyst Fernando Castrillon, the quest for a degree of peace of mind is in sync with the Lacanian goal of psychoanalysis, which "is to bring the patient to confront the elementary coordinates and deadlocks of his or her desire (adapted from Slavoj Žižek's, How to Read Lacan)".[93] The aim of psychoanalysis, says Castrillon, "is to lead the analysand to recognize his/her desire and by doing so to uncover the truth about his/her desire". Or put somewhat differently, as Lacanian analyst Yehuda Israely noted, "The question that marks termination of the analysis is: 'Have you lived the desire that inhabits you?'"; "The aim of treatment is to consolidate a reality in which patients can function as subjects" (Israely, 2018, pp. xviii, 7). Adapting to social or consensual reality, however, is entirely a matter of one's idiosyncratic trajectory (it is not the Lacanian focus), but a modicum of peace of mind can be a practical outcome once one knows the truth of one's desires (Castrillon, n.d).

Whether one calls it peace of mind, flourishing, happiness, health, etcetera, what all of these master narratives demand is a longstanding treatment that rakes over the details of one's personal life. Peace of mind is probably not a general state of mind but a state that one resides in and out of depending on the totality of circumstance of one's life. This being said, there are those few people who seem to have great resiliency such that their homeostasis or allostasis (i.e., core values) remains more or less intact, despite the challenges that a person has in a lifetime.

35. Success and material possessions

> (II–8). He [Hillel] used to say: The more flesh, the more worms; the more possessions, the more anxiety; the more women, the more sorcery; the more female slaves, the more lewdness; the more male slaves, the more robbery; the more Torah, the more life; the more contemplation, the more wisdom; the more counsel, the more understanding; the more righteousness, the more peace. One who has acquired a good reputation has it for himself. One who has acquired for himself Torah, has acquired for himself life eternal.
>
> (Bokser, 1983, p. 235)

There are many subthemes to this mishna, though there is one overarching theme which I will comment on, namely the "dangers of success" and a "lifestyle of spending" (Kravitz & Olitzky, 1993, p. 23). Sacks and Angel (2015) succinctly elaborate the larger point of this mishna:

> The acquisition of excessive material assets is illusory. A person may feel successful by having more possessions, yet these very possessions detract

from the pursuit of a happy and meaningful life. One should not lose sight of the ultimate goal of life: to live wisely, righteously, and compassionately. The study of the observance of Torah are the keys to a good reputation in the world, and blessing in the World-to-Come.

(pp. 38, 41)

Thus, "the more flesh, the more worms" refers to the fact that many of the possessions that a person accumulates bring a number of problems with them. For example, inordinate weight, or obesity as it is now called, has the side effect of being very unhealthy. Likewise, when one dies, literally, the more flesh the more worms have to feed on. Also, the more wealth one has, the more one tends to worry about losing it. The more women, the more sorcery appears to relate to the then belief that women could be sorcerers and therefore the polygamy of the time was ill-advised (polygamy was prohibited in 1000 CE by Rabbi Gershom).[94] That is, many wives meant many rivals who might use sorcery to compete for their husband's attention (Kravitz & Olitzky, 1993). In addition, the more female slaves, the more there was a possibility of promiscuity on the part of the male slave owners, and the more male slaves, the more there was the potential for robbery and theft.

In the minds of the Rabbis, a contented and purposeful life is one that is lived wisely (e.g., skillfully), righteously and compassionately, and to the believer this was instantiated by the study of Torah, which maximized life-affirmation as one strove to be near to God through mitzvah observance—the use of one's intellect for contemplation that tended to bring about increased wisdom; the more one listened to the wise counsel of others, the more understanding of a situation and its dynamics one usually acquired; likewise, the more one lived a life of righteousness (e.g., do justice, love mercy and walk humbly with your God), the more peace and peace of mind. And finally, "one who has acquired for himself Torah, has acquired for himself life eternal" indicates that he personifies all the other characterological assets mentioned in the aforementioned list of instantiations. That is, one who has acquired for himself Torah, its knowledge and wisdom translated into action in the real world, has acquired for himself life eternal (a belief that was common in the era this was written and still is among devout Jews).

What does psychoanalysis make of the aforementioned observations about life-conduction?

Undoubtedly, the obsessive quest, for example, of wealth, social status and sexual pleasure (Berkson, 2010) represents a person's attempt to look to the external world for meaning and satisfaction ("the more possessions, the more anxiety"). This centripetal effort is bound to fail in the long run, for it never satisfies the hunger for external affirmation. One thinks of the narcissistic personality disorder where the person relates to others as if they were satellites in his orbit, squeezing the lemon and throwing away the rind. Such people with inordinate narcissism display vanity, they are privilege-seeking and have inflated assumptions of superiority over others or absolute grandiosity. In addition, such people are very reactive to slight or insult, sometimes expressing narcissistic rage (intense anger at assaults on the self-esteem) (Person, Cooper & Gabbard, 2005). While nearly everyone has a need for a modicum of external reward, such as pride in one's successes, the narcissist's way of being-in-the-world operates along the aforementioned malignant coordinates.

In contrast, the centrifugal-oriented person who is motivated by internalized beliefs and values, such as autonomy, integration and humanity, is more willing and able to sustain himself in a reasonable manner, such as through love and work as Freud famously said, passionate creativity and the like. That is, he tends to have strongly felt, flexibly and creatively applied, transcendent-pointing moral beliefs and values. An example of this is given by Bettelheim from his experiences in the Nazi concentration camps.

According to Bettelheim, it was the non-political, non-religious middle-class prisoners that had the greatest difficulty responding to the initial period of internment because these prisoners had lost the world that their self-respect and self-esteem was based on. Their self-esteem had heavily relied on a status and respect that came with their positions, their jobs, on being head of a family, or similar external factors. Without their external structures to prop them up, they collapsed into despair soon after their arrival at the camps (Bettelheim, 1960, pp. 120–122). Says Bettelheim

> It can become completely shattering to a person's integration when the system of beliefs on which he relied for integration … not only lets him down, but worse, is about to destroy him psychologically and physically. Then nothing seems left that can offer protection. Furthermore, we now no longer can feel confident that we will be able to ever again know reliably what to trust, and what to defend against.
>
> (1979, p. 10)

In other words, such inmates, without their familiar world of meaning—their social position, prestige and power to command—without a sense of their world as orderly, stable, continuous and comprehensible, were unable to maintain their prior narrative of self-identity. Their security of their being was threatened, and their sense of self was shattered (Weinstein, 1980, pp. 8, 18). Moreover, as Erich Fromm has pointed out, without the props on which their self-esteem and sense of identity rested, these non-political, non-religious middle-class inmates collapsed "morally like a deflatable balloon" (Fromm, 1973, p. 86). In a word, these inmates felt humiliated. In contrast, as I said earlier (entry #29), the religious and politically committed prisoners had deeply internalized, strongly felt, flexibly and creatively applied, transcendent-pointing moral beliefs and values, allowing them to sustain their autonomy, integration and humanity, at least relatively speaking. Creativity is very important in all of this, for as Winnicott noted, "it is creative apperception more than anything else that makes the individual feel that life is worth living" (1971, p. 71).

36. Torah and the natural world

> (III–9). Rabbi Jacob said: He who studies while traveling on a journey and in the very midst of his studies interrupts himself to admire the scenery, saying, How beautiful is this tree, how fair is this field, such a person has brought injury upon his soul.
>
> (Bokser, 1983, p. 239)

This Ethic appears to put two dimensions of human experience in contradiction. Studying Torah as revelation and acknowledging the beauty of nature, God's signature. How do the Rabbis reconcile these two well-intentioned actions? According to Sacks and Angel (2015)

> One should study Torah as a manifestation of God's will; one should admire nature as a reflection of God's wisdom and creative powers. Torah and nature are complementary paths to God. One must not "interrupt" between them by seeing them as distinct and separate domains.
>
> (Ibid., p. 68)

The fact is that the Rabbis created blessings when coming upon the beauty of the natural world; in their minds, this was God's world. For example, there is a blessing for viewing a beautiful, towering mountain and the like. However, in this Ethic there is a cautionary note, which is not to worship beauty rather than the Almighty. "Worship of beauty puts no demands on us, whereas God's commandments do" (Berkson, 2010, p. 109). Greenberg (2016) notes

> It is a mitzvah to admire nature and even to saying a blessing over beautiful, natural phenomena such as a rainbow, or when the trees first blossom in the spring, or when tasting a fruit. However, here the sin is to break off from Torah study in order to appreciate beauty, thus pitting God's beautiful revelation against God's beautiful nature.... The two do not contradict each other since they have one Creator. Each should be accorded its own respect and studied in its own time.
>
> (p. 127)[95]

Psychoanalysis has something to add to these interpretations of the Ethics in terms of the hard-to-pin-down phenomena of spirituality. Does all desire and pleasure (e.g., studying Torah and enjoying natural beauty) need to be directed toward attaining unity with the universe at large? (Akhtar, 2009). Such that there is an overcoming of one's inordinate narcissism or self-centric subjectivity into a person who is by disposition other-directed, other-regarding and other-serving, this being a crucial point of access to closeness to the Almighty. Indeed, as Huston Smith, the great religious scholar noted, hard-wired into the human condition is a yearning for "more" than the world of everyday experience can satisfy. The reality that often inspires and fulfills the human yearning for "more" and for self-transcendence is God, regardless of the name that is used (e.g., a Higher Being, A Realm, a Force, a Reality etcetera). In this context, says Smith, since God's nature is fundamentally unintelligible at this time, God is best viewed as a direction ("to God" as Levinas says) rather than an object. In fact, suggests Smith, one can make a strong argument that the desire for knowledge of the right direction, for orientation in life, is stronger than sexual instinct, the drive for power and the lust for material possessions (Smith, 2001, pp. 3, 26).

It is also worth noting that at first reading this aphorism appears to be very severe in terms of the superego—that is, all that really matters is the study of Torah. However, perhaps what is most interesting about the aforementioned Ethic is the interpretation that many of the Rabbis give to it (e.g., Greenberg, 2016; Sacks & Angel, 2015; Yanklowitz, 2018); namely, that the ideal approach to life is to blend both the love of Torah and the love of nature, each in its own time. As Ecclesiastes famously noted, "Everything has its season, and there is time for everything under the heaven".

What the psychoanalyst may see in this Ethic and its rabbinic interpretations is the fact that what matters most in terms of an art of living is an amalgamation of the intellectual domain (studying Torah) and the more emotional domain (enjoying nature's beauty). Indeed, psychoanalysis, at least as I understand it, involves the blending of the intellectual understanding and the emotional understanding (i.e., emotional or personal truths) of a particular issue that is in sharp focus. For while psychoanalysis is an intellectual activity of a sort (e.g., it involves skillful conceptual/symbolic thinking), its main focus, what tends to help people change as they see fit, is the right intervention that targets the emotional meaning of what is being spoken about. Intellectualization is one of the main defenses that neurotic analysands use. It has been defined as "the binding of the instinctual drives to intellectual activities [e.g., "abstract discussions and speculations about philosophic and religious topics" in adolescence], especially in order to exert control over anxiety and reduce tension" (Moore & Fine, 1990, p. 101). From my experience with a number of patients who were devout Jews, they all had notable tendencies to use intellectualization as a way of protecting themselves from distressing emotions.[96] Being raised in a rule-bound traditional world that idealizes intellectual attainment, as in the study of Talmud,[97] made them at least in part somewhat estranged from their emotional lives, which to my way of thinking was crucial for them to honestly and wholeheartedly engage.

Thus, what is mainly mutative in psychoanalysis is the transformation of the emotional domain, and so psychoanalysis gives greater weight to emotional understanding than intellectual understanding, at least in terms of what helps the patient modify what he believes he needs and wants to change in himself. In a word, in the beginning, the infant is a sentient, sensuous being before he is a thinking one. In psychoanalysis, emotional experience and change trump intellectual experience and change.

37. Truth

> (IV–16). Rabbi Judah said: Be cautious in teaching others, for even an unintentional error in teaching is tantamount to a deliberate transgression.
>
> (Bokser, 1983, p. 245)

Teaching is about so-called truth-telling, even though some scholars believe what constitutes truth is radically perspectival. Notwithstanding the problem of relativism, which undermines the notion of objective truth, the Rabbis believed that one should teach one's students (and oneself) the truth as one knows it to be. This includes emotional or personal truths. This requires accuracy, completeness and weighing the evidence about a contested matter etcetera. Perhaps it is better to do what the late philosopher Richard Rorty did; namely, to speak about "usable truths" as opposed to The (unconditional) Truth (e.g., integrated linear truths). In this view, there is no "immaculate perception" but rather the "gray haziness of uncertainty"—that is, "reality-as-it-is perceived" (Wallenfang, 2021, pp. 60, 62). This being said, the Rabbis were concerned that a person may unintentionally speak a falsehood by, say, "inadvertently giving improper advice" (Twersky, 1999, p. 237). Speaking an unintentional falsehood, giving what turns out to be bad advice, is judged to be as bad as a deliberate sin, an admittedly very high bar to get over. As the Rabbis saw it, inadequate or defective knowledge is not an acceptable defense, "because if one did not know, then one should have known before giving advice to others" (ibid.). Who among us has not given what we took to be good and sound advice only to find out that our advice was ill-conceived, ill-advised and ill-fated? Kravitz and Olitzky (1993) conclude:

> Rashi and Bartinoro take Rabbi Yehudah's statement as a warning to scholars that care must be exercised in the analysis of law lest decisions be made that could allow that which is prohibited. God will then treat indolence as insolence.
>
> (p. 64)

The point here is that extreme care should be taken when one studies Torah and especially when it comes to making judgments about legal matters. That is, carelessness or forgetfulness can contribute to giving incorrect legal decisions. Interestingly, through mistakes in study, one might not only permit that which God has forbidden, but one might also forbid something which is permitted. Either way, one is guilty (Sacks & Angel, 2015). The Rabbis are saying that being a teacher carries with it huge responsibilities, and that is why in the rabbinic world a rabbi/teacher only becomes a rabbi/teacher by being ordained by another rabbi/teacher, one who understands the gravity of the responsibility.

The Rabbi's standard, that an inadvertent mistake is as bad as an intentional one, strikes me, qua analyst, as rather harsh. For motivation is what is crucial here; does the person make a mistake on purpose, maliciously, or is it unintentional and seemingly at the time good and sound advice? Motivation really does matter. To want to hurt or to want to heal. This has obvious ramifications in terms of guilt and responsibility both in the clinical context and in real life. For it is nearly impossible not to make some unintentional mistakes even with the best of intentions.

Psychoanalysis is also about truth-telling, about finding/creating usable truths in terms of the art of living a good life. It centrally involves teaching, the analyst trying to teach the analysand a different way of looking at his life and especially his problems in living. That is, psychoanalysis attempts to assist the analysand to feel, think and act differently, more rationally and realistically, based in part on confronting the lies he tells himself. As Freud noted in *The Future of an Illusion*, psychoanalysis is an "education to reality" ("Men cannot remain children for ever; they must in the end go out into 'hostile life'" (1927b, p. 49). Exactly how this plays out in the consultation room is of great technical concern.

For example, psychoanalysis does not assume there is one Truth that is deduced by the majority opinion as in the Talmud, as if truth was determined by a vote. Truth in the clinical setting is a question of narrative truth—that is, the analysand decides, with some help from the analyst, what is the usable truth on a particular issue. Thus, truth in analysis is situational truth; it is context-dependent and setting-specific. What is "right" in one situation may not be in another. Social psychologists have made this point quite convincingly in their studies of how environmental circumstances impact in "real time" how a person behaves, like in, say, the famous Milgram obedience to authority experiments. In other words, social psychology, especially the "classic" experiments, have shown how situational forces shape moral behavior (Marcus, 2020).

Psychoanalysis also tends not to give advice in the clinical setting for many reasons. Firstly, because practical advice has often been given by others and has usually been rejected by the analysand for one reason or another. Rather, what has to be explored are the defenses and motivations for not being able to follow sometimes an obvious solution, and understanding this in the context of a pattern of behaviors is crucial. Secondly, another reason that advice giving is usually shunned by analysts is that it undermines the analysand's sense of autonomy, since the analysand is in a partially regressed state in the transference (i.e., regression in service of the ego), and hence they are more vulnerable to being influenced or to rejecting the advice, not based on the value of the advice per se but as, say, a neurotic re-enactment of past relationships. Every word that the analyst says is carefully weighed by him in terms of its content, form and timing, how it is likely to land in terms of the analysand's inner experience, and hopefully receptivity. Psychoanalysts take their pedagogic role very seriously, but it shuns straightforward advice-giving.

In terms of self-revelation in the form of teaching the analysand, it is a subject that analysts also take earnestly. That is, the analyst tends to remain impartial (an ideal that is never fully realized) so as not to burden the analysand with the analyst's problems in living and other personal considerations etcetera. Giving advice, for example, frequently requires the person giving the advice to make an analogy to his own life, which can be very tricky indeed, especially when the patient is in a transference. Another important issue pertinent to giving advice and the like was raised by Akhtar (2009) in terms of the analyst's self-disclosure for the sake of advancing the analysis. He notes that

> The issue of self-disclosure is more complex than whether to reveal a piece of information about oneself to one's analysand or not. It involves other questions—what to disclose? How much to disclose? When? To Whom? To what end? And, finally, how to determine whether one's decision has been appropriate.
>
> (p. 258)

The aforementioned questions put into sharp focus the fact that self-disclosure, perhaps a subspecies of advice giving, has to be done with great care.[98] Thus, for psychoanalysis, extreme caution by the analyst about imposing their view or opinion is built into the process. Put differently, the issue of imposing one's will on the regressed analysand is rejected, often replaced by the virtue of silence. The Rabbis may have been aware of this when they wrote, "All my life I was raised among scholars and I found that no virtue becomes a man more than silence" (Bokser, 1983, p. 233, III–17).

38. Emotional intelligence

> (IV–23). Rabbi Simeon ben Elazar said: Do not attempt to appease your friend at the time of his anger; do not begin to console him while his beloved lies dead before him; do not question him for particulars at the time he makes a vow; and do not try to face him in the hour of his disgrace.
>
> (Bokser, 1983, p. 245)

"Ripeness is all" says Shakespeare in King Lear. Indeed, this mishna speaks to the need for maturity and skillful timing when it comes to making an intervention to someone who is angry, bereft, making a vow (i.e., rejecting or taking on some singular duty) or ashamed. As is common knowledge, when someone is very angry, it is near impossible to get them to do anything besides vent their anger, hopefully in not a destructive fashion. Likewise, it would be premature to tell someone whose loved one has just died that they should get over it or move on (moving forward, yes, moving on, no). Indeed, who has not condemned those news reporters who shove a microphone in the face of a bereaved parent whose child has just died, say, from a shooting, asking them how they feel, and not felt that this was unbelievably inappropriate? In a similar manner, when a person makes a vow of, say, dieting or a pledge to exercise, to be dismissive of such a pledge or in some other way meddle in the person's decision is to be disrespectful to that person (Greenberg, 2016). It may also make him feel unhelpfully guilty. And finally, when one has been publicly shamed, disgraced or embarrassed, the Rabbis believed that it was not in the person's best interests to force oneself upon the shamed person, for "your words may turn into criticism and, intentional or not, into mockery, thus adding insult to injury" (ibid., p. 221). Moreover, sometimes visiting a person in his hour of legitimate shame (as opposed to neurotic shame) makes him feel even more ashamed. Effective social skills and good emotional intelligence (Yanklowitz, 2018) really do matter when it comes to interpersonal relationships. All in all, the Rabbis believed that Hillel's comment to a proselyte that the essence of the Torah was "Love your neighbor like yourself", which Hillel interpreted as meaning "Do not do anything to another person that you would not wish done to you", should be one's guiding ethical optic (Twersky, 1999, p. 254).

Psychoanalysis regards the issue of timing to be a very serious one in the treatment setting. That is, knowing when and how to make a helpful comment takes years of experience to get good at. This skill requires judging when the analysand's receptivity is most fertile, which often is very hard to discern. This capacity requires not only empathy, "the imagining of another's subjective experience through the use of one's own subjectivity" (Person, Cooper & Gabbard, 2005, p. 551), but also "experiencing the other side", as Martin Buber called it, "to feel an event from the side of the person one meets as well as from one's own side" (Friedman, 2002, p. 102).[99]

Most importantly, a psychotherapist has to have the discipline of thought and action to let an analysand live the emotion in the "here and now", to not rush them away from the feeling of, say, anger, grief, guilt or shame. Such a capacity displays the utmost respect for the analysand, for his inner world. Take, for example, the attempt to "appease" an analysand who is angry. Such efforts to pacify/placate an analysand by agreeing to his demands can easily backfire in that the analysand may feel like his anger is justified, rather than being misplaced based on false assumptions or from some other ill-conceived consideration. By giving in to the analysand's demands, one is not setting adequate standards or rules of engagement, thus missing an opportunity for the analysand to critically reflect on the unreasonableness of his anger. Such anger can be especially intense when there is a transference in play, especially a negative one, where anger from the past, for example, "old" anger toward the parents is being re-enacted with the analyst. When an analyst tries to "console" an analysand who has lost a loved one, the latter may feel that the efforts at consolation are phony. In addition, the analyst's response may not correlate with the analysand's experience, reflecting the analyst's inaccurate empathy. Allowing the analysand to dwell in his lamenting state for a while appears to be the more prudent course of action. To "question" an analysand when he is making a pledge is to possibly undermine the analysand's autonomy/agency and faith in himself. While deconstructing the pledge about, say, losing weight is a necessary thing to do, at the time the analysand is making the pledge, one is better off affirming the healthy aspects of the analysand's decision. Finally, to attempt to "face" an analysand when he feels legitimate shame is possibly to further humiliate him. Rather, the analyst would want to "sit" with the patient who has to "sit" with his shame and know that firstly it can be lived with and tolerated then later understood.

Overall, then, what matters most in psychoanalysis is the analyst be willing and able to engage the analysand in the present, cultivating the emotional atmosphere (e.g., of trust) for the analysand to dwell in the "here and now" emotion until he is ready to move forward. When an analyst cannot adequately do this, it usually reflects some kind of countertransference limitation, especially truncated ties to empathy.

39. Asceticism

> (VI-4). This is the way of those who are devoted to the study of the Torah: If necessary, eat bread with salt, drink your water by measure, sleep on the ground, live a hard life, but toil in the Torah. If you will do this, you will be happy, and all will be well with you. You will be happy in this world; and all will be well with you in the world to come.
>
> (Bokser, 1993, p. 254)

Chapter 6 of the Ethics is an editorial add-on to the original Pirkei Avot.[100] It comprises the weekly study portion of the Ethics for the sixth and last Shabbat between Passover, the liberation from Egyptian slavery, and Shavuot, the giving of the Torah. In general, its focuses on the religious person's joys and rewards of Torah study in this world and the next (Greenberg, 2016).

While in general Judaism rejects asceticism as a way of life (and its opposite, crass opulence), this Ethic is regarded as a minority perspective, in favor of a degree of asceticism as one engages in serious Torah study. Some, like Rashi, have attempted to alleviate the obvious meaning of this Ethic by claiming that even if one was as poor and vulnerable to adversity as described, one would still be duty-bound to study Torah. Be that as it may, this Ethic clearly advocates an ascetic lifestyle as "the way of those who are devoted to the study of the Torah". Twersky (1999) tells us,

> The mishna does not actually mean that one must live on the meagerest of subsistence in order to excel in Torah. Rather, he must be ready to do so if circumstances necessitate such austerity. If he cannot make peace with living on the bare essentials, he may be distracted from his Torah studies in order to better his condition. If, however, one is able to subsist on the bare necessities, greater comforts will not distract him.
>
> (p. 349)

While Twersky initially says that this Ethic is not meant to be taken literally, he than argues that "perhaps this mishnah was meant to be taken literally after all", citing the lack of great rabbinical creativity in the USA due to too cushy a lifestyle (i.e., lack of work ethic and going soft) (ibid.). I believe that this Ethic can reasonably be taken literally, for a degree of spartan-like living may help potentiate serious Torah study. For example, Hillel, the prototype of Torah acumen, chopped wood for a living, earning very little each week. Half of his earnings went to assisting his family, while the other half went to the gatekeeper to the study hall (ibid., p. 350).[101]

What is the psychoanalytic view of asceticism, severe self-discipline and avoidance of all forms of indulgence? For many people inclined to asceticism, the main issue is their precarious relationship to pleasure, viewing it as a corrupting force to the soul. In this view, allowing oneself certain pleasures is seen as "bad", and the beginning of a "slippery slope" to wanton debauchery. Often the fear is of the breakthrough into consciousness and behavior of anti-social impulses. So, for example, a teenager who suddenly becomes a vegetarian may be defending himself against oral sadistic wishes (e.g., biting and the upsurge of ambivalence) directed at one of his parents, siblings or other significant others, or the denial of the upsurge of sexual wishes, such that they have to reject any pleasure-giving behavior like eating meat.

Asceticism often has masochistic components to it, in particular moral masochism. Moral masochism originates in a person's sense of unconscious guilt, which leads to long-term self-denigration, self-punishment and self-destructiveness. In terms of the above example, denying oneself the pleasure, say, of eating meat becomes the unconscious punishment. As Rycroft further notes, following Freud, moral masochism describes the proclivity to succumb to one's own sadistic superego. The superego obtains its moral force from instinctual aggressive energy, which is released by taking it out on the vulnerable ego (Rycroft, 1995). Asceticism can also be entwined with anhedonia, the difficulty in experiencing pleasure or joy in those activities that generally are viewed as pleasurable and joyful.

Thus, what the Rabbis are recommending seems to represent an all or nothing view of Torah study versus the instinctual life. Such that rather than integrating these wishes into their lives they are condemned, rejected and seen as bad and a distraction from Torah study. In other words, the individual is stopped from being in touch with their aggressive and sexual wishes rather than there being a more wholesome integration of all parts of the personality.

40. Piety

> (VI–5). Do not aspire to grandeur and do not be covetous for honor. Let your deeds exceed your learning; crave not after the table of kings, for your table is greater than theirs, and your crown is greater than theirs. And your Employer may be depended on to compensate you for your labors [karmic consequences are in play].
>
> (Bokser, 1993, p. 254)

The first sentence of this Ethic indicates that the pious Jew should not be seduced by the material acquisitions associated with fame and fortune, nor should he be jealous or envious of what others have acquired. Rather one should stay existentially centered on serving the Almighty (we have seen this teaching earlier, entry #19). Also, the idea here is that there is a danger of becoming so enamored with the importance of Torah learning, in striving for honor, recognition and/or rule over others, that the positive impact of Torah learning for its own sake drops away (Greenberg, 2016).

"Let your deeds exceed your learning" refers to the truism that what matters in terms of Torah living is the deployment of these ethical precepts in everyday life: Greatness is not determined by the amount of power, fame or wealth acquired, rather greatness is achieved by perfecting one's spiritual and moral way of being-in-the-world. Therefore, "a life dedicated to Torah learning is greater than the life of a king" (ibid., p. 315). Sacks and Angel (2015) put the point just right:

> Many are simply drawn into the [rat] race because they have not thought through their philosophy of life or do not have the independence of spirit to stand up to their values and ideals. They are driven by conformism or spiritual apathy. They surrender their freedom and autonomy in order to play the game of life according to the rules of the rat race.
>
> (p. 163)

From a psychoanalytic point of view, the likely take-home point of this Ethic is that one would be better off appreciating what you have, and by doing so you do not have to be jealous or envious of others. To accomplish this requires an inner center of gravity that enables the individual to focus on their own strengths and even weaknesses. The analytic process is aimed at the ability to gradually uncover the sources of conflicts and defensive maneuvers used, in order to reach a point where there can be an appreciation of the underlying motivations and ultimately strengths in the individual's personality. The work done in this process to ameliorate the harshness of the superego and be less self-critical further enhances this ability. As the analysand becomes more empathic and more sympathetic to their younger selves, they are able to recognize the feelings and wants that led to their present discomfort and not condemn themselves, thus enhancing their self-esteem. This aforementioned process of self-exploration takes the focus away from comparing themselves to others, which is the source of so much misery, and instead allows for the appreciation of who one is.

41 and 42. The court system and justice

> (1–8). Judah ben Tabbai and Simeon ben Shatah received the traditions from them. Judah ben Tabbai said: Let not the judge play the part of the counselor; when two litigants stand before you, suspect both of being in the wrong; and when they leave after submitting to the court's decree, regard them both as guiltless.
>
> (Bokser, 1993, p. 232)

> (1–9). Simeon ben Shatah said: Search the witnesses thoroughly and be cautious with your own words lest you give them an opening to false testimony.
>
> (Ibid., p. 233)

Both of these mishnas are concerned with the court system. The Rabbis were fervently devoted to creating a just and merciful legal system. In fact, Levinas noted, "the harmony achieved between so much goodness and so much legalism constitutes the original note of Judaism" (1990, p. 19). The aforementioned mishnas are not laws, but rather give an ethical basis for the development of law, the Halacha (Berkson, 2010). Freud had a similar perspective when he wrote, "The first requisite of civilization, therefore, is that of justice—that is, the assurance that a law once made will not be broken in favor of an individual" (1930, p. 95).

In the first mishna, it says that a judge should not act like an advocating lawyer (or appear to be), but rather he should be neutral and tolerant, receptive to all aspects of a case. The judge should also assume that both litigants are guilty; in other words, he should be impartial (or impartial-like) and skeptical toward both parties. Also, once the (civil) case is over and the litigants have accepted the verdict, the judge should treat each party as an upright citizen (Greenberg, 2016). Yanklowitz (2018) aptly summarizes the meaning of this mishna:

> We should always demand reason and evidence and never merely rely on piety or wisdom of the authorities. Every person has intellectual challenges, as well as psychological blind spots. To treat both parties in conflict equally is a matter of justice that requires us to be aware of our biases. We must admit that we all—even unconsciously—judge based on

> appearance, age, race, intellect, and so on. Understanding these biases is the first step.
>
> (p. 31)

The second mishna puts forth a principle of exacting and thorough cross-examination to get to the truth (e.g., no leading questions, no deliberate ambiguity), bearing in mind the propensity of parties to distort the truth in their favor or blatantly lie. In other words, we should not speak in a way that promotes distortion or lying on the part of others. That the cross-examination should be exhaustive and clear is a view that suggests in general that "people must think carefully before speaking, and must speak carefully so as not to be misunderstood" or worse (Sacks & Angel, 2015, p. 17). For example, the Rabbis are here speaking about something beyond the aforementioned meaning; namely, gossiping, "speaking evil of another and bringing shame on the person is akin to murder" (Yanklowitz, 2018, p. 32; see entry #17, the Chofetz Chaim on gossip). Likewise, one must

> give the best of ourselves, even if it would seem to run counter to our personal bottom line. It is all too easy to stretch the meaning of our words and actions to gain a client, to gain a friend, to gain favor.
>
> (Ibid., p. 33)

On the face of it, these mishnas don't have much to do with psychoanalysis. However, we can make two brief points that highlight the confluence of thinking here but also elucidate and elaborate on these mishnas. With regard to the first mishna, the analyst should remain "neutral" in the psychoanalytic encounter. By this is not meant that the analyst doesn't have feelings and thoughts that are pertinent to the treatment, but he must never impose these feelings and thoughts on the analysand who is amidst a transference or transference neurosis (emergencies are exceptions). In other words, his countertransference must be kept under his control. As Akhtar notes, notwithstanding Freud's use of the "mirror" and "surgeon" metaphors (Freud, 1912, pp. 115,118) to depict the analyst's overall attitude toward the analysand, Freud did not practice neutrality in the sense of being detached and aloof: Rather, he practiced "Neutrality, characterized by a non-judgmental and non-critical attitude, was always coupled with earnest interest, compassion, and 'sensitivity to the patient's developmental potentialities'" (2009, p. 187. Akhtar is quoting H. Blum). In other words, Freud was well aware that absolute neutrality was neither possible nor desirable in an analysis that usually goes on for years. The largely North American Relational/intersubjective school of psychoanalysis, with its "two person psychology"[102] (i.e., psychological processes are dialectically created between analyst and analysand) and the co-produced nature of psychoanalytic information (especially countertransference), has put these considerations as the main thrust of the analytic process.[103]

Following Hoffer (1985), psychoanalytic neutrality is perhaps best formulated as composed of three domains: neutrality with regard to feeling; neutrality with regard to the analysand's conflicts and deficits; neutrality with regard to the power imbalance in the analyst/analysand relationship (Akhtar, 2009). As Hoffer (1985) noted,

> We must not allow our means, our theory of cure, to obscure our ends, the elucidation of conflict. The analyst's best position from which to respond to the analysand's needs is a neutral position in relation to the conflicts brought into the analytic situation.
>
> (p. 790)

The overall point is that Freudian psychoanalysis is in sync with the first mishna; it argues that the analyst should for the most part not impose his beliefs on the analysand, nor should he reflexively educate, advise or inflict his values upon the analysand emanating from some kind of countertransference reaction (Moore & Fine, 1990).

The second mishna connects to the notion of countertransference, the analyst's transference to the analysand. The idea here is the analyst must not "lead" the vulnerable analysand with his words, because of his own issues—that is, he should not engage in leading questions or deliberate ambiguity in order to provoke the analysand to respond in a certain way that more reflects the analyst's conflicts and difficulties rather than the analysand. He should choose his words wisely and time them to have maximum positive impact. Thus, with some guidance from the analyst, the analysand should arrive at his own insights largely from his own efforts.

43. Free will

> (III–19). Everything is foreseen, yet freedom of choice is given. The world is judged mercifully, yet all is in accordance with the preponderant quality of work.
>
> (Bokser, 1983, p. 241)

This mishna raises what for the *homo religious* is a timeless paradox; namely, God's foreknowledge of events against human freedom (Kravitz & Olitzky, 1993). Twersky deconstructs the difficult paradox just right:

> We believe that God has Omniscient knowledge, and knows everything that was, that is, and that will ever be. We also believe that man has total freedom of will[104] in ethical and moral matters, and at any moment is absolutely free to choose whether to do right or wrong. The obvious difficulty is that if God knows what I am going to do tomorrow, how can it be that I will have the freedom tomorrow to make a choice? If I do other

than what God knows, then His knowledge is not perfect, which is impossible. On the other hand, if I must do what He knows I will do, then I do not have the freedom to do otherwise.

(1999, p. 181)

This paradox has troubled theologians throughout the ages, and there is no satisfying solution that I am aware of which reconciles the matter. As Greenberg notes, God's knowledge may be perfect, but He also endowed human beings with the freedom to act:

> The limits of logic and reason should be recognized, especially given the limits of the human mind. Furthermore, life experiences, and indeed all of reality, should be accepted in their complexity and often contradictory states rather than be filtered or denied due to philosophical or ideological blinders.... Consistency [said Emerson] is the hobgoblin of little minds.
>
> (2016, pp. 151–152)

Even the great Maimonides was not able to sort out the paradox. He argued that while it is essentially beyond our comprehension, he still maintained we must maintain the paradox in a dialectical tension and focus on our freedom to choose good or bad, right or wrong. In other words, to do otherwise. As Greenberg concludes, the main thrust of this mishna is to "make room for the pluralism of God's creation and human understanding" (ibid., p. 152).

Psychoanalysis, especially a version that has a postmodern sensibility, views consciousness in a similar manner as this mishna suggests. For example, as Bass (1998) has noted, Freud was against the idea of a psychoanalytic Weltanschauung (worldview) in part because it is antipsychoanalytic—that is, it went against the basic thrust of psychoanalysis, which following Freud is that "it cannot be systematic".[105] Philosophers, theologians and psychotics, according to Freud, strive for systematicity, but psychoanalysis should not—in part because it fundamentally concerns itself with "unconscious energic processes" that by definition are contradictory, paradoxical and ambiguous, and therefore must challenge our habitual conscious patterns of organizing data. In other words, for Bass, like Freud, to seek out or create a Weltanschauung is to succumb to an "illusory wish fulfillment". A commitment to such systematization is not only a form of imprisonment, but it also misses some of the essential themes of psychoanalysis that suggest what Freud thought constituted aspects of the human condition; for example, that human consciousness is inescapably ambiguous and contradictory. Psychoanalysis, says Bass, must push against the tendency to mold itself into the habitual patterns of conscious experience, against Weltanschauungen; it should strive to be more like an endless movement that perpetually undoes itself (Marcus & Rosenberg, 1998, editor's introduction, pp. 412–413).[106]

Another aspect of psychoanalysis which has some bearing on this mishna is the notion that while analysands in principle have a choice in terms of how they live their lives, often their choices are not determined by consciously held views but rather are motivated by their unconscious mind and traumatic history. In other words, such analysands can be described as having a choice only superficially speaking, for in a certain sense their choices are governed by aspects of their neurotic mind which are out of awareness. Neurosis, by definition, limits the options in terms of ego flexibility and other considerations; it shrinks and narrows one's way of being-in-the-world.

As French analyst André Green noted, "Being sane was having the possibility of being free. If the unconscious took hold of a person, then we have the pathology of freedom" (1999, p. 18).[107]

As to the last sentence of the mishna, for the believing Jew, as for other religious people, the world is judged in terms of God's mercy (His goodness and compassion), and in accordance with the amount of good and compassionate deeds that one performs (notice that the emphasis is on deeds not beliefs, though studying Torah ideally provides one with the motivation and direction for righteous action). Put differently, there is the belief that if one behaves righteously then one will be rewarded in this world or the next (a debatable claim for some, such as the secular analyst/analysand). As Berkson (2010) notes, there are two elements of God's mercy in judging human beings. The first element is the possibility of repentance, *teshuvah*. According to the Rabbis, says Berkson, even if people are wicked all their lives, they will in principle be forgiven by God if they genuinely repent. The other aspect of God's mercy in judging human beings is that when our deeds are for the most part balanced God will nevertheless judge us meritorious. This being said, the matter is hardly straightforward. As Yanklowitz (2018) notes, "If God is a judge of truth and justice, how can God also be merciful, compassionate, and all-loving?"; "here too, this paradox is true: God is both the God of truth and justice and the God of mercy, compassion, and love" (p. 174). Unambiguous absolute Truth is impossible for humans to fathom, and there lies the rub. The believer lives with this dialectical tension; the non-believer views these paradoxes as evidence of the absurdity of this form of life conduction. For the secular psychoanalyst, while there are no absolute moral truths in the clinical situation (i.e., truths are context-dependent and setting-specific), if an analysand believes in absolute moral truths, the goal is to help him hold such a view in a manner that is non-oppressive, that doesn't transform him into an oppressor himself (Roberts, 2023).

Notes

1 This refers to the chapter and number of the particular Ethic in Bokser's translation.
2 In Jewish tradition, the Great Assembly refers to an assembly of about 120 scribes, sages and prophets from the conclusion of the Biblical prophets to the time of the evolution of Rabbinic Judaism, delineating a transition from the

prophetic to the Rabbinic era. They lived in a period of about two hundred years, concluding in 70 CE.

3   In the Talmud, typical acts of lovingkindness include visiting the sick, offering hospitality to strangers, providing a suitable outfit and dowry for a poor bride, and caring for the orphaned (Bokser, 1989, p. 44).

4   As Jungian analyst Murray Stein (1998) noted, "the archetypes are formative factors that exist in a realm beyond the range of the human psyche, which Jung calls 'spirit'"(p. 45).

5   Symington's notion of revelation appears to be rather limited and literal. For Martin Buber (a believing Jewish humanist/philosopher/theologian) and Gabriel Marcel (a believing Catholic humanist/philosopher/theologian), revelation does come from "without" but not the way Symington implies, as if man were a vessel that is filled or simply a mouthpiece of God. Rather, says Buber, "revelation seizes the human elements that are at hand and recasts them: it is the *pure shape of the meeting*" (Buber, 1967, p. 135). Likewise, for Marcel, revelation is only conceivable to the extent that it is addressed to a person who is engaged (existentially available) with the fullness of his whole being, who participates in the mystery of being. Revelation subverts the person's self-enclosed way of being-in-the-world. It is a disruptive force which crashes through the rationalistic perspective (Rotenstreich, 1968).

6   In a letter to his friend and collaborator Wilhelm Fliess, Freud mentioned "in passing that psychoanalysis was akin to the ancient mystery rites" (Eigen, 1998, p. 13).

7   Wallwork (1991) agrees with Phillips, "psychoanalysis is inherently a psychology of morals" (p. 283).

8   Elsewhere, Phillips describes the different theories of psychoanalysis as "morality plays".

9   Bollas (1987) had an interesting discussion of the dynamics of lying in the clinical context (pp. 173–188).

10 It is not perfection that the devout Jew is after; it's betterment. God is not looking for us to be perfect; perfection is a human construct. Even in Genesis, the best work that God has ever done, God says "it was very good, *tov meod*". God never says or looks for perfection.

11 What constitutes the "whole self" is of course hard to define. Moreover, judging when the whole self (as opposed to part of the self) is allegedly operating is a complex and tenuous activity. And what about discerning "a divided self" as William James famously put it? Put differently, as Bollas (1987) notes, in analysis "the analyst restores to the patient what I believe we can term genuine or true subjectivity" (p. 63), a questionable notion if one considers the postmodern critique of essentialism. Bollas also uses the term "true self" (p. 73).

12 Altruism as a term was first used by the French philosopher Auguste Compte in the middle of the 1800s (Phillips & Taylor, 2009).

13 Rycroft notes that the superego is not the conscience (1995, pp. 177–178). Freud sometimes correlates the superego with the "demands of the conscience", though he conceptualizes the conscience as one of the functions of the superego (1930, p. 127).

14 It is worth mentioning that a rabbi is, at heart, a teacher who learned tradition from his teacher, who learned from his teacher. This is what is meant by "get yourself a teacher"; find someone who understands the tradition/religion/community you belong to so you can also belong to that tradition through a life-affirming train of succession.

15 Hans Loewald indicates that ideally the analyst "is more experienced, more knowledgeable, and more mature in regard to the emotional than" the analysand himself (1991, p. 141). Likewise, Loewald uses the words the "analyst's objectivity"

in describing the analyst's way of being in terms of the transference neurosis (Lear, 1996, pp. 689).

16 In Marcus (2021), I take up how Martin Buber viewed teaching/education, this being an example that constitutes the best of great teaching.

17 Homer has claimed that "today over 50% of the world's psychoanalysts practice some form of Lacanian analysis, and the Lacanian orientation predominates in many parts of the globe" (Homer, 2016, p. 112). Unfortunately, Homer does not indicate how he came to this 50% figure.

18 The rabbinic tradition of "friend" is also one who "pushes against you" to help you become the best version of yourself. That is, to see more clearly and not get mired in your own way of thinking. That is, the best friend, the best *havruta* (study partner) is the one who helps you "see the other side".

19 Freud, in another context, in a letter to Ferenczi, made a similar point: "Tell me how someone makes love, and I will tell you everything about their character" (Phillips & Taylor, 2009, p. 73).

20 In another saying in the Ethics, it recommends that one should "greet every person with a cheerful countenance" (Bokser, 1983, p. 233).

21 Following S.D. Luzzatto, a modern Italian Jewish philosopher, who regarded the source of ethical activity in compassion and righteousness, Rotenstreich defined compassion and righteousness succinctly. "Compassion is the desire to alleviate the burden of pain and sorrow in our fellow man", while "righteousness is the desire to be the true judge in the rival claims between man and man" (Rotenstreich, 1968, p. 33).

22 See my book on work, *The Psychoanalysis of Career Choice, Job Performance and Satisfaction: How to Flourish in the Workplace* (Marcus, 2017).

23 Psychoanalysis, or at least my version of it, would not be troubled by sadomasochism in the bedroom, providing it was between consenting adults.

24 Hillel is depicted as a devoted supporter of peaceful conduct, a lover of all people, a hardworking student, a convincing and ready teacher, and a man of comprehensive and cheerful faith in God. "In short, he appears as the model of the ideal Jewish sage". Hillel is the most quoted Talmudic sage in the Ethics (Goldin, 2023, n.p.). Arguably, one of the reasons that Hillel achieved such an exalted role was because he was "pushed", in the best sense of the word, by Shammai, his alter-ego in study. (Shammai was a first-century scholar of the Mishna who was known for his strict literal interpretation of the Law). Hillel was the more lenient and tolerant of the two, thereby living the dictum to not dominate the other.

25 In Pythagoras's academy, the student was not allowed to speak for five years, actually three to five years depending on their educational status, as he was not viewed as learned in listening to the master's speech.

26 It is important to note that in the most extreme situation of the Nazi concentration and death camps, an inmate who was a "lone wolf", a solitary person who was only out for himself, usually did not survive with his autonomy, integration and humanity relatively intact.

27 The study began in 1938 and followed more than 700 people throughout their lives, eventually expanding to include their offspring.

28 As David Brooks notes, "there are mountains of evidence to show that intimate relationships, not career, are at the core of life, and that those intimate relationships will have a downstream effect on everything else you do" (2023a, p. 3). For example, one study done at the University of Chicago "found that marriage was 'the most important differentiator' between happy and unhappy people. Married people are 30 points happier than the unmarried" (ibid.).

29 As Daniel Goleman (2019) noted in his introduction to Frankl's book (2019), Frankl (commenting on Hillel's famous saying, entry #4) believed that each one of us has our special purpose and that serving others enhances, if not ennobles it: "The scope and range of our actions matter less than how well we respond to the specific demands of our life circle" (p. 11).

30 Gobodo-Madikizela's (2016, p. 432) notion of "empathic care", conceived "as a starting point for understanding the emergence of forgiveness [and genuine remorse] and reconciliation [in apartheid South Africa] in survivor-perpetrator dialogue", has some family resemblance to what Buber was getting at.

31 Winnicott noted, also somewhat enigmatically, that "madness is the need to be believed". Phillips does a good job of unpacking this notion (2021c, pp. 114–118).

32 Empathy and altruism are usually associated with compassion, but they are generally regarded as somewhat different from it by empirical researchers. Wallwork (2005) notes that an analyst should exemplify "empathic respect" toward an analysand. He writes that "empathy alone, without respect, is too close to sympathy, which involves compassionate identification with the other's plight in a way that can feel false or even arrogant and presumptuous to the recipient, evoking suspicion of inauthenticity". Moreover, says Wallwork, "sympathy also connotes agreement with the sufferer's explanation of his or her problems which the analyst rebuffs" (p. 290). Ogden (1999, 2022), however, sees an important role for compassion in the analyst's way of comporting himself.

33 In a later saying from Rabbi Yose, it is written, "Respect the possessions of your friend as you do your own" (Bokser, 1983, p. 236). Also worth mentioning is that Rabbi Eliezer's caution to respect the honor of a friend may be related to his tragic experiences in defying his rabbinic colleagues, when they outvoted him in the academy (i.e., majority ruled), which ultimately brought upon him his excommunication (ibid., p. 237).

34 This notion has a family resemblance to mentalization: "the imaginative interpretation of others' and one's own mental state"; "the impulse to seek to understand to imagine other people's thoughts" (Fonagy & Campbell, 2016, pp. 115, 123).

35 Wallwork cites Freud (1930, pp. 109–145) to support his claims.

36 Wallwork is quoting from Freud (1933a, p. 212).

37 Eigen found that living this way was not productive, rather he lives each day as if it's his first (Bagai, 2023). While Ecclesiastes believed that there was nothing new under the sun, Rabbi Abraham Isaac Kook, the late Ashkenasi Chief Rabbi of British Mandatory Palestine, noted that there was nothing old under the sun.

38 This is often true of the Rabbis of the Mishneh and the Talmud. But this is what contributed to the rise of Hassidism, where psychological insights were considered integral to understanding the Torah, or put another way, the Torah offers us some very deep psychological insights, but we have to have the psychological wherewithal to read them into the text.

39 Psychoanalysis has a concept called "feel the thought", which is a complicated "act, constituted not only through the linking of emotion with cognition, but also when we are able to embody a lived object relationship that links self and other, affect and object, past and present" (Sekoff, 1999, p. 123). As Sekoff notes in his discussion of French analyst André Greene's writings, "Green helps us to see that all 'felt thoughts' are both shadow and light, that is, the presence of our psychic experience rests on a penumbra of absence" (ibid.). A. Ferro believes that "the ultimate goal of analysis is to enrich—or in some cases to supply for the first time—the equipment for metabolising formerly unthinkable emotion and affective states" (2009, p. 178). These considerations call to mind Bollas's notion of "unthought known"—that is, "the infant's unconscious, learned assumptions

40 about the nature of reality, based fundamentally on experiences that register in the mind before the advent of language" (Nettleton, 2017, p. 27; Bollas, 1987).
40 In fact there is an Ethic that says, "This world is like a vestibule before the world to come. Prepare yourself in the vestibule [e.g., strive for goodness] so that you may enter the main chamber" (Bokser, 1983, pp. IV–21).
41 In a certain sense, a belief in the world to come offers the believer a "second chance" to get things right. The Rabbis also believed that each person's soul can live through many incarnations, which also influenced their thinking on what constitutes reward and punishment.
42 This statement excludes "evil" people like Hitler, Stalin and Mao.
43 Lamed-vav is also how to spell the Hebrew word lev, which means heart.
44 According to rabbinic tradition, Moses was the most humble man ever to have lived, according to the Torah, but one can arguably claim that he did not have a "reduced view of his own significance".
45 The Rabbis in the Talmud stressed that we have to acknowledge that all we have and are is because of God's beneficence; this is a recurring theme in much of the Jewish liturgy as well, liturgy that was created by the Rabbis during the Mishnaic and Talmudic era.
46 As Gaskill (2014) noted, "It may sound a bit silly, but actually saying goodbye to the objects you've chosen to let go of can help bring a sense of closure—not only to the lightening of your space, but to the emotions you are choosing to let go of, too". In other words, saying goodbye to sentimental objects can be a compelling moment for the owner of the item.
47 Of course there are those reasonable individuals who feel that there is not a profound order in the cosmos that has meaning for themselves. That the structure of things is not purposive (Williams, 1993). Such a point of view raises numerous issues and problems in terms of life-conduction that are beyond the scope of this book. Resignation without despair is probably the best one can do in these circumstances (the opposite being melancholic resignation to the *what is*) (Prager, 2016, p. 73).
48 And let us remember the rabbinic adage that a person should always carry two notes; in one pocket, the note should say "I am but dust and ashes", and in the other pocket, the note should say, "for me the world was created". It is living in that in-between space where both are true that may be the "real" goal.
49 Shammai (the House [school] of Shammai) was a first-century scholar of the Mishna who was known for his strict literal interpretation of the Law in contrast to Hillel (the House of Hillel), who was more flexible in his interpretations.
50 According to Derrida (2000) the opposite of hospitality is hostility, though he also says that "we do not know what hospitality is" (p. 6). See Still (2013) for an interesting study of Derrida and hospitality.
51 It is interesting to note that the contemporary Jewish philosopher Hermann Cohen began his essay on the Jewish question with the striking phrase, "We are again obliged to bear witness" (Poma, 2007, p. 83).
52 A related behavior to gossip is keeping a secret, which for most people is near impossible. In fact as Freud noted, even if a person is silent, he will almost always give the secret a way via unconscious signs.
53 From the rabbinic perspective, not only can we not speak negatively against others, but we should also not say good things, because that could lead the person we're talking with to say something negative. The rabbinic idea is that speaking about people is wrong; talk about ideas, the Torah, but talking about people is considered gossip.

54 Sass and Woolfolk (1988) provide a set of serious criticisms of Spence's work. They believe that his "presuppositions are incompatible with fundamental tenets of contemporary hermeneutic thought as expressed in the philosophies of Heidegger, Gadamer, and the later Wittgenstein" (p. 429). Freud indicated "that psycho-analytic treatment is founded on truthfulness. In this fact lies a great part of its educative effort and its ethical value" (1915b, p. 164).

55 As Hanly points out, correspondence theory alleges that truth is comprised of the degree of correspondence between the object and its description, "it assumes that under normal conditions the human mind is able to gain knowledge of objects by means of observation and its experimental refinement. This observational knowledge can then be used to test beliefs and theories". A coherence theory of truth embraces the view "that of the question: *What objects does the world consist of*? only makes sense within a theory or description … Truth … is some sort of idealized rational acceptability—some sort of ideal coherence of beliefs with each other and with our experiences as *those experiences are themselves represented in our belief system*—and not correspondence with mind-independent or discourse-independent 'states of affairs'" (Hanly is quoting from H. Putnam (Hanly, 1990, p. 374)). Freud wrote, "the criterion of truth—[is] correspondence with the external world … correspondence to reality" (1933b, p. 176).

56 In contrast, Freud wrote in a letter to Jung, "to salve my conscience, I often tell myself: above all, don't try and cure, just learn and earn some money! These are the most useful conscious aims" (Phillips, 2021b, p. 156).

57 Thus, for the Rabbis, we need the evil impulses, going back to Eden. Everything was perfect in Eden, but Adam and Eve weren't happy living in a perfect world. If the happy/good impulses were satisfied, Adam and Eve would never have given in to the evil impulses.

58 For a brief but interesting psychoanalytic treatment of gratitude, see Lear (2022). As Lear points out, "very little has been written on gratitude", especially in terms of gratitude as a "fundamental attunement of being" (pp. 119, 142).

59 Akhtar, Kramer, & Parens (1995) present the views of eight analysts on the subject of intense aggression.

60 Freud notes that "all neurotics" "take exception to the fact *that inter urinas et faeces nascimur* [we are born between urine and faeces]" (1930, p. 106).

61 A compromise formation is "the ego's solution to a problem presented by the competing demands of id, superego, the repetition compulsion, and external reality" (Person, Cooper, & Gabbard, 2005, p. 549). A repetition compulsion is a proclivity to engage in repetition of patterns of behavior or re-create circumstances that are typically painful or self-destructive (ibid., p. 558).

62 As Stolorow notes, Freud believed later in his life in the death instinct such that the aim was to guide what is living back into an inorganic state. Thus, "the aim of all life is death" (1920, p. 38), and all the phenomena of life are simply "detours" on the way to this final aim. The death instinct has been rejected by most analysts, though Kleinians believe that aggression is a projection of the person's innate self-destructive drive (Rycroft, 1995).

63 Because these forces within us are so hard to control/conquer, the Rabbis in the Talmud have a long argument about whether it's better to have been born or never to have been born. If the fear of death is so overwhelming, maybe it's better not to have been born. The final decision is that it's better to not have been born, but since you're here, you have to make the best of it and fight the good fight over the dark and negative impulses.

64 Rashi, is an acronym for Rabbi Shimon ben Yitzchak, a prolific commentator who lived in France during the twelfth century and wrote all-inclusive and wide-ranging commentaries on the Talmud and Hebrew Bible.
65 Wisdom is, however, mentioned by two analysts in passing in Wallwork (2005) and Lear (2005).
66 See Busch (2019) for a useful exploration of the "analyst's reverie" and Brenner (2000) on "evenly suspended attention". Brenner notes that an analyst ought to "listen to every aspect of a patient's conflicts, to the sexual and aggressive wishes, to the anxiety associated with those wishes, to the defenses against them, and to the demands and prohibitions" that Freud "subsumed under the heading of the superego" (p. 547).
67 It is interesting to note that for the Rabbis we are all created in the Image of God, and *imitatio Deo*, emulating God is what we aspire to. Following this logic, it's not only us who has to conquer negative emotions, but God does too. God gets so angry, God destroyed the world with a Flood, and afterwards, God promised that God would never do that again. The Torah is replete with times that Moses begged God to quell God's anger and not destroy the people. In other words, that's how hard it is to overcome these powerful emotions. In the rabbinic mind, even God wrestles with this.
68 Psychoanalysis has used other terms that have a family resemblance to self-control, such as self-regulation; it "refers to the tendency and a capacity for maintaining or restoring the baseline functional integrity during environmental perturbations" (Akhtar, 2009, p. 260. Akhtar is quoting from Robert Emde).
69 For example, in positive psychology, the term "self-regulation" is often used synonymously with self-control. It has been defined as "how a person exerts control over his or her own responses so as to pursue goals and live up to standards" (Peterson & Seligman, 2004, p. 500). Self-regulation "means different things to different people" (Carver & Scheier, 2016, p. 3), while Berkman notes, "the dominant models lack specificity regarding exactly how self-regulation actually works" (2016, p. 451). "Self-discipline" is another synonym for self-control, and it refers "to making oneself do things that one does not want to do and restraining temptation" (Peterson & Seligman, 2004, p. 500). Others use self-control to specifically refer "to controlling one's impulses so as to behave in a moral fashion" (ibid.). In his final book before his death, Mischel defined self-control as "the ability to delay immediate gratification for the sake of future consequences" (2014, p. 3). Overall, "research has yet to resolve how self-control should be best conceptualized and measured empirically" (Rocque, Posick & Piquero, 2016, p. 522). See Marcus (2020) for a discussion of self-control versus lack of self-control, in the context of Walter Mischel's famous Marshmallow Experiment.
70 Busch (2019) notes that the goal of analysis is to help the analysand gain "the freedom to free associate, and to reflect upon the associations to begin to understand their meaning" (p. 86).
71 The question of the goals of psychoanalysis is a complex one and to a large extent depends on which version of psychoanalysis one is allied with. Put differently, the goals of analysis when one is lodged in a Freudian outlook is different than a Kohutian or Lacanian one etc. For example, for Freud the origin of the unconscious and the entirety of psychological life is the body and the drive emanates from it. For Lacan, the origin of the unconscious is the other—that is, the unconscious is the discourse of the other (Yadlin-Gadot & Hadar, 2023, pp. 3, 15). Each one of these theories puts forth a markedly different "language game".
72 Seven is a number that indicates completeness or wholeness in biblical and rabbinic writings

(Greenberg, 2016, p. 253). Seven also carries with it significant meaning in the Kabbalistic tradition of the sixteenth-century *Tzefat*.

73 As I have noted earlier, in the case of analysis, it is the analysand and not the analyst who embodies the "wisdom" so to speak—that is, he is the main repository of unconscious meanings, hence the analyst lets the analysand begin the session as he free associates.

74 What's mine is mine and what's yours is yours follows an earlier dictum—who is happy? The one who is happy with one's lot. The person who doesn't want more than she/he has—that is, doesn't want your stuff—is the happy person.

75 An interesting Lacanian observation that has a family resemblance to this quotation is, "love is giving what one doesn't have to someone who doesn't want it" (Yadlin-Gadot & Hadar, 2023, p. 118–119).

76 The rabbinic view of *tzedkah* is not a conventional notion of charity. The word *tzedkah* comes from the root *Tzedek*, justice. In other words, giving to those who have less than you have is a way of "kind of" evening out the playing field, of righting an injustice of those having less than others. While we should be satisfied with what we have, we should not be satisfied with others who have way less than we have.

77 A yoke has also been used in the Bible as a conceptual metaphor for servitude, oppressiveness, bondage or burdensomeness.

78 See Marcus (1999) for a comparison between the believers and non-believers in the Nazi camps. As Jennifer Ring notes, Hannah Arendt makes an interesting observation that "thinking philosophically was no guarantee of being able to act responsibly in the world" (she probably had Heidegger in mind). In fact "she referred to intellectuals' inability to act as a 'deformacion professionelle', a sort of occupational hazard of scholarly life" (2003, p. 68). Moreover, says Ring, Arendt believed "that the intellectual community was more likely to find a rationale for cooperating with the Nazis than ordinary people" (ibid.).

79 It is important to appreciate the context of Wiesel's remarks, for as far as I can tell, they have a somewhat rhetorical quality. Wiesel made his comments as part of his improvised reply to a controversial lecture given by Richard Rubenstein to the question of "What can be told, what can be written, where must silence be kept, what can be witnessed only by living?" (the quote is cited by the editors, p. 269).

80 Psychoanalyst André Green, however, believes that ideology is important to the analytic process: "Again … we are confronted with our ideology of what psychoanalysis is for. What is its aim?" (Green, 1995). Likewise, in his discussion of Loewald, Fogel (1991, p. 6) discusses the former's "values and ideologies" that permeate his clinical work. This being said, as psychoanalyst Marion Milner noted, "Psychoanalytic treatment is an antidote to indoctrination; it is an enquiry into how people influence each other, into the individual's history of living in other people's regime" (Phillips, 2021b, p. 7).

81 The ontological refers to the Being of a specific being. For example, what distinguishes Dasein from all other specific beings (ontically) is that it considers the question of its Being (ontological level).

82 According to Aristotle, jealousy is a reasonable emotion and is deployed by reasonable people, while envy is dishonorable and is deployed by the dishonorable, for the one makes him acquire good things by jealousy, while the other prevents his neighbor from attaining them through envy. Rycroft (1995) also distinguishes envy from jealousy.

83 Lust includes inordinate eating and drinking to the Rabbis (Kravitz & Olitzky, 1993).

84 Some people have an "open" marriage or partnership—that is, a relationship in which both people agree that each may have sexual relations with others. To the religious Jew, this is an abomination; to the psychoanalyst it would be "acceptable".

85 Winnicott famously wrote a dedication in *Playing and Reality*: "To my patients who have paid to teach me" (Phillips, 2021b, p. 36).
86 The Rabbis are saying that pleasure and joy are real, and valued, and an important part of life. However, in their view, it depends on what you're getting pleasure from. Even a physical pleasure, like sex, is lauded under the right circumstances, such as marriage, *mikvah* (purifying ritual bath), etc. The Rabbis do not eschew pleasure and joy; on the contrary, when done "right", it's what we were created for.
87 López-Carvo has characterized Freud's approach as a "psychology of impulses", Klein's as a "psychology of affects" and Bion's as a "psychology of intuition" (2016, p. 76).
88 Put somewhat differently, "Man identifies himself with God by becoming himself" (Rotenstreich, 1968, p. 126).
89 These two Rabbis may be acronyms, though it is not known who these statements actually apply to (Berkson, 2010). They are frequently lumped together.
90 Psychoanalyst Martin Bergmann (1999) agreed with Foucault when he wrote, "What is more likely is that Freud be compared to Plato as one who gave rise to a complex history of ideas that would in time develop in many directions. The complexity of Freud's work is responsible for the fact that already there are many interpretations of its meaning" (p. 200).
91 According to tradition, Aaron would also bring together two parties by indulging in small white lies. He'd tell one person, "X is so upset that there's tension between the two of you", even if X hadn't said that. And then he'd go to the other person and say, "Y is so upset that there's tension between the two of you", even if Y hadn't said that. That's how far Aaron would go to bring peace between people. Aaron understood that peace isn't like some objective Truth; if two people can find/create peace, in whatever form that takes for them, then peace has been found/created.
92 Homeostasis emanates from "the recognition that in infancy homeostatic processes are mutually regulated" (Modell, 1999, p. 79).
93 Lacan noted that the objective of psychoanalysis was that "the subject should come to recognize and to name his desire" (Lichtenstein, 2018, p. 70). Thus, as Israely points out, the question for the analysand is, "How does the symptom maintain his desire and jouissance?"; "At the end of treatment", says Israely, "the symptom no longer represents an illness but is a structure that supports the subject" (Israely, 2018, pp. 39, 61).
94 It was not until Israel became an independent nation in 1948 that Sephardic Jews were included in that prohibition (Kravitz & Olitzky, 1993, p. 23).
95 As Maggie Lange notes in Katy Kelleher's book *The Ugly History of Beautiful Things: Essays on Desire and Consumption*, Kelleher interprets our capacity to locate beauty as a wish to emotionally connect to the physical world and an opportunity for revelation (The Week, 2023b, p. 22).
96 In *Moses and Monotheism*, Freud spoke about the "omnipotence of thoughts", a phrase which may well apply to my patients (1939, p. 113).
97 Freud described this tendency as a "process of thinking [that] becomes hypercathected and eroticized" (1926, p. 119).
98 Self-disclosure has been extensively discussed by Relational-inspired analysts; see, for example, Kuchuck (2021).
99 In Ethic entry #6, I take up the difference between empathy and experiencing the other side.
100 Chapter 6 is known as *Kinyan Torah*, Acquiring Torah or the "Chapter of Rabbi Meir", after the first quoted author. These wisdom sayings are not taken from

the mishna but are from the *Baraita*—that is, Torah wisdom sayings by Rabbis of the mishnaic period that were not included into the final version of the mishna compiled by Rabbi Judah ha-Nasi. A lot of the material in this chapter is a repetition and/or in the spirit of earlier chapters.

101 The one ascetic that is sanctioned in the Torah is the Nazirite, who takes a three-fold vow: Not to drink wine, not cut one's hair, not to be "defiled" by a corpse. But even this vow to be a Nazirite is typically only for thirty days, then the person reverts back to normal life.

102 One person psychology, associated with classical Freudian theory, assumes that psychological processes are in the patient's mind; they are not context-dependent and setting-specific—that is, they are not co-produced in a dialectical manner by the analyst and analysand. In one person psychology, the analyst is a detective attempting to unmask unconscious wishes via dreams and free association; in two person psychology it is a joint journey of discovery (Polmear, 2016, p. 227).

103 For a plausible integration of the classical and intersubjective approaches, see Dunn (1995).

104 As Williams (1993) notes, "there is a problem of free will only for those who think that the notion of the voluntary can be metaphysically deepened" (p. 168).

105 In this context, says philosopher Emil L. Fackenheim, "a Weltanschauung requires: cosmic scope, internal coherence … and a sincere commitment on the part of devotees" (1996, p. 155).

106 Another way of saying this, with a religious sensibility, is that "a closed system cannot endure transcendence" (Rotenstreich, 1968, p. 162).

107 Freud noted a similar point: "The inhibition upon life of those who are dominated by neurosis and their incapacity for living constitute a most important factor in human society and we may recognize in their condition a direct expression of their fixation to an early portion of their past" (1939, p. 77).

Chapter 3

Conclusion

The Ethics of the Fathers is a blueprint for living as a religious Jew, to creatively live "the earthly path of revelation" as the Jewish philosopher Franz Rosenzweig described it (Gordon, 2007, p. 140). It uses categories and interpretations of what constitutes a *homo religious* at his best, shaping imagination and perception of reality (Bokser, 1989). In particular, it emphasizes the importance of righteous action and behavior above all else, even above the study of Torah. "Do justice, love mercy, and walk humbly with your God", says Michah, the watchword of righteousness (and of course, exactingly doing the *mitzvot*, commandments, the way to get near to God). In this context, ethics can be simply defined as being "concerned with values and principles held in depth, a dimension into which specific, relative, and variable norms sink their roots" (Zoja, 2007, p. xviii). As Sacks (2023b) indicated, while the French philosopher Jean-Francois Lyotard once defined postmodernism as "the death of the metanarrative", suggesting that we don't have or don't need the big stories any more, the ones that tell us who we are, where we came from and what we are called on to do the Rabbis have generated just such a religious metanarrative for the believer, including an embedded notion of human subjectivity. In their view, "without memory there is no identity, and without identity we are cast adrift into a sea of chance, without compass, map or destination" (ibid., p. 2).[1] Such a view is in sync with Jean-Paul Sartre who noted,

> A man is always a teller of tales. He lives surrounded by his stories and the stories of others, he sees everything that happens to him through them, he tries to live his own life as if he were telling a story.
> (Brooks, 2023c, p. A24)[2]

Psychoanalysis too has a wide range of master narratives that each include a notion of human subjectivity, mainly geared to the non-believer and secular intellectual. In other words, we have two different worldviews (i.e., different language games),[3] one religious and one that is largely secular (e.g., Freud believed in the scientific worldview, the "scientific spirit", "intellect" and "reason" (1933b, p. 171)), though they have in common a notion of spirituality, one that is lodged in the belief in self-transformation and self-transcendence (with or without God). A few prominent analysts have integrated religious notions into their largely secular thinking. For example, as early as 1953, Hans Loewald, a Freudian with revisionist tendencies, opined that the "mature individual" is

> able to reach back into his deep origins and roots of being [his "soul" as Buber/Marcel might say] find[ing] in himself the oneness from where he stems [the ultimate "ground" of his being] and understand[ing] this in his freedom as his bond of love with God [with the noncorporeal "whole" cosmic consciousness, ethicality].
>
> (Loewald, 1953)

Loewald's "god-talk" is his way of describing the cosmic vision and oceanic sentiment, its associated ethical outlook, and the analytical goal of helping analysands become "spiritual beings", as he called them, to achieve the "highest form of awareness … the freedom for faith and love" (ibid., pp. 13, 14, 15).[4] Loewald never backed off this point of view, as far as I know. And more recently, hybrid psychoanalyst Michael Eigen wrote in his book *Faith*,

> I feel that what you call that other dimension [the spiritual/divine] is here, always here. Whatever you call God or spiritual reality is right here, in our lives. We are creating it and it is creating us through the way we are with each other, how we make each other feel. Do our interactions make a more kindly world or a less kindly world? It reminds me of what Judaism says—that my words are creating angels and devils.
>
> (Eigen, 2014, pp. 98–99)[5]

Finally, Otto Kernberg noted in 2018,

> I think that the people who believe in God have grace, that it is a strength of spiritual determination to have a realistic relation to a higher entity that dictates personal morality. I don't have such a belief in a personal God, but I admire and respect people who have it. It's a grace. It's a state of grace.
>
> (Velde & Hegger, 2018, p. 144)

Thus, it would appear, to quote Rabbi Abraham Isaac Kook, "Religious faith … is a [felt] response of God's presence" (Bokser, 2006, p. 35).[6]

In this conclusion, I want to mainly suggest ways that psychoanalysis, as a theory and practice, can enhance our understanding of the Ethics. Rather than repeat what has been said in the bulk of this book, the details of a particular ethic viewed with a psychoanalytic lens, I will provide a few generalities that boil down to five key points.

First, psychoanalysis respects what people rationally and reasonably believe about living a good life. However, it emphasizes the role of unconscious processes and "apprehended willing" as Freud called it (1916–17, p. 22) in motivating human behavior. This view is compatible with the latest research findings "that only about 5% of mental life is considered conscious" (Tye, 2023, p. 123).[7] Moreover, as the Lacanians have pointed out, "the bulk of mental life always escapes representation" (Yadlin-Gadot & Hadar, 2023, p. 42). As I have said, the Rabbis blueprint for living assumed that for the most part human behavior was governed by rational and reasonable considerations. That is, the Rabbis are concerned with conscious acts of a responsible and autonomous subject. So, for example, in a number of the Ethics, the Rabbis appeal to conscious emotions and virtues that are, in theory, in conflict with profounder meanings and motivations. Moral decision making is governed by conscious and unconscious considerations, considerations that can undermine consciously held propositions that are a screen for deleterious narcissism and/or aggression. The Rabbis of the Ethics do not consider the latter from what I can discern, at least it is not their main focus in the Ethics.[8]

Second, psychoanalysis has taught us that a person's way of managing his conscious and unconscious emotions, including in moral decision making, may depend on his character structure or personality dynamics and defenses (Wallwork, 1999), and internal mental structures (intrapsychic structures) (Lear, 2003). For example, a borderline or narcissistic personality will quite likely approach the problem of living a good life markedly differently than, say, a neurotic person (e.g., someone with an obsessional or hysterical personality) or someone who is "higher" functioning. And a "normal" person also differs from the aforementioned in his moral decision making. This is in part due to differences in reality testing.[9] As Mendelson (1974) noted,

> Even the average normal human being develops subtly individual perspective on reality that is a consequence of his unique life experiences. There are, furthermore, no objectively calibrated models of reality by which to measure precisely the accuracy of someone's reality testing.
>
> (p. 89)

For the Rabbis, these psychological categories and interpretations are not typically in play.

Third, psychoanalysis provides a more in-depth and nuanced understanding of emotions such as jealousy, envy, anger, shame and guilt than is typically the case in the Ethics. By more precisely defining the person's emotional truths, the average person can better know himself and ideally become more skilled at making moral decisions. For example, as Phillips and Taylor (2009) point out, loving-kindness, a critically important personal asset in the Ethics, can be disguised egoism. Kindness can also be a camouflaged form of sexuality or aggression, both of which are lodged in covert selfishness. Says Phillips and Taylor,

> Insofar as kindness is a sexual act it is seen as seduction ("I am being very nice to you so I can get to have sex/and or babies"), or as a defense against the sexual event ("I'll be so kind to you that you will forget about sex and we can do something else together"), or as a way of repairing the supposed damage done by sex ("I'll be nice to you to make up for all my harmful desires"). Insofar as kindness is an aggressive act it is seen as a placation ("I feel so aggressive toward you that I can only protect both of us by being very kind"), or a refuge ("My kindness will keep you at arm's length"). "One can always for safety, be kind", as Maggie Verver says to her father in Henry James's *The Golden Bowl*.
>
> (pp. 111–112)

This being said, the Rabbis of the Talmud were impressed with the profoundly significant role that emotions play in everyday life. This included wisdom being instantiated by a person having the capacity to control unwieldy emotions enough to act as a resource to demonstrate goodness—that is, the principal demand was ethical, to act with compassion and loving-kindness toward God's creatures (Bokser, 1951).

Fourth, psychoanalysis emphasizes the importance of awareness about how destructive we humans are. As Eigen further notes, "psychoanalysis puts a barium tracer on our sense of destructiveness" (Eigen, 2014, p. 96). While the Rabbis use the concept of the *yetzer-hara* (the evil urge), they do not give enough credence to the power of human destructiveness, including its infantile origins. Though the Ethics is written by, and is meant for the devout believer, psychoanalysis can help illuminate what psychologically motivates faith and what undermines its credibility for how the individual engages in living a good life.[10] In particular, psychoanalysis emphasizes the role of ambivalence and conflict in human motivation. The Rabbis tended to believe that all the believer had to do was to will himself into living a good life, giving less attention in terms of what makes this so difficult for the average person. As Freud wrote, "Men have gained control over the forces of nature to such an extent that with their help they would have no difficulty in exterminating one another to the last man" (1930, p. 145).

Fifth, from a psychoanalytic point of view, the Ethics contains too much superego morality. That is, there are too many inhibiting demands, "thou shalt" and "thou shalt not", at the expense of one's psychology (e.g., self-regard and self-concept), making reasonable, wholesome living near impossible. Put differently, the Rabbis are in "overdrive" when it comes to what "must" and "mustn't" be done to live a good life as they define it. Perhaps the Ethics are best viewed as aspirational. Psychoanalysis puts into sharp focus what the person loses in terms of his psychology by being governed by superego moralism, namely the renunciation of instinct, which could lead to neurotic inhibitions, compromise formations and the like. As Adam Phillips noted, "a person becoming more independent of the superego" means he is inclined to live "a life less organized around censorship and self-punishment. It involves widening the field of perception" (2021b, pp. 160–161). This being said, it is not clear how one can diminish the superego moralism without undermining the whole religious structure.

Finally, the Rabbis indicate, or at least strongly imply, that the overarching goal of the Ethics, and studying and living Torah, is holiness ("the remarkable concept of holiness", Freud called it (1939, p. 120)). Holiness is a complex subject, and there are many definitions of it in Judaism and religion in general. Levinas, for example, suggests that "holiness ... the supreme perfection ... which cedes one's place to the other" is what characterizes "humanity" at its best (Levinas, 2001, p. 183). For Buber, holiness meant enacting in the concrete situation we find ourselves an open, receptive dialogue with God—that is, "hallowing the everyday", hallowing one's life through efforts to make himself responsible to what is holy (Friedman, 1986, p. 131). Indeed, as Katz (2006) noted, Buber (and Marcel) emphasized that the I-Thou encounter summoned one to ontic and fundamental moral obligations to the other: "Responsibility presupposes one who addresses me primarily, that is, from a realm independent of myself, and to whom I am answerable" (Buber, 1965, p. 17). Likewise, for Marcel, such holy people were "creators", they were discernible

> by the radiance of charity and love shining from their being, they add a positive contribution to the invisible work which gives the human adventure the only meaning which can justify it. Only the blind may say with the suggestion of a sneer that they have produced nothing.
>
> (2001, p. 45)

Psychoanalysis has had almost no interest in using holiness as a viable concept into the theoretical or clinical context, though I believe this may be a notion worth judiciously integrating into its theory and technique.[11] There are of course exceptions which suggest what experientially is required to be holy or move toward holiness. Eigen (2012) briefly mentions his personal experience of the holy. He notes, "A sense of the Good, Beauty, Holy, Justice intertwined, opposed to, fused with destruction. That we recoil at this notion indicates that we are afraid to let in fully our experiential capacity" (p. 74). Elsewhere, Eigen opines on the notion of holiness in terms of "sainthood":

> It is as if Levinas and Wittgenstein declare sainthood a necessity, a privileged and necessary part of self-image ... they affirm or reaffirm sainthood as a necessary human direction, a fertile reality. Modern psychology gives us so many parts of selves, and how the saint takes a legitimate place in self-conception as psychic force, template, archetype, tendency.
>
> (2005, p. 209)

One possible reason why psychoanalysis does not use holiness as an overarching goal, even the sophisticated versions of holiness, Levinas, Buber and Marcel put forth, is that it is so rare for a human to configure himself as such. Moreover, in some instances, to strive for holiness means a high degree of instinctual renunciation that can undermine a person's psychic development. Put simply, as some would have it, it is just too damn hard and costs too much (psychologically) to live a holy life. Thus, following Freud, psychoanalysis uses the category of "happiness" as constituting the good life. Human beings, above all else, says Freud, strive for happiness: "What do people show by their behavior to be the purpose and intention of their lives", they "strive after happiness; they want to become happy and to remain so" (Freud, 1930, p. 76).[12] Deep and wide love and creative and productive work is the way to achieve a modicum of happiness. Psychoanalysis puts forth some compelling reasons for why typically people do not behave in a holy manner; for example, they have powerful, if not troubling sexual and aggressive feelings that get in the way.

Lastly, I have attempted to suggest that psychoanalysis can be an insightful interpretive tool in unpacking the Ethics, thus providing another illuminating gloss on this classic of practical wisdom. I have tried to reveal aspects of the Ethics that are often overlooked and/or underappreciated and that have relevance to a secular and religious analysand's outlook and behavior. I have also suggested that psychoanalysis can be enhanced by entering into dialogue with the Ethics and possibly incorporating aspects of its insights into its theory and practice.

While not my focus, in the future psychoanalysis can ideally help explain how the Ethics gets into people's heads (e.g., how it is internalized and animating as an authoritative mini-guide in all domains of life), how rabbinic authority is projected onto and into the Ethics (e.g., how rabbinic authority becomes idealized as an aesthetic-symbolic other), how the Ethics functions to create and/or satisfy demands and desires (e.g., why most religious Jews "love" the Ethics, why its symbols and ideas impact the way Jews experience and narrate reality) and, most importantly, how many aspects of the Ethics are unconscious, repressed and irrational (e.g., what unconscious wishes the Ethics stimulates and how it tends to guide behavior) (Caudill, 2016, p. 366). These are only some of the questions that psychoanalysis can further explore beyond what I have illuminated. My hope is that this book will encourage others to move the conversation wider and deeper.

Notes

1 This being said, cultural identity is a "matter of becoming" says British Marxist sociologist Stuart Hall. That is, while cultural identity originates from many histories, those that are personal and collective, identity is not some intrinsic essence, anchored in the past; it has to be created and transformed (Hoy, 2023).

Psychoanalytic versions of identity that have been influenced by poststructural and postmodern considerations have "decentered" conventional notions of identity.

2 In her epilogue to the second edition of her book *The Politics of Postmodernity* (2002), Linda Hutcheon alleged, "Let's just say it: it is over ... The postmodern movement has passed" (Lev, 2023, p. 34).

3 Traditional Judaism and psychoanalysis represent two perspectives on living a good life. As Sacks and Angel note, "One should not lose sight of the ultimate goal of life: to live wisely, righteously, and compassionately" (2015, p. 41). Indeed, mainstream psychoanalysis does not usually describe the ultimate goal of life this way. In contrast, as Adam Phillips notes, the psychoanalytic aims include "the relative freedom to love and work, the achievement of the depressive position, the capacity to play, the flourishing of one's true self" (1999, p. 163). Moreover, André Green includes, for example, "increas[ing]" the "feeling of freedom" and "finding that life is worth living" (ibid., p. 164). Perhaps there is a way to integrate the two perspectives. Finally, Adam Phillips (2021a) notes, "Freud is implicitly invoking psychoanalysis here as a secular theology, asking what meaning we can give to pleasure and suffering now if there is no God, no provisional design, and no sacred ethical framework" (p. 63).

4 Loewald's reference to faith has a family resemblance to Eigen's definition of psychoanalytically-based faith: "By the area of faith I mean to point to a way of experiencing that is undertaken with one's whole being, all out, 'with all one's heart, with all one's soul, and with all one's might'" (Daws, 2023, p. 52).

5 See Marcus (2021, pp. 194–195) for other examples of religious notions integrated into mainstream psychoanalysis.

6 As Eigen notes, "Religion is not just one dimension of our life; it is a different way of living" (Daws, 2023, p. 118).

7 Ogden (2022), quoting Laplanche and Pontalis, notes, "If Freud's discovery had to be summed up in a single word, that word without doubt would have to be 'unconscious'" (p. 121). This being said, the term unconscious has been psychoanalytically defined and described in a variety of different ways depending on where one is located theoretically. For example, for Lacan, the Freudian unconscious is not "an organic entity", but rather it "is a system of meanings that have become repressed as a result of the wish not to know" (Israely, 2018, p. 2). Likewise, as Chodorow has noted, those versions of psychoanalysis that have been influenced by poststructural and postmodern considerations have subverted the conventional notions of self (e.g., the "decentered-self"), responsibility, autonomy, agency, decision making (i.e., personal choice), reason/rationality and the like. "We do not control our own lives in the most fundamental sense" (Chodorow, 1989, p. 154).

8 The Rabbis of the Talmud were aware that the unconscious performs its delicate operations in everyday behavior such as in dreams (Bokser, 1951).

9 Reality testing is the "capacity to distinguish between mental images and external percepts, between phantasy and external reality, to correct subjective impressions by reference to external facts" (Rycroft, 1995, p. 153). "Reality testing is far more than an intellectual or cognitive function", says Loewald. "It may be understood more comprehensively as the experiential testing of fantasy—its potential and suitability for actualization—and testing of actuality—its potential for encompassing it in, and penetrating it with, one's fantasy life" (1991, p. 149).

10 Kuisis (2004) claims that psychoanalysis is an effective tool for analyzing the developmental stages of religious belief, in understanding how it functions for an individual or community, and in helping differentiate pathology from authentic spirituality.

11 Marcus (2008) applies Levinas's notion of holiness, being-for-the-other, especially before oneself, to psychoanalytic theory and technique. Lev (2023) describes what

he calls "spiritually sensitive psychoanalysis", providing a good summary of the analysts who have attempted to integrate the spiritual/religious domain into their work. However, Lev does not list holiness in his index, though he does quote Eigen, who wrote, "Therapy is a holy business for me and was so from my first session" (p. 79).

12 The Rabbis opined about human happiness elsewhere in the Talmud etcetera, but usually happiness is conflated with holiness. That is, someone who lives a holy life is quite likely to be happy in general, for it meaningfully affirms his raison d'être. As Rabbi Abraham Isaac Kook noted, "It is neither the environment nor particular actions which form the basis for the inner treasure of the soul's happiness. It is rather the greatness of the self, the inner holiness and purity, the firmness of will and the potency of thought. The environment and the actions take a secondary place before the spiritual power when it rises to a high place" (Bokser, 2006, p. 183).

References

Akhtar, S. (2009). *Comprehensive Dictionary of Psychoanalysis*. London: Karnac.
Akhtar, S., Kramer, S., & Parens, H. (1995). (Eds.). *The Birth of Hatred: Developmental, Clinical, and Technical Aspects of Intense Aggression*. Northvale: Jason Aronson.
Algoe, S.B., Gable, S.L., & Maisel, N. (2010). It's the little things: Everyday gratitude as a booster shot for romantic relationships. *Personal Relationships*, 17: 217–233.
Alvarez, A. (2012). *The Thinking Heart: Three Levels of Psychoanalytic Therapy with Disturbed Children*. London: Routledge.
Améry, J. (1980). *At the Mind's Limits: Contemplations by a Survivor on Auschwitz and its Realities*. Trans. A. Rosenfeld & S.P. Rosenfeld. Bloomington: Indiana University Press.
Bagai, R. (2023). *Commentaries on the Work of Michael Eigen: Oblivion and Wisdom, Madness and Music*. Abingdon: Routledge.
Bass, A. (1998). Sigmund Freud: The question of a weltanschauung and of defense. In P. Marcus & A. Rosenberg (Eds.), *Psychoanalytic Versions of the Human Condition: Philosophies of Life and their Impact on Practice* (pp. 412–446). New York: New York University Press.
Bellah, R.N., Madsen, R.Sullivan, W.M., Swidler, A., & Tipton, S.M. (1986). *Habits of the Heart: Individualism and Commitment in American Life*. New York: Harper & Row.
Berg, J.M., Grant, A.G. & Johnson, V. (2010). When callings are calling: Crafting work and leisure in pursuit of unanswered occupational callings. *Organization Science*, 21(5): 973–994.
Berenbaum, M. (1994). *Elie Wiesel: God, the Holocaust and the Children of Israel*. New York: Behrman.
Bergmann, M.S. (1999). The dynamics of the history of psychoanalysis: Anna Freud, Leo Rangell, and André Green. In G. Kohon (Ed.), *The Dead Mother: The Work of André Green* (pp. 193–204). London: Routledge.
Bergmann, M.S. (1987). *The Anatomy of Loving: The Story of Man's Quest to Know What Love Is*. New York: Fawcett Columbine.
Berkman, E.T. (2016). Self-regulation training. In K.D. Vohs & R.F. Baumeister (Eds.), *Handbook of Self-regulation: Research, Theory, and Applications* (3rd ed.) (pp. 440–457). New York: Guilford.
Berkson, W. (2010). *Pirke Avot: Timeless Wisdom for Modern Life*. Philadelphia: The Jewish Publication Society.
Bernstein, J. (2023). The irrepressible Sigmund Freud. *New York Times*, Sunday Styles, March 26 2023, 10.

Bettelheim, B. (1979). *Surviving and Other Essays.* New York: Knopf.
Bettelheim, B. (1960). *The Informed Heart: Autonomy in a Mass Age.* Glencoe: The Free.
Binswanger, L. (1963). Trans. J. Needleman. *Being in the World.* New York: Basic Books.
Bokser, B.Z. (2006). *The Essential Writings of Abraham Isaac Kook.* Teaneck: Ben Yehuda Press.
Bokser, B.Z. (1989). *The Talmud: Selected Writings.* New York: Paulist Press.
Bokser, B.Z. (1983). *The Prayer Book: Weekday, Sabbath and Festival.* Translated and arranged by Ben Zion Bokser. New York: Behrman House Publishing.
Bokser, B.Z. (1951). *The Wisdom of the Talmud.* Scotts Valley: CreateSpace.
Bollas, C. (1987). *In the Shadow of the Object: Psychoanalysis of the Unthought Know.* New York: Columbia University Press.
Brenner, C. (2000). Brief communication: Evenly hovering attention. *Psychoanalytic Quarterly*, 69: 545–549.
Brooks, D. (2023a). Marriage, not career, brings happiness. *New York Times*, Sunday Opinion, August 20 2023, 3.
Brooks, D. (2023b). People are more generous than you may think. *New York Times*, Friday Opinion, September 1 2023, A19.
Brooks, D. (2023c). A theory of Musk's maniacal drive. *New York Times*, Friday Opinion, September 22 2023, A24.
Buber, M. (1967). *A Believing Humanism: My Testament, 1902–1965.* New York: Simon & Schuster.
Buber, M. (1965). *The Knowledge of man: A Philosophy of the Interhuman.* M. Friedman (Ed.), Trans. M. Friedman & R.G. Smith. New York: Harper & Row.
Busch, F. (2019). *The Analyst's Reveries: Explorations in Bion's Enigmatic Concept.* London: Routledge.
Cain, S. (1979). *Gabriel Marcel.* South Bend: Regnery/Gateway.
Carver, C.S., & Scheier, M.F. (2016). Self-regulation of action and affect. In K.D. Vohs & R.F. Baumeister (Eds.), *Handbook of Self-Regulation: Research, Theory, and Applications* (3rd ed.) (pp. 3–23). New York: Guilford.
Castrillon, F. (n.d). Lacanian psychoanalysis. Available at: https://drcastrillon.com/lacanian-psychoanalysis/ (Accessed May 7 2023).
Caudill, D. (2016). Law and psychoanalysis. In A. Elliott & J. Prager (Eds.), *The Routledge Handbook of Psychoanalysis in the Social Sciences and Humanities* (pp. 364–379). Abingdon: Routledge.
Chaim, Chofetz (Kagan, Y.M.) (1975). *Guard Your Tongue.* Union City: Gross Bros.
Chasseguet-Smirgel, J. (1985). *Creativity and Perversion.* New York: W.W. Norton & Company.
Cherry, K. (2022). Compassion vs. empathy: What's the difference?. Available at: https://www.verywellmind.com/compassion-vs-empathy-what-s-the-difference-7494906. (Accessed December 11 2022).
Chodorow, N.J. (1989). *Feminism and Psychoanalytic Theory.* New Haven: Yale University Press.
Compton, W.C., & Hoffman, E. (2012). *Positive Psychology: The Science of Happiness and Flourishing.* Los Angeles: Sage.
Daws, L. (2023). *Michael Eigen: A Cotemporary Introduction.* London: Routledge.
Derrida, J. (2000). Hospitality. Trans. B.S. Stocker & F. Morlock. *Angelaki: Journal of Theoretical Humanities*, 5(3): 3–18, doi:10.1080/09697250020034706.

Dimen, M. (2016). Psychoanalysis and sexuality. In A. Elliott & J. Prager (Eds.), *The Routledge Handbook of Psychoanalysis in the Social Sciences and Humanities* (pp. 397–415). Abingdon: Routledge.
Dunn, J. (1995). Intersubjectivity in psychoanalysis: A critical review. *International Journal of Psychoanalysis*, 76: 723–738.
Edelson, M. (1988). *Psychoanalysis: A Theory in Crisis*. Chicago: University of Chicago Press.
Eigen, M. (2018). *The Psychotic Core*. Abington: Routledge (first published in 1986).
Eigen, M. (2014). *Faith*. London: Karnac.
Eigen, M. (2012). *Kabbalah and Psychoanalysis*. London: Routledge.
Eigen, M. (2005). *Emotional Storm*. Middletown: Wesleyan University Press.
Eigen, M. (1998). *The Psychoanalytic Mystic*. London: Free Associations.
Elliot, A. (1994). *Psychoanalytic Theory: An Introduction*. Oxford: Blackwell Publishing.
Elliott, A., Prager, J. (2016). Introduction. In A. Elliott & J. Prager (Eds.), *The Routledge Handbook of Psychoanalysis in the Social Sciences and Humanities* (pp. 1–9). Abingdon: Routledge.
Emmons, R.A., & Mishra, A. (2011). Why gratitude enhances well-being: What we know, what we need to know. In K.M. Sheldon, T.B. Kashdan, & M.F. Stegar (Eds.), *Designing Positive Psychology: Taking Stock and Moving Forward* (pp. 248–262). New York: Oxford University Press.
Erikson, E.H. (1964). *Insight and Responsibility*. New York: Norton.
Erikson, E.H. (1959). *Identity and the Life Cycle: Selected Papers* (Psychological Issues, Vol. 1, No. 1, Monograph 1). New York: International Universities Press.
Eskreis-Winkler, L., Gross, J.J., & Duckworth, A.I. (2016). Grit: Sustained self-regulation in the service of superordinate goals. In K.D. Vohs & R.F. Baumeister (Eds.), *Handbook of Self-Regulation: Research, Theory, and Applications* (3rd ed.) (pp. 380–395). New York: Guilford.
Etezady, M.H., Blon, I., & Davis, M. (Eds.). (2018). *Psychoanalytic Trends in Theory and Practice: The Second Century of the Talking Cure*. New York: Lexington Books.
Fackenheim, E.L. (1996). *Jewish Philosophers and Jewish Philosophy*. M.L. Morgan (Ed.). Bloomington: Indiana University Press.
Fackenheim, E.L. (1987). *What is Judaism: An Interpretation for the Present Age*. New York: Summit Books.
Ferro, A. (2009). *Mind Works*. London: Routledge.
Ferro, A., & Civitarese, G. (2018). *The Analytic Field and Its Transformations*. London: Routledge.
Fine, R. (1979). *History of Psychoanalysis*. New York: Columbia University Press.
Fogel, G.I. (Ed.). (1991). *The Work of Hans Loewald: An Introduction and Commentary*. Northvale: Jason Aronson.
Fonagy, P., & Campbell, C. (2016). Attachment theory and mentalization. In A. Elliott & J. Prager (Eds.), *The Routledge Handbook of Psychoanalysis in the Social Sciences and Humanities* (pp. 115–131). Abingdon: Routledge.
Forester, J. (2000). What kind of truth. In P. Brooks & A. Woloch (Eds.), *Whose Freud? The Place of Psychoanalysis in Contemporary Culture*. New Haven: Yale University Press, 311–323.
Foucault, M. (1990). *The Use of Pleasure*. New York: Vintage Books.

Foucault, M. (1989). The ethics of the concern for self as a practice of freedom. In S. Lotringer (Ed.), *Foucault Live: Collected Interviews, 1961–1984* (pp. 432–449). New York: Semiotexte.

Foucault, M. (1984). What is an author? In P. Rabinow (Ed.), *Foucault Reader* (pp. 101–120). New York: Pantheon.

Fowler, J. (2021). Philanthropy daily. Available at: https://philanthropydaily.com/author/jfowler (Accessed June 7 2023).

Frankl, V.E. (2019). *Yes to Life in Spite of Everything*. Boston: Beacon.

French, S. (2023). The importance of being there. *The New York Times*, Monday Opinion, September 25 2023, A25.

Freud, S. (1939/1934–38). *Moses and Monotheism: Three Essays.* S.E.23: 1–137.

Freud, S. (1933a/1932). *Why War.* S.E.22: 196–215.

Freud, S. (1933b/1932). *New Introductory Lectures on Psycho-Analysis.* S.E.22: 1–182.

Freud, S. (1930/1929). *Civilization and its Discontents.* S.E.21: 59–145.

Freud, S. (1927a). *Post-script to a Discussion of Lay Analysis in S.E.*, 20: 251–258.

Freud, S. (1927b). *The Future of an Illusion.* S.E.21: 3–58.

Freud, S. (1926). *In Inhibitions, Symptoms and Anxiety.* S.E.20: 75–174.

Freud, S. (1923). *The Ego and the Id.* S.E.19: 3–66.

Freud, S. (1921). *Group Psychology and the Analysis of the Ego.* S.E.18: 65–143.

Freud, S. (1920). *Beyond the Pleasure Principle.* S.E.18: 1–64.

Freud, S. (1916–17/1915–1917). *Introductory Lectures on Psycho-Analysis.* S.E.15: 9–483.

Freud, S. (1915a). *Thoughts for the Times on War and Death.* S.E.14: 273–307.

Freud, S. (1915b [1914]). *Observations on Transference-Love: Further Recommendations on the Technique of Psychoanalysis III.* S.E.12: 157–173.

Freud, S. (1912). *Recommendations to Physicians Practising Psycho-Analysis.* S.E.12: 109–120.

Freud, S. (1905). *Three Essays on the Theory of Sexuality.* In The Standard Edition of the Complete Psychological Works of Sigmund Freud (henceforth *S.E.*), Trans J. Strachey with A. Freud assisted by A. Stratchey and A. Tyson, 24 volumes (1953–1974). London: Hogarth, S.E.7:130–243.

Freud, S. (1895/1985). *The Complete Letters of Sigmund Freud to Wilhelm Fliess: 1887–1904.* J. Masson (Ed.). Cambridge: Harvard University Press.

Freyer, D.R. (2004). *The Intervention of the Other: Ethical Subjectivity in Levinas and Lacan.* New York: Other Press.

Friedman, M.S. (2002). *Martin Buber: The Life of Dialogue* (4th ed.). London: Routledge.

Friedman, M.S. (1986). *Martin Buber and the Eternal.* New York: Human Sciences Press.

Fromm, E. (1973). *The Anatomy of Human Destructiveness.* Greenwich, CT: Fawcett Crest Books.

Fromm, E. (1956). *The Art of Loving: An Enquiry into the Nature of Love.* New York: HarperColophon Books.

Fromm, E. (1947). *Man for Himself: An Inquiry into the Psychology of Ethics.* New York: Henry Holt.

Garone, S. (2021). 8 Physical and mental health benefits of silence, plus how to get more of it. Available at: https://www.healthline.com/health/mind-body/physical-and-mental-health-benefits-of-silence#takeaway (Accessed December 7 2022).

Gaskill, L. (2014). 10 steps for saying goodbye to sentimental objects. Available at: https://www.houzz.co.uk/magazine/lifestyle-10-steps-that-will-help-you-let-go-of-sentimental-objects-stsetivw-vs~34319178 (Accessed May 5 2023).

Gobodo-Madikizela, P. (2016). Psychoanalysis and reconciliation. In A. Elliott & J. Prager (Eds.). *The Routledge Handbook of Psychoanalysis in the Social Sciences and Humanities* (pp. 416–434). Abingdon: Routledge.

Goffman, E. (1961). *Asylums*. New York: Anchor Books.

Goldin, Judah (2023). "Hillel". *Encyclopedia Britannica*. Available at: https://www.britannica.com/biography/Hillel (Accessed March 24 2023).

Goleman, D. (2019). Introduction. In Viktor E. Frankl, *Yes to Life in Spite of Everything* (pp. 1–18). Boston: Beacon.

Gordon, P.E. (2007). Franz Rosenzweig and the philosophy of existence. In M.L. Morgan & P.E. Gordon (Eds.). *The Cambridge Companion to Modern Jewish Philosophy* (pp. 122–146). Cambridge: Cambridge University Press.

Green, A. (1999). Interview. In G. Kohon (Ed.), *The Dead Mother: The Work of André Green* (pp. 10–15). London: Routledge.

Green, A. (1995). Has sexuality anything to do with psychoanalysis? *International Journal of Psycho-Analysis*, 76: 871–883.

Greenberg, I.Y. (2016). *Sage Advice: Pirkei Avot. With translation and Commentary.* Jerusalem: Maggid Books.

Greenberg, J.R., & Mitchell, S.A. (1983). *Object Relations in Psychoanalytic Theory.* Cambridge: Harvard University Press.

Grossman, V. (2023). *The Week*. 5 December 2023, 17.

Hadot, P. (1995). *Philosophy as a Way of Life.* Oxford: Blackwell.

Hale, N.G. (1995). *The Rise and Crisis of Psychoanalysis in the United States.* New York: Oxford University Press.

Hale, N.G. (1971). *James Jackson Putnam and Psychoanalysis: Letters Between Putnam and Sigmund Freud.* Trans. J.B. Heller. Cambridge: Cambridge University Press, 163–164.

Hanly, C. (1993). Ideology and psychoanalysis. *Canadian Journal of Psychoanalysis*, 1 (2): 1–17.

Hanly, C. (1990). The concept of truth in psychoanalysis. *International Journal of Psychoanalysis*, 71: 374–384.

Heery, M., & Bugental, J.F.T. (2005). Meaning and transformation. In E.V. Deurzen & C. Arnold-Baker (Eds.). *Existential Perspectives on Human Issues* (pp. 253–264). Houndmills: Palgrave Macmillan.

Heilman, S. (1973). *Synagogue Life: A Study of Symbolic Interaction.* Chicago: University of Chicago Press.

Hinshelwood, R.D. (1991). *A Dictionary of Kleinian Thought.* London: Free Association Books.

Hoare, C.H. (2001). *Erikson on Development in Adulthood: New Insights from the Unpublished Papers.* Oxford: Oxford University Press.

Hoffer, A. (1985). Toward a definition of psychoanalytic neutrality. *Journal of the American Psychoanalytic Association*, 33: 771–795.

Homer, S. (2016). Jacques Lacan Freud's French interpreter. In A. Elliott & J. Prager (Eds.), *The Routledge Handbook of Psychoanalysis in the Social Sciences and Humanities* (pp. 97–114). Abingdon: Routledge.

Hoy, J.C. (2023). Matters of becoming. *New York Times Book Review*, May 21 2023, 14.

Israely, Y. (2018). *Lacanian Treatment: Psychoanalysis for Clinicians*. London: Routledge.

Iverach, L., Menzies, R.G., Menzies, R.E. (2014). Death anxiety and its role in psychopathology: Reviewing the status of a transdiagnostic construct. *Clinical Psychology Review*, 34: 580–593.

Jacobs, J. (2023). Pirkei Avot: Ethics of Our Fathers. Available at: www.myjewishlearning.com/article/pirkei-avot (Accessed January 4 2023).

Johnson, A.G. (1995). *The Blackwell Dictionary of Sociology: A User's Guide to Sociological Language*. Oxford: Blackwell.

Jones, E. (1953–1957). *The Life and Work of Sigmund Freud* (3 vols.). New York: Basic Books.

Jones, J.W. (1991). *Contemporary Psychoanalysis: Religion, Transference and Transcendence*. New Haven: Yale University Press.

Jung, C.G. (1966). *Practice of Psychotherapy: Vol. xvi, The collected works of C G. Jung*. G. Adler & R.F.C. Hull, Eds. & Trans. Princeton, NJ: Princeton University Press.

Katz, S. (2006). Martin Buber in retrospect. In M. Zank (Ed.), *New Perspectives on Martin Buber* (pp. 255–266). Tubingen: Mohr Siebeck.

Kaufman, W.E. (1992). *Contemporary Jewish Philosophies*. Detroit: Wayne State University Press.

Keen, S. (1967). *Gabriel Marcel*. Richmond: John Knox Press.

Klein, M. (1957). Envy and gratitude. In *Envy and Gratitude and Other Works—1943–1963* (pp. 176–235). New York: Free Press, 1975.

Klein, M. (1931). A contribution to the theory of intellectual inhibition. In *Love, Guilt and Reparation and Other Works—1921–1945* (pp. 236–247). New York: Free Press, 1975.

Klosterman, C. (2006). *A Decade of Curious People and Dangerous Ideas*. New York: Scribner.

Knafo, D., & Moscovitz, S. (2018). Contemporary Freudian approaches. In M. Charles (Ed.), *Introduction to Contemporary Psychoanalysis* (pp. 9–32). London: Routledge.

Kohut, H. (1971). *The Analysis of the Self: A Systematic Approach to the Psychoanalytic Treatment of Narcissistic Personality Disorders*. Madison: International Universities Press.

Kramer, K.P., & Gawlick, M. (2003). *Martin Buber's I and Thou: Practicing Living Dialogue*. New York: Paulist Press.

Kravitz, L., & Olitzky, K.M. (1993). *Pirke Avot: A Modern Commentary on Jewish Ethics*. New York: UAHC Press.

Kristoff, N. (2023). How we can fix our loneliness epidemic. *The New York Times*, Thursday Opinion, September 7 2023, A27.

Krystal, H. (1988). *Integration and Self Healing: Affect, Healing and Alexithymia*. London: Routledge.

Kuchuck, S. (2021). *The Relational Revolution in Psychoanalysis and Psychotherapy*. London: Confer Books.

Kuisis, R.G. (2004). Book review of Ancient Religious Wisdom, Spirituality and Psychoanalysis. *Division of Psychoanalysis (Division 39)*. Available at: https://www.division39.org/pub_reviews_detail_book_id_96.html.

Kulp, J. (2023). English explanation of Pirkei Avot 4:15. Available at: https://www.sefaria.org/English_Explanation_of_Pirkei_Avot.4.15?lang=bi&with=About&lang2=en (Accessed January 3 2023).

Lasch, C. (1991). *The Culture of Narcissism: American Life in an Age of Diminishing Expectations.* New York: W.W. Norton & Company.

Lear, J. (2022). *Imagining the End: Mourning and Ethical Life.* Cambridge: Harvard University Press.

Lear, J. (2005). Philosophy. In E.S. Person, A.M. Cooper, & G.O. Gabbard (Eds.). *Textbook of Psychoanalysis* (pp. 513–523). Washington, DC: American Psychiatric Publishing.

Lear, J. (2003). The idea of a moral psychology: The impact of psychoanalysis on philosophy in Britain. *International Journal of Psychoanalysis,* 84(5): 1351–1361.

Lear, J. (1996). The introduction of Eros: Reflections on the work of Hans Loewald. *Journal of the American Psychoanalytic Association,* 44: 673–698.

Lev, G. (2023). *Spiritually Sensitive Psychoanalysis: A Contemporary Introduction.* London: Routledge.

Levi, P. (1988). *The Drowned and the Saved.* New York: Summit Books.

Levinas, E. (2001). *Is it righteous to be? Interviews with Emmanuel Levinas.* J. Robbins (Ed.). Stanford: Stanford University Press.

Levinas, E. (1990). *Difficult Freedom: Essays on Judaism.* Trans. S. Hand. Baltimore: Johns Hopkins.

Levinas, E. (1987). *Time and the Other (And Additional Essays).* Trans. R. Cohen. Pittsburgh: Duquesne University Press.

Levinas, E. (1985). *Ethics and Infinity.* Trans. R. Cohen. Pittsburgh: Duquesne University Press.

Levinas, E. (1981). *Otherwise than Being or Beyond Essence.* Trans. A. Lingis. The Hague: Martinus Nijhoff.

Levinas, E. (1976). *Proper Names.* Trans. M.B. Smith. Stanford: Stanford University Press.

Levinas, E. (1969). *Totality and Infinity: An Essay on Exteriority.* Trans. A. Lingis. Pittsburgh: Duquesne University Press.

Lichtenstein, D. (2018). Lacan and the evolution of Hermes. In M. Charles (Ed.), *Introduction to Contemporary Psychoanalysis: Defining Terms and Building Bridges* (pp. 52–72). London: Routledge.

Lilius, J.M., Kanov, J., Dutton, J.E., Warline, M.C. & Maitlis, S. (2012). Compassion revealed: What we know about compassion at work (and where we need to know more). In: K.S. Cameron & G.M. Spreitzer (Eds.), *The Oxford Handbook of Positive Organizational Scholarship* (pp. 273–287). Oxford: Oxford University Press.

Loewald, H. (1991). Psychoanalysis as an art and the fantasy character of the psychoanalytic situation. In G.I. Vogel (Ed.), *The Work of Hans Loewald: An Introduction and Commentary* (pp. 128–152). Northvale: Jason Aronson.

Loewald, H. (1970). Psychoanalytic theory and psychoanalytic process. In *Papers on Psychoanalysis* (pp. 277–301). New Haven: Yale University Press.

Loewald, H. (1953). Psychoanalysis and modern views on human existence and religious experience. *Journal of Pastoral Care,* 7(1), 1–15.

López-Carvo, R.E. (2016). Wilfred Bion and psychoanalysis. In A. Elliott & J. Prager (Eds.). *The Routledge Handbook of Psychoanalysis in the Social Sciences and Humanities* (pp. 76–96). Abingdon: Routledge.

Malach-Pines, A., & Yafe-Yanai, O. (2001). Unconscious determinants of career choice and burnout: Theoretical model and counseling strategy. *Journal of Employment Counseling*, 38: 170–184.

Maranges, H.M., & Baumeister, R.F. (2016). Self-control and ego depletion. In K.D. Vohs & R.F. Baumeister (Eds.). *Handbook of Self-Regulation: Research, Theory, and Applications* (3rd ed.) (pp. 42–61). New York: Guilford.

Marcel, G. (2001). *Mystery of Being: Volume II. Faith and Reality.* South Bend, IN: St. Augustine's Press, 1951.

Marcel, G. (1995). *The Philosophy of Existentialism.* New York: Carol Publishing.

Marcel, G. (1973). *Tragic Wisdom and Beyond.* Evanston, IL: Northwestern University Press.

Marcel, G. (1964). *Creative Fidelity.* Trans. R. Rosthal. New York: Farrar, Straus and Giroux.

Marcus, P. (2021). *Psychoanalysis as a Spiritual Discipline: In Dialogue with Martin Buber and Gabriel Marcel.* London: Routledge.

Marcus, P. (2020). *Psychoanalysis, Classic Social Psychology and Moral Living: Let the Conversation Begin.* London: Routledge.

Marcus, P. (2019). *The Psychoanalysis of Overcoming Suffering: Flourishing Despite Pain.* London: Routledge.

Marcus, P. (2017). *The Psychoanalysis of Career Choice, Job Performance and Satisfaction: How to Flourish in the Workplace.* London: Routledge.

Marcus, P. (2010). *In Search of the Good Life: Emmanuel Levinas, Psychoanalysis, and the Art of Living.* London: Karnac.

Marcus, P. (2008). *Being For The Other. Emmanuel Levinas, Ethical Living and Psychoanalysis.* Milwaukee: Marquette University Press.

Marcus, P. (2003). *Ancient Religious Wisdom, Spirituality, and Psychoanalysis.* Westport: Praeger.

Marcus, P. (1999). *Autonomy in the Extreme Situation: Bruno Bettelheim, the Nazi Concentration Camps and the Mass Society.* Westport: Praeger.

Marcus, P., & Rosenberg, A. (Eds.). (1998). *Psychoanalytic Versions of the Human Condition: Philosophies of Life and their Impact on Practice.* New York: New York University Press.

Martinuzzi, B. (2013). The third ear: A powerful tool to becoming a better listener. Available at: https://www.americanexpress.com/business/articles (Accessed January 6 2023).

McCammon, C. (2018). Domination. Available at: https://plato.stanford.edu/entries/domination/ (Accessed November 24 2022).

McCullough, M.F., & Carter, E.C. (2013). Religion, self-control, and self-regulation: How and why are they related. In K.I. Pargament (Editor-in-Chief). *APA Handbook of Psychology, Religion, and Spirituality: Vol. 1, Context, Theory, and Research* (pp. 123–138). Washington, DC: American Psychological Association.

McGuire, W. (Ed.). (1974). *The Freud/Jung Letters.* Princeton: Princeton University Press.

McNutty, G. (2018). Passive, assertive or aggressive? How to figure out your communication style. http://www.dramandahale.com/blog/passive-assertive (Accessed August 29 2023).

Mendelson, M. (1974). *Psychoanalytic Concepts of Depression* (2nd edition). Flushing: Spectrum Publications.

Mischel, W. (2014). *The Marshmallow Test: Mastering Self-control.* New York: Little, Brown and Company.

Modell, A. (1999). The dead mother syndrome and the reconstruction of trauma. In G. Kohon (Ed.), *The Dead Mother: The Work of André Green* (pp. 76–86). London: Routledge.

Monte, C.F. (1980). *Beneath the Mask: An Introduction to Theories of Personality* (2nd edition). New York: Holt, Rinehart and Winston.

Moore, B.E., & Fine, B.D. (Eds.) (1990). *Psychoanalytic Terms & Concepts.* New Haven: The American Psychoanalytic Association and Yale University Press.

Morgan, M.L. (2011). *The Cambridge Introduction to Emmanuel Levinas.* Cambridge: Cambridge University Press.

Nehamas, A. (1998). *The Art of Living: Socratic Reflections from Plato to Foucault.* Berkeley: University of California Press.

Nettleton, S. (2017). *The Metapsychology of Christopher Bollas.* Abington: Routledge.

Neubauer, P. (1982). Rivalry, envy, and jealousy. *Psychoanalytic Study of the Child*, 37: 121–142.

Ogden, T.H. (2022). *Coming to Life in the Consulting Room: Toward a New Analytic Sensibility.* London: Routledge.

Ogden, T.H. (2016). *Reclaiming Unlived Life: Experiences in Psychoanalysis.* London: Routledge.

Ogden, T. (1999). Analysing forms of aliveness and deadness—Countertransference. G. Kohon (Ed.), *The Dead Mother: The Work of André Green* (pp. 128–148). London: Routledge.

Olyan, S.M. (2017). *Friendship in the Hebrew Bible.* New Haven: Yale University Press.

O'Malley, J.B. (1984). Marcel's notion of the person. In P.A. Schilpp & L.E. Hahn (Eds.). *The Philosophy of Gabriel Marcel* (pp. 275–294). La Salle: Open Court.

Ornstein, P. (1998). Heinz Kohut's vision of the essence of humanness. In P. Marcus & A. Rosenberg (Eds.). *Psychoanalytic Versions of the Human Condition. Philosophies of Life and Their Impact on Practice* (pp. 206–232). New York: New York University Press.

Patterson, E.M. (1984). The holocaust as sin: Requirements in psychoanalytic theory for human evil and mature morality. In S.A. Luel & P. Marcus (Eds.), *Psychoanalytic Reflections on the Holocaust: Selected Essays* (pp. 71–91). New York: University of Denver and KTAV Publishing.

Pawelczynska, A. (1979). *Values and Violence in Auschwitz: A Sociological Analysis.* Trans. C.S. Leach. Berkeley: University of California Press.

Pearson, C. (2023). The emotional relief of forgiving someone. *The New York Times*, Sunday Opinion, May 2 2023, D7. Available at: https://www.nytimes.com/2023/04/28/well/forgiveness-mental-health.html.

Person, E.S., Cooper, A.M, Gabbard, G.O. (2005). (Eds.). *Textbook of Psychoanalysis.* Washington, DC: American Psychiatric Publishing.

Peterson, C., & Seligman, M.E.P. (2004). *Character Strengths and Virtues: A Handbook and Classification.* Oxford: Oxford University Press.

Phillips, A. (2021a). *On Getting Better.* New York: Picador.

Phillips, A. (2021b). *The Cure for Psychoanalysis.* London: Confer Books.

Phillips, A. (2021c). *On Wanting to Change.* New York: Picador.

Phillips, A. (1999). Taking aims: André Green and the pragmatics of passion. In G. Kohon (Ed.), *The Dead Mother: The Work of André Green* (pp. 163–172). London: Routledge.

Phillips, A. (1994). *On Flirtation*. Cambridge: Harvard University Press.

Phillips, A., & Taylor, B. (2009). *On Kindness*. New York: Picador.

PJ Library (n.d.). You never know: A legend of the Lamed-Vavniks. Available at: https://pjlibrary.org/books/you-never-know-a-legend-of-the-lamed-vavniks/if520 (Accessed January 7 2023).

Polmear, C. (2016). British psychoanalysis in the 20th century. In A. Elliott & J. Prager (Eds.), *The Routledge Handbook of Psychoanalysis in the Social Sciences and Humanities* (pp. 225–241). Abingdon: Routledge.

Poma, A. (2007). Hermann Cohen: Judaism and critical idealism. In M.L. Morgan & P.E. Gordon (Eds.), *The Cambridge Companion to Modern Jewish Philosophy* (pp. 80–101). Cambridge: Cambridge University Press.

Prager, J. (2016). Donald Winnicott and psychoanalysis. In A. Elliott & J. Prager (Eds.), *The Routledge Handbook of Psychoanalysis in the Social Sciences and Humanities* (pp. 58–75). Abingdon: Routledge.

Rangell, L. (1963). On friendship. *Journal of the American Psychoanalytic Association*, 11: 3–54.

Redjebov, E. (2022). The psychology of giving: Why do people give to charity? Available from: https://rallyup.com/blog/the-psychology-of-giving-why-do-people-give-to-charity/ (Accessed February 1 2023).

Rees, S. (2023). Understanding why people give (Hint: It's not what you think!). Available at: https://getfullyfunded.com/why-people-give/ (Accessed February 1 2023).

Reik, T. (1983). *Listening with the Third Ear*. New York: Farrar, Straus and Giroux.

Reik, T. (1949). *Of Love and Lust: The Psychoanalysis of Romantic and Sexual Relations*. London: Routledge, 2017.

Renik, O. (1993). Analytic interaction: Conceptualizing technique in light of the analyst's irreducible subjectivity. *Psychoanalytic Quarterly*, 62(4): 553–571.

Ring, J. (2003). *Holocaust Literature. An Encyclopedia of Writers and Their Work*. S.L. Kremer (Ed.). Volume 1. (pp. 67–75). New York: Routledge.

Robbins, J. (Ed.). (2001). *Is it Righteous to be? Interviews with Emmanuel Levinas*. Stanford: Stanford University Press.

Roberts, S. (2023). Obituary of Timothy Keller. *New York Times Obituaries*, May 20 2023, B11.

Rocque, M., Posick, C., & Piquero, A.R. (2016). Self-control and crime: Theory, research, and remaining puzzles. In K.D. Vohs & R.F. Baumeister (Eds.), *Handbook of Self-regulation: Research, Theory, and Applications*. (3rd ed.) (pp. 514–532). New York: Guilford.

Rotenstreich, N. (1968). *Jewish Philosophy in Modern Times: From Mendelssohn to Rosenzweig*. New York: Holt, Rinehart and Winston.

Roth, P.A. (1998). The cure of stories, self-deception, danger situations, and the clinical role of narratives in Roy Schaefer's psychoanalytic theory. In P. Marcus & A. Rosenberg (Eds.). *Psychoanalytic Versions of the Human Condition* (pp. 306–331). New York: New York University Press.

Rudavsky, T. (2007). Feminism and modern Jewish philosophy. In M.L. Morgan & P.E. Gordon (Eds.), *The Cambridge Companion to Modern Jewish Philosophy* (pp. 324–348). Cambridge: Cambridge University Press.

Ruti, M. (2009). *A World of Fragile Things: Psychoanalysis and the Art of Living*. Albany: State University of New York Press.
Rycroft, C. (1995). *A Critical Dictionary of Psychoanalysis*. London: Penguin.
Sacks, J. (2023a). Shabbat announcements. *Great Neck Synagogue*, March 25 2023, 1–2.
Sacks, J. (2023b). Shabbat announcements. *Great Neck Synagogue*, April 6 2023, 1–2.
Sacks, J. (2023c). Shabbat announcements. *Great Neck Synagogue*, May 6 2023, 1–2.
Sacks, J. (2023d). Shabbat announcements. *Great Neck Synagogue*, August 3 2023, 1–2.
Sacks, J., & Angel, M.D. (2015). *The Koren Pirkei Avot*. Jerusalem: Koren Publishers.
Sagal, P. (2023). What do you know? *New York Times Book Review*, August 6 2023, 13.
Sass, L., & Woolfolk, L. (1988). Psychoanalysis and the hermeneutic turn: A critique of narrative truth and historical truth. *Journal of the American Psychoanalytic Association*, 36: 429–454.
Sekoff, J. (1999). The undead: Necromancy and the inner world. In G. Kohon (Ed.). *The Dead Mother: The Work of André Green* (pp. 109–127). London: Routledge.
Selig, B., & Rosof, L. (2001). Normal and pathological narcissism. *Journal of the American Psychoanalytic Association*, 41: 933–959.
Slochower, J. (2018). D.W. Winnicott: Holding, playing and moving toward mutuality. In M. Charles (Ed.), *Introduction to Contemporary Psychoanalysis: Defining Terms and Building Bridges* (pp. 97–117). London: Routledge.
Smith, H. (2001). *Why Religion Matters: The Fate of the Human Spirit in an Age of Disbelief*. New York: Harper San Francisco.
Smith, S.B. (2007). Leo Strauss and modern Jewish thought. In M.L. Morgan & P.E. Gordon (Eds.), *The Cambridge Companion to Modern Jewish Philosophy* (pp. 147–169). Cambridge: Cambridge University Press.
Somerstein, L. (2014). Ethics of the Fathers. In D.A. Leeming (Ed.), *Encyclopedia of Psychology and Religion*. Boston, MA: Springer. https://doi.org/10.1007/978-1-4614-6086-2_217.
Sophocles (2009). *Oedipus the King: Electra*. E. Hall (Ed.), Trans. H.D.F. Jitto. Oxford: Oxford University Press.
Spence, D. (1982). *Narrative Truth and Historical Truth: Meaning and Interpretation in Psychoanalysis*. New York: W.W. Norton.
Sprengnether, M. (2016). Literature and psychoanalysis. In A. Elliott & J. Prager (Eds.), *The Routledge Handbook of Psychoanalysis in the Social Sciences and Humanities* (pp. 300–313). Abingdon: Routledge.
Stein, M. (1998). Jung's vision of the human psyche and analytic practice. In P. Marcus & A. Rosenberg (Eds.), *Psychoanalytic Versions of the Human Condition: Philosophies of Life and their Impact on Practice* (pp. 37–63). New York: New York University Press.
Stewart, P., & Strathern, A. (2004). *Witchcraft, Sorcery, Rumors, and Gossip*. Cambridge: Cambridge University Press.
Still, J. (2013). *Derrida and Hospitality: Theory and Practice*. Edinburgh: Edinburgh University Press.
Stolorow, R. (1973). Perspectives on death anxiety: A review. *Psychiatric Quarterly*, 47: 473–486.
Strauss, C., Taylor, B.L., Gu, J., Kuyken, W.Baer, R., Jones, F., Cavanagh, K. (2016). What is compassion and how can we measure it? A review of definitions and measures. *Clinical Psychology Review*, 47: 15–27. https://doi.org/10.1016/j.cpr.2016.05.004.

Stulberg, B. (2023). Stop resisting change. *The New York Times*, Sunday Opinion, September 3 2023, 10.

Stux, R. (2022). 4 quotes by Carl Jung that might transform your life. Available at: https://medium.com/illumination/4-quotes-by-carl-jung-that-might-transform-your-life-3a1673aedfbc (Accessed May 7 2023).

Symington, N. (2012). The essence of psycho-analysis as opposed to what is secondary. *Psychoanalytic Dialogues*, 22: 395–409.

Symington, N. (1994). *Emotion and Spirit: Questioning the Claims of Psychoanalysis and Religion*. New York: St. Martin's Press.

Szalai, J. (2023). Use your disillusion. *New York Times Book Review*, January 22 2023, 10.

The Week (2023a). A psychiatrist's prescription for happiness. February 3 2023, 10.

The Week (2023b). Review of reviews: Books. March 2 2023, 22.

Treanor, B. (2006). *Aspects of Alterity: Levinas, Marcel, and the Contemporary Debate*. New York: Fordham University Press.

Todd, S. (2003). *Levinas, Psychoanalysis, and Ethical Possibilities in Education*. Albany: SUNY Press.

Tustin, F. (1981). A modern pilgrim's progress: Reminiscences of personal analysis with Dr. Bion. *Journal of Child Psychotherapy*, 7: 175–192.

Twersky, A.J. (1999). *Visions of the Fathers: Pirkei Avos with an Insightful and Inspiring Commentary*. Brooklyn: Shaar Press.

Tye, S. (2023). Book review of Interpersonal Neurobiology and Clinical Practice. *Psychoanalytic Review*, 110(1), March, 121–127.

Velde, N.V.D., & Hegger, A. (2018). 'I do not have such a belief myself': An interview with Otto Kernberg on psychoanalysis, religion and belief in God. *Psyche & Geloof*, 29(2): 143–148.

Vogel, G.I. (1991). *The Work of Hans Loewald: An Introduction and Commentary*. Northvale: Jason Aronson.

Volkan, V.D. (2020). *Large-Group Psychology: Racism, Societal Divisions, Narcissistic Leaders and Who We Are*. Bicester: Phoenix House.

Volkan, V.D. (2005). Politics and international relations. In E.S. Person, A.M. Cooper, & G.O. Gabbard (Eds.), *Textbook of Psychoanalysis* (pp. 525–533). Washington, DC: American Psychiatric Publishing.

Wallenfang, D. (2021). *Emmanuel Levinas and Variations on God with Us*. Eugene: Cascade Books.

Wallwork, E. (2005). Ethics in psychoanalysis. In E.S. Person, A.M. Cooper, & G.O. Gabbard (Eds.), *Textbook of Psychoanalysis*(pp. 281–297). Washington, DC: American Psychiatric Publishing.

Wallwork, E. (1999). Psychodynamic contributions to religious ethics: Toward reconfiguring "Askesis". *The Annual of the Society of Christian Ethics*, 19: 167–189.

Wallwork, E. (1991). *Psychoanalysis and Ethics*. New Haven: Yale University Press.

Watson, B. (1968). *The Complete Works of Chuang Tzu*. New York: Columbia University Press.

Weinstein, F. (1980). *The Dynamics of Nazism*. New York: Academic Press.

Wiesel, E. (1974). Talking, and writing and keeping silent. In F.H. Littell & H.G. Locke (Eds.), *The German Church Struggle and the Holocaust* (pp. 269–277). Bloomington: Wayne State University Press.

Wikipedia (2022). *Perkei Avot*. Updated January 25 2022. Retrieved April 18 2023.

Williams, B. (1993). *Shame and Necessity*. Berkeley: University of California Press.

Winnicott, D.W. (2015). *Human nature*. Abingdon: Routledge, 1988.
Winnicott, D.W. (1971). *Playing and Reality*. London: Tavistock.
Winnicott, D.W. (1958). The capacity to be alone. *International Journal of Psychoanalysis*, 39: 416–420.
Wright, T. (2007). Self, other, text, God: The dialogical thought of Martin Buber. In M.L. Morgan & P.E. Gordon (Eds.), *The Cambridge Companion to Modern Jewish Philosophy* (pp. 102–121). Cambridge: Cambridge University Press.
Xiaogan, L. (1993). *Taoism, in Our Religions*. S. Sharma (Ed.). San Francisco: Harper.
Yadlin-Gadot, S., & Hadar, U. (2023). *Lacanian Psychoanalysis: A Contemporary Introduction*. Abingdon: Routledge.
Yanklowitz, S. (2018). *Pirkei Avot. A Social Justice Commentary*. New York: Central Conference of American Rabbis.
Zoja, L. (2007). *Ethics and Analysis: Philosophical Perspectives and their Application in Therapy*. College Station, TX: A&M University Press.

Index

Footnotes will be denoted by the letter 'n' and Note number following the page number.

Aaron (brother of Moses) 90, 117n91
Abtalyon 17
Adam and Eve 114n57
affection 15
afterlife *see* world to come
aggression 10–11, 15, 30; internalized 53; real or imagined 92; turning against the self 39, 58
Akhtar, S. 11, 14–15, 19, 23, 32, 43, 49–51, 53, 54, 57, 81, 100, 106, 107, 114n59, 115n68
Algoe, S.B. 70
Allen, W. 61
allostasis 91
altruism 11–12, 13, 74, 110n12, 112n32; *see also* compassion; empathy
altruistic surrender 11
Alvarez, A. 23
American Perspectives Survey 25
Améry, J. 67, 77, 78, 79
Analects of Confucius 2
analysand 7n14, 9–10, 22–24, 27, 28, 31, 39, 40, 51, 61, 63–65, 71, 93, 102, 104–107, 110n15, 112n32, 115n70, 116n73, 117n93, 118n102; and analyst 9, 12–13, 22–24, 72, 87, 106, 107, 116n73, 118n102; becoming spiritual beings 120; Catholic 67; co-produced narrative 50; interaction with analyst 12–13; neurotic 97; receptivity 101; regressed 100; religious 4, 124; secular 4, 34, 36, 75, 109, 124; self-aware 24; as spiritual beings 120; teaching 99, 100
analyst(s): and analysand 12–13, 22–24, 72, 87, 106, 107, 116n73, 118n102;

choosing 12–13; knowing when to speak 28; personal psychology 13; sharing of theoretical principles 1; as teacher 12; truth-telling, sensing 10
anarchy 34
Angel, M.D. 5, 10, 13–14, 16, 20, 21, 32, 38, 42, 44, 48, 50, 52, 55, 58, 60, 64, 68, 70, 71, 73, 77, 80, 81, 83, 86, 88, 90, 93–94, 96, 97, 104, 106, 125n3
anger 16, 30, 63, 65, 95, 100, 121; expressing 39; of God 115n68; intense 101–102; repressed 33; unconscious 31; unreasonable 101; *see also* aggression
anhedonia 103
Aquinas, T. 48–49
Arendt, H. 116n78
Aristotle 89, 116n82
art of living 4, 6n13, 7n14
artificial intelligence (AI) 75
asceticism 102–103
assertive behavior 21, 33
attachment 75
Augustine, Saint 36, 48–49
Auschwitz 78
authentic spirituality 125n10
Axial period 9

Bagai, R. 5, 72, 112n37
Balzac, H. de 81
Bartinoro 58, 98
Bass, A. 108
Baumeister, R.F. 68
beauty, worship of 96
behavior, unwilling to change 24
being-in-the-world 14, 20, 34, 43, 49, 50, 72, 87, 104

belief/value structure 77–80
Bellah, R.N. 19; *Habits of the Heart* 18
ben Dosa, Rabbi Hanina 60, 61
ben Elazar, Rabbi S. 100
ben Gamaliel, Rabban Simeon 47
ben Hahinai, Rabbi Hanina 57, 58
ben Hakeneh, Rabbi Nehunia 77
ben Heresh, Rabbi Mattithyah 40
ben Jacob, Rabbi E. 37
ben Mahalalel, Akavyah 54
ben Perahya, J. 12
ben Shatah, S. 105
ben Tabbai, J. 105
ben Yitzchak, Rabbi Shimon (Rashi) 58, 70, 90, 98, 102, 115n64
ben Yohanan, Yose (of Jerusalem) 43
ben Zoma 63, 68, 70
benefit of the doubt, giving 15–17
Berenbaum, M. 29
Berg, J.M. 19
Bergmann, M.S. 85, 117n90
Berkman, E.T. 115n69
Berkson, W. 2, 5, 22, 44, 48, 49, 60, 64, 65, 68, 82, 87, 94, 105, 109, 117n89
Bernstein, J. 6n2
Bettelheim, B. 66, 77–79, 95
biblical friendship 13, 14
Binswanger, L. 9
Bion, W.R. 12–13, 27, 65
birth trauma 56
Blon, I., *Psychoanalytic Trends in Theory and Practice* 1
Blum, H. 106
Bokser, B.Z. 3, 6n7, 8, 10, 12, 21, 22, 24, 28, 30, 32, 34, 35, 37, 40, 42, 43, 47, 51, 57, 60, 63, 71, 72, 74, 77, 80, 88, 90, 93, 96, 98, 100, 102, 104, 107, 109n1, 110n3, 111n20, 112n33, 113n40, 119, 122
Bollas, C. 23, 54, 110n9, 110n11, 113n39
Brenner, C. 115n66
broaden and build theory (Frederickson) 45
Brooks, D. 76, 111n28
Buber, M. 5, 14, 21, 26–29, 69, 70, 79, 87, 101, 110n5, 111n16, 112n30, 120, 123, 124; I-Thou/I-It distinction 7n16, 41, 83, 84, 88
Buddha 13, 31, 75
Bugental, J.F.T. 12
Busch, F. 115n66, 115n70

Cain, S. 45
calling (career) 18, 19
Campbell, C. 112n34
Camus, A. 56
career choice 18–19
Carry, P. 56
Carter, E.C. 67
Carver, C.S. 115n69
Castrillon, F. 93
Caudill, D. 124
Chaim, Chofetz 47, 106
charity 12, 74–76
Chasseguet-Smirgel, J. 2
Cherry, K. 29
Chodorow, N.J. 125n7
Christian Bible 29
Church Fathers 89
Civitarese, G. 72
cliques 46
cognitive dissonance 40
Cohen, H. 113n51
Coltart, N. 9
communication: assertive 33; passive 33; silence as 23; verbal 71–72; *see also* gossiping; talking, compulsive
community 24–28
compassion 16–17, 28–29, 111n21, 122; *see also* altruism; empathy
compromise formation 114n61
Compte, A. 110n12
Compton, W.C. 29, 69, 70
concentration camps 66, 77, 78, 95, 111n26, 116n78
conflict 3, 49, 51, 107, 122; avoiding or postponing 33, 42, 68; and controls 35; emotional 11; high-conflict parties 90, 105; Hobbesian view of 35; infantile 56; intergroup and intragroup 26, 51, 91; intrapsychic 65; Oedipal 52, 80; open 47; resolution of 91
conflicted altruism 11
contemplation 23
Cooper, A.M 38, 52, 53, 61, 64, 66, 80, 84, 91, 92, 95, 101, 114n61
correspondence theory 49, 114n55
cosmic vision 120
countertransference 6n11, 102, 106, 107; *see also* transference/transference neurosis
court system 105–107
creativity 23, 95–96; intersubjective 44; passionate 95; rabbinical 103

critical attitude 17
culture 5, 35, 79, 124n1

Dasein 116n81
David and Jonathan 82, 83
Davis, M., *Psychoanalytic Trends in Theory and Practice* 1
Daws, L. 125n4, 125n7
de Sade, Marquis 81
death 54–57
death anxiety 56, 57, 114n63
death instinct 54
decentered-self 125n7
decision making, moral 10, 121
dehumanization 67
delusion 31
Derrida, J. 7n16, 113n50
Deuteronomy 8
Dimen, M. 81
domination 19–20
domineering personality 20
doubt 16
dream analysis 65, 71
Duckworth, A.I. 68
Dunn, J. 118n103

Ecclesiastes 97, 112n37
Edelson, M. 1
ego 11, 20, 23, 27, 31, 41, 46, 54
ego crisis 62
ego integrity 62
ego strength 62
Eigen, M. 41, 79, 110n6, 112n37, 122, 123, 125n4, 125n6, 126n11; *Faith* 120
Elazar, Rabbi 74
Eliezer, Rabbi 28, 30, 112n33
Elliott, A. 6n1
Emde, R. 115n68
Emmons, R.A. 70
emotional intelligence 29, 31, 100–102
empathy 22, 26, 27, 28, 30, 112n32; *see also* altruism; compassion
Encyclopedia of Psychology and Religion 2
envy 51–54, 69, 80
Epictetus (Stoic philosopher) 23
Erikson, E.H. 3, 18, 34, 42, 62, 92
Eros 51
Eskreis-Winkler, L. 68
Etezady, M.H., *Psychoanalytic Trends in Theory and Practice* 1
ethical subject 14

Ethics of the Fathers (Talmud tractate) 2–3; aspirational 122; as a blueprint for living 119; commentaries 10, 12, 74–75; dialogue with 124; modern commentaries 5; Rabbis of *see* Rabbis; superego morality 122; time of writing 5; translation of 6n7; *see also individual Ethic such as* lovingkindness
everyday interactions 20
evil 38, 39–40, 51, 113n42
evil eye 51, 52
existentialism 7n16, 56
Exodus 8

Fackenheim, E.L. 6n1, 36, 44, 118n105
faith 34, 125n4
fallacy of translatability 7n17
fantasy 12, 23, 54, 57, 125n9
feminism 44
Ferenczi, S. 6n10, 50, 81, 111n19
Ferro, A. 72, 112n39
Fine, B.D. 52, 81, 84, 97
Fine, R. 84
five books of Moses 8
Fliess, W. 110n6
Fogel, G.I. 116n80
Fonagy, P. 112n34
Forester, J. 10
forgiveness 16–17
Foucault, M. 3, 4, 89
Fowler, J. 76
Frankl, V.E. 26, 112n29
Frederickson, B. 45
free association 3, 6n10, 64, 65, 71
free will 107–109, 118n104
free-flowing interchanges 64, 71
French, S. 25
Freud, A. 11
Freud, S. 1–2, 5–6n1, 6n8, 9, 11, 12, 14, 15, 18, 19, 31, 35, 39, 56, 63, 66, 73, 87, 91, 95, 106, 111n19, 112n35, 112n36, 113n52, 114n56, 117n90, 117n97, 121, 122, 124; *Civilization and its Discontents* 7n14, 10–11, 30, 79; Freudian worldview 92, 115n71; *Future of an Illusion* 3, 6n3; *The Future of an Illusion* 34, 99; Guilty Man 35; *Moses and Monotheism* 117n96; Tragic Man 35; *Why War* 30
Freyer, D.R. 2
Friedman, M.S. 27, 101, 123
friend 14, 111n18

friendliness 14, 15
friendship 13, 14, 15
Fromm, E. 6n11, 7n14, 53, 73–74, 95
frustration 31

Gabbard, G.O. 38, 52, 53, 61, 64, 66, 80, 84, 91, 92, 95, 101, 114n61
Gable, S.L. 70
Galileo 89
Garone, S. 23
Gaskill, L. 113n46
Gawlick, M. 27
gender bias 44
generative altruism 11, 13, 74
generativity 34
generosity 72–74; creative 45; of spirit 17
Genesis 8, 110n10
Gershom, Rabbi 94
Gobodo-Madikizela, P. 112n30
God: anger of 115n68; belief in 34, 39; fear of 60; Image of God 115n67; listening to 65; reverence for 60; turning away from 36; will of 56
Goffman, E. 46, 79
Goldin, J. 111n24
Goleman, D. 112n29
good deeds 37–39
good life 6n6, 17, 29, 85–88, 125n3; and happiness 124
Gordon, P.E. 119
gossiping 46–47, 113n52, 113n53
grace 74
Grant, A.G. 19
gratitude 53, 63–70
greed 31, 51–54
Green, A. 109, 112n39, 116n80, 125n3
Greenberg, I.Y. 5, 12, 15, 16, 22, 24–25, 31, 35–38, 40–42, 44, 47, 49, 51, 54, 55, 58, 64, 65, 70–73, 75, 80, 82–83, 86, 90, 97, 102, 104, 105, 108
Greenberg, J.R. 1
grit 68
Gross, J.J. 68
Grossman, V. 8
group psychology 25
guilt 17, 38, 42, 57, 58, 77, 84, 99, 101, 105, 121; Freud's Guilty Man 35; unconscious 103

Hadar, U. 115n71, 115n75, 121
Hadot, P. 3, 7n14
ha-Kapor, Rabbi Elazar 28, 80

Halacha 105
halakhah (Jewish law) 44
Hale, N.G. 1
Hall, S. 124n1
ha-Nasi, Rabbi J. 3, 85–86
Hanina, Rabbi 34
Hanly, C. 49, 79, 114n55
happiness 68, 124, 126n12
Harvard Study of Adult Development 25, 75
Hassidism 112n38
hatred 31, 52, 54
hearing 22–24
heaven 34, 56, 66, 97
Hebrew Bible 8, 29, 73
Heery, M. 12
Hegger, A. 120
Heideggar, M. 116n78
Heilman, S. 46
Heschel, A.J. 6n1
Hillel (biblical commentator) 21, 22, 24, 90, 93, 101, 111n24, 113n49
Hinshelwood, R.D. 52, 53
Hitler, A. 113n42
Hoare, C.H. 3
Hobbes, T. 35
Hoffer, A. 107
Hoffman, E. 29, 69, 70
holiness 8, 123, 124, 125n11, 126n11; holy person 21
Holocaust 39, 66, 77, 78, 91, 95
homeostasis 91–92, 117n92
Homer 89
Homer, S. 13, 89, 111n17
homo religious 107
homo viator (spiritual wanderer) 88
homosexuality 15
honor 30, 36, 43, 47, 63, 70, 80, 81, 82, 85, 104, 112n33
hope, versus optimism 43
hospitality 43–47
Hoy, J.C. 124n1
human condition 63, 74, 92
Humanism 36; "Jewish Humanism" 4
humility 35–37, 55
Hutcheon, L., *The Politics of Postmodernity* 125n2

'I' statements 33
id 11
identity: conventional notions 125n1; cultural 124n1; group 35;

psychoanalytic versions 125n1; self-identity 95
idleness 57–59
ignorance 73
incest 15
inclusion 27
inclusiveness 26
insight 61
intellectualization 97
Ishmael, Rabbi 42
Israel 29, 117n94
Israely, Y. 1, 117n93
I-Thou/I-It distinction (Buber) 7n16, 41, 65, 83, 84, 88
Iverach, L. 57

Jacob, Rabbi 96
Jacobs, J. 3
James, H., *The Golden Bowl* 122
James, W. 15, 110n11
jealousy 52, 69, 80–82, 116n82
Jesus Christ 12
"Jewish Humanism" 4
Johnson, A.G. 79
Johnson, V. 19
Jones, E. 18
Jones, J.W. 87
Joshua, Rabbi 28, 51
joy 117n86
Judah, Rabbi 98
Judaism 123; Rabbinic 10, 44, 90, 109n2; and Torah study 11; traditional 125n3; *see also* Mishnah (written account of Jewish oral law); Rabbis; Talmud; Torah
judgements 16, 26, 27
Jung, C.G. 12, 24, 114n56
justice 47–51; and court system 105–107; and truth 48, 49, 50, 51, 109

Kagan, Rabbi Yisrael Meir, *Guard Your Tongue* 46
Kant, I. 48–49
karma 34
Katz, S. 123
Kaufman, W.E. 88
Keen, S. 83
Kelleher, K., *The Ugly History of Beautiful Things* 117n95
Kernberg, O. 120
kindness 29, 121, 122
Kinyan Torah 117n100

Klein, M. 15, 38, 52, 53, 69, 83–84, 87; Kleinian worldview 92
Klosterman, C. 17
Knafo, D. 1
Kohut, H. 21, 35, 87, 92; Kohutian worldview 92, 115n71
Kook, Rabbi A.I. 112n37, 120, 126n12
Kramer, K.P. 27
Kramer, S. 114n59
Kravitz, L. 5, 51, 55, 64, 65, 70, 73, 80, 82, 89, 90, 93, 98, 107, 117n94
Kristoff, N. 25
Krystal, H. 31
Kuchuck, S. 13
Kuisis, R.G. 125n10
Kulp, J. 41

Lacan, J. 13, 87, 111n17, 117n93, 125n7; worldview 93, 115n71
Lamed-Vavniks, legend of 36, 113n43
Lange, M. 117n95
Lasch, C. 9, 70
Lear, J. 111n15, 114n58, 115n65, 121
Lev, G. 125n11, 126n11
Levi, P. 66, 67, 77, 78, 79
Levinas, E. 4, 5, 6n5, 7n16, 13, 14, 21, 34, 39, 41, 62, 63, 73, 74, 83, 123, 124; *Totality and Infinity* 7n16
Leviticus 8
Lichtenstein, D. 5n1, 117n93
life cycle 62
life-affirmation 39, 51, 86, 94, 110n14
life-conduction 94
Lilius, J.M. 45
listening 22–24, 30, 65
Loewald, H. 1, 6n11, 49, 110n15, 116n80, 120, 125n4, 125n9
loneliness epidemic 25
López-Carvo, R.E. 117n87
love 82–85; and forgiveness 16–17; and jealousy 81; mature 85; platonic 15; self-love 14, 36; of wisdom 4; wisdom of 4; of work 17–18
lovingkindness 60–63, 110n3, 121, 122
lust 81, 82, 116n83; for material possessions 97
Luzzatto, S.D. 111n21
Lyotard, J-F. 119

McCammon, C. 20
McCullough, M.F. 67
McGuire, W. 4

McNutty, G. 33
Maimonides 36, 65, 89, 108
Maisel, N. 70
Malach-Pines, A. 18
man-woman friendships 15
Maranges, H.M. 68
Marcel, G. 5, 7n16, 21, 29, 43, 44–45, 69, 70, 79, 83, 87, 88, 110n5, 120, 123, 124; *Mystery of Being* 7n16
Marcus, P. 9, 46, 56, 74, 79, 83, 87, 108, 111n16, 115n69, 125n5, 125n11; *Ancient Religious Wisdom* 1; *Psychoanalysis as a Spiritual Discipline* 1; *The Psychoanalysis of Career Choice, Job Performance and Satisfaction* 111n22
Marshmallow Experiment 115n69
Martinuzzi, B. 23
Marx, K. 89
Maslow, A. 69
masochism 20, 103
master narratives 92
material possessions: lust for 97; and success 93–96
mature altruism 11–12, 13
Mendelson, M. 121
mentalization 112n34
Menzies, R.E. 57
Menzies, R.G. 57
Middle Group of the British psychoanalysts 9
Milner, M. 116n80
Mischel, W. 115n69
Mishnah (written account of Jewish oral law) 3, 37, 44, 71, 90, 100, 105–107, 111n24, 112n38, 118n100; charity 74–75
Mishra, A. 70
Mitchell, S.A. 1
mitzvot 85, 86, 94, 119
Modell, A. 50, 117n92
Monte, C.F. 62
Moore, B.E. 52, 81, 84, 97
moral outlook 8–12
moral psychology 66
morality 66, 69; of an analysand 9; personal 120; practical 4; superego 122, 123
morality plays 87, 110n8
Morgan, M.L. 63
Moscovitz, S. 1
Moses 8, 113n44

motivation 122
Murdoch, I. 37

narcissism 9, 10, 11, 17, 19, 20, 29, 36; and anger 31; culture of 70; inordinate 94, 96; of minor differences 26; narcissistic personality disorder 94; narcissistic rage 17, 31; robust and healthy 21; *see also* self-interest
narrative truth 49, 50, 72, 99
natural world, and the Torah 96–98
negative emotions 53
Nehamas, A. 7n14
neighbor, loving as yourself 14, 30–31, 101
Nettleton, S. 113n39
Neubauer, P. 52
neurosis 24, 97, 100, 109, 114n60, 118n107, 121, 122; conflict 26, 27, 29, 40, 41; neurotic shame 101; transference neurosis 1, 64, 65, 106, 111n15
Nietzsche, F. 48, 66
nightime 57–59
nirvana 17
Nittai the Arbelite 12
Numbers 8

object relations 56, 63, 92; mature 29, 30
objective truth 47, 50, 98, 117n91
Oedipal complex 1, 42, 61, 84; conflict 52, 80
Ogden, T.H. 65, 72, 112n32, 125n7
Olitzky, K.M. 5, 51, 55, 64, 65, 70, 73, 80, 82, 89, 90, 93, 98, 107, 117n94
Olyan, S.M. 13
O'Malley, J.B. 88
one person psychology 118n102
optimism, versus hope 43
original goodness 21
original sin 56
originalism 49
Ornstein, P. 35
over-talking 23, 24

paranoid-schizoid position 84
Parens, H. 114n59
passions 3, 63, 65, 66
passivity 32–34
Passover 102
Patterson, E.M. 56
Pawelczynska, A. 78–79
peace 47–51, 90–93; and truth 49, 50, 51

peace of mind 92
Pearson, C. 17
Person, E.S. 38, 52, 53, 61, 64, 66, 80, 84, 91, 92, 95, 101, 114n61
Peterson, C. 115n69
phenomenology 7n16
Phillips, A. 6n10, 9, 12, 13, 19, 27, 50, 87, 110n7, 110n8, 110n12, 111n19, 112n32, 114n56, 121, 122–123, 125n3
piety 104–105
Piquero, A.R. 66, 115n69
Pirkei Avot See Encyclopedia of Psychology and Religion
platonic love 15
pleasure 117n86
politicians 20
Polmear, C. 28
polygamy 94
Poma, A. 113n51
Posick, C. 66, 115n69
positive emotions 53
postmodernism, as death of the metanarrative 119
power 2, 18, 34, 47, 49, 64, 78; in camps 78; desire for 81; expanding 19; of God 39; raw 20; reflected 20; of sin 47; social 20; struggles 42
practical wisdom 124
Prager, J. 6n1, 113n47
prayer 6n9, 22; prayer books 2
procrastination 28
proto-altruism 11
Proverbs 60, 63
Psalms: Psalm 111:10 60; Psalm 128:2 63
psychoanalysis: aims of analytic treatment 39; as culturally aging 1; defining 3–5, 9; emotions, managing 121; Freud on benefits of 1–2; Freudian-based 6n2; goals 11, 117n93; and good life, living 121; mainstream 62, 66, 74, 125n5; master narratives 119; moral activity, seen as 9; narrative of self-identity 9; and religious belief 125n10; spiritual exercise, perceived as 3, 4, 9; spiritually sensitive 126n11; talking cure, seen as 23; as a technology of the self 3, 4; as a theory in crisis 1; *see also* transference
psychoanalyst *see* analyst(s)
psychoanalytic reductionism 5
psychoanalytic theory 9

psychological multiple determination 22
psychologism 79
psychotherapy 12, 64; primary 1
psychotic altruism 11
public officials 20
Putam, H. 114n55
Putnam, J.J. 5
Pythagoras 111n25

Rabbinic Judaism 10, 90
Rabbis 5, 6n5, 7n19, 51, 90, 94, 113n41, 117n86, 119, 121, 122, 123; on benefits of silence 22; on community 25; creativity 103; of the Ethics 11, 23, 121; the intellectual, overvaluing 31; and listening 24; and moral outlook 11; Rabbinic Judaism 10, 44, 109n2; of Talmud 112n38, 113n45, 125n8, 126n12; and wisdom 13, 15, 16; on work 20; *see also* Abtalyon; ben Dosa, Rabbi Hanina; ben Hahinai, Rabbi Hanina; ben Heresh, Rabbi Mattithyah; ben Jacob, Rabbi E.; ben Yitzchak, Rabbi Shimon (Rashi); Eleizer, Rabbi; Eliezer, Rabbi; ha-Kapor, Rabbi Elazar; ha-Nasi, Rabbi J.; Hanina, Rabbi; Ishmael, Rabbi; Jacob, Rabbi; Joshua, Rabbi; Judah, Rabbi; Kagan, Rabbi Yisrael Meir; Kook, Rabbi A.I.; S'forno (Italian rabbi); Shemaya; Simeon, Rabbi; Tarfon, Rabbi; Yannai, Rabbi
rage, narcissistic 17, 31
Rangell, L. 14, 15
Rashi (Rabbi Shimon ben Yitzchak) 58, 70, 90, 98, 102, 115n64
reality: Freud on 6n8; testing 125n9
reciprocity 70
Redjebov, E. 76
Rees, S. 76
Reik, T. 18, 23, 81
Renik, O. 13
repentance 37–39, 89, 109
resentment, giving up 17
resignation 34
reward 3, 6n9, 85, 86, 89, 95; external 95; financial 75, 76; in the world to come 32, 34, 38, 40
Ricoeur, P. 7n16
Rilke, R.M. 26
Ring, J. 116n78
Robbins, J. 83

Roberts, S. 109
Rocque, M. 66, 115n69
Rorty, R. 98
Rosenberg, A. 79
Rosenzweig, F. 119
Rosof, L. 11, 74
Rotenstreich, N. 4, 79, 110n5, 111n21, 117n88, 118n106
Roth, P.A. 87
Rudavsky, T. 44
rules of engagement 34–35
Ruti, M. 7n14
Rycroft, C. 15, 38, 50, 54, 81, 84, 103, 110n13, 114n62, 125n9

Sacks, J. 5, 7n17, 8, 10, 13–14, 16, 20, 21, 32, 38, 42, 44, 48, 50, 52, 55, 58, 60, 61, 64, 68, 70, 71, 73, 77, 80, 81, 83, 86, 88, 90, 93–94, 96, 97, 104, 106, 119, 125n3
sadomasochism 20, 111n23
Sagal, P 61
Sandler, J. 65
Sartre, J.-P. 7n16, 24, 56, 119
Sass, L. 114n54
Scheier, M.F. 115n69
secular analysand 4, 34, 36, 75, 109, 124
secular equivalent 36, 57, 76
secular intellectual 66, 119
secular theology 125n3
secular thinking 120
secular worldview 119
Sekoff, J. 112n39
self-actualization 69
self-awareness 89
self-centeredness 22
self-centric subjectivity 96–97
self-control 63–70
self-discipline 103, 115n69
self-esteem 19, 20, 21, 31, 33, 41, 95
self-identity 95
self-interest 10, 11, 21–22
self-love 14, 36
self-mastery 4, 66, 68, 89, 90
selfobjects 92
self-regulation 46, 66, 67, 68, 115n68, 115n69
self-respect 20
self-revelation 100
self-transcendence 4, 89, 90, 97, 120
self-transformation 120
self-understanding 4, 89, 90

Selig, B. 11, 74
Seligman, M.E.P 115n69
separation 59
Sephardic Jews 117n94
sexism 44
sexuality 81, 97, 116n84; aim-inhibited 15
S'forno (Italian rabbi) 15
Shakespeare, W. 100
shame 21, 71, 81, 106, 121; legitimate 101, 102; neurotic 101
Shammai (House of Shammai) 90, 111n24, 113n49
Shemaya 17
Shma (prayer) 22
silence: in consultation room 22, 23, 28, 100, 113n52; as listening 22; of parent 23; positive aspects 23; "silent treatment" 23
Simeon, Rabbi 28
Simeon the Just (Jewish High Priest) 8
sin 24, 55, 60–63; fear of 60, 61–62; original sin 56
slavery 94, 102
Slochower, J. 69
Smith, H. 97
Smith, S.B. 6n12
social isolation 25
social learning 63–70
Socrates 60
Sodom 72, 73
Somerstein, L. 2
Sophocles 26
soul 11, 47, 58, 90, 96, 103, 113n41, 120, 126n12
Spence, D. 49
spiritual exercise 3, 4, 9
splitting 52, 53, 84, 85
Sprengnether, M. 6n1
Stalin, J. 113n42
Stein, M. 6n11, 110n3, 110n4
Stewart, P. 46
Still, J. 113n50
Stoicism 68
Stolorow, R. 56, 57, 114n62
Strathern, A. 46
Strauss, C. 17
Strauss, L. 6n12
Stulberg, B. 91, 92
Stux, R. 24
subjectivity 119
sublimation 65, 81
submissiveness 42–43

success, and material possessions 93–96
suffering 6n3, 29; and evil 39–40; useless 39
superego 12, 17, 26, 35, 38, 39, 62, 97, 110n13
superego morality 122, 123
Symington, N. 3–4, 9, 110n5
Szalai, J. 37

talking, compulsive 23, 24
Talmud 8, 49, 110n3, 122; *Ethics of the Fathers* as tractate of 2, 4; Lamed-Vavniks, legend of 36, 113n43; Rabbis of 48, 113n45, 125n8, 126n12; source of wisdom 6n5
Tarfon, Rabbi 32
Taylor, B. 12, 27, 110n12, 111n19, 121
teacher, finding 12
technology of the self 3, 4
Thanatos 51
Thantophobia 55
theodicy 39, 40
time 32–34
Todd, S. 27
Torah 8, 43, 58, 88–90, 118n101; living 123; and the natural world 96–98; observance of 94; sacred quality of 89; self-perfection, personifying 10; study of 11, 24, 34, 58, 88, 94, 96, 97, 98, 102, 103, 119; yoke of 77, 115n77
transference/transference neurosis 1, 6n11, 64, 65, 99, 106, 111n15
trauma 56, 91
Treanor, B. 7n16
trust 16
truth 4, 18, 27, 47–51, 93, 98–100, 106; absolute 48, 109; abstract 48; biblical sense 48; coherence view of 49, 114n55; and correspondence theory 114n55; emotional 31, 61, 98, 121; historical 50; and justice 48, 49, 50, 51, 109; linear 98; moral 109; narrative 49, 50, 72, 99; objective 47, 50, 98, 117n91; one Truth 99; and peace 49, 50, 51; personal 31, 97, 98; in psychoanalysis 49; seeking 71; situational 99; socially constructed 49; truth-telling 9, 48, 50, 98, 99; unconditional 98; unrecognized 61; usable 71, 72, 98, 99; verbal communication 71
Tustin, F. 27–28

Twersky, A.J. 5, 37–38, 74–75, 80, 98, 102–103, 107–108
Tye, S. 121
tzedkah 115n76
Tzefat (Kabbalistic tradition) 115n72

unconscious, the 18, 121, 125n7; homosexual tendencies 15
United States Constitution 49

Velde, N.V.D. 120
verbal communication 71–72
violence 16, 34; psychological 38; *see also* aggression; anger
Vogel, G.I. 1
Volkan, V.D. 35, 91
Voltaire 17

Waldinger, R. 25
Wallenfang, D. 98
Wallwork, E. 4, 30, 110n7, 112n32, 112n35, 112n36, 115n65
Watson, B. 32
Weinstein, F. 95
Weltanschauung *see* worldviews
Wiesel, E. 29, 77, 78, 79, 116n79
Wikipedia 6n9
Williams, B. 6n5, 39, 113n47, 118n104
Winnicott, D.W. 12, 13, 27, 40, 50, 51, 59, 69, 79, 96, 112n31; *Playing and Reality* 117n85
wisdom 12–17, 115n73; classical Jewish wisdom literature 6n4; concept 62; and humility 60; of love 4; practical 124
Wittgenstein, L. 123
women, historical context 44
Woolfolk, L. 114n54
work 17–20; love of 17–18
world to come 56, 94; reward in 32, 34, 38, 40
worldviews 108; Freudian 92, 115n71; Kleinian 92; Kohutian 92, 115n71; Lacanian 93, 115n71; life-affirming 86; rabbinic 3; scientific 119; secular 119
worship: of beauty 96; divine 10
Wright, T. 87
wu-wei (inaction) 32

Xiaogan, L. 32

Yadlin-Gadot, S. 115n71, 115n75, 121
Yafe-Yanai, O. 18

Yanklowitz, S. 5, 11, 15, 17–18, 34–35, 40, 55, 58, 59, 64, 70, 77, 80, 88, 97, 101, 105, 106
Yannai, Rabbi 39, 40
yetzer-hara (the evil urge) 11, 65, 122
Yohanan, Rabban 28, 29

yoke metaphor 77, 115n77
Yose, Rabbi 112n33

Zoja, L. 29, 48, 119

For Product Safety Concerns and Information please contact our EU
representative GPSR@taylorandfrancis.com
Taylor & Francis Verlag GmbH, Kaufingerstraße 24, 80331 München, Germany

www.ingramcontent.com/pod-product-compliance
Lightning Source LLC
Chambersburg PA
CBHW050539300426
44113CB00012B/2176